CHRISTMAS
with Jinny Beyer

CHRISTMAS
with Jinny Beyer

DECORATE YOUR HOME FOR THE HOLIDAYS WITH BEAUTIFUL QUILTS,
WREATHS, ARRANGEMENTS, ORNAMENTS, AND MORE

✦ JINNY BEYER ✦

Rodale Press, Inc.
Emmaus, Pennsylvania

© 1996 by Jinny Beyer

Photographs © 1996 by Rodale Press, Inc.

All rights reserved. No part of this publication may be re-produced or transmitted in any form or by any means, electronic or mechanical, including photocopy, recording, or any other information storage and retrieval system, without the written permission of the publisher.

The author and editors who compiled this book have tried to make all of the contents as accurate and as correct as possible. Patterns, illustrations, photographs, and text have all been carefully checked and cross-checked. However, due to the variability of materials, personal skill, and so on, neither the author nor Rodale Press assumes any responsibility for any injuries suffered or for damages or other losses incurred that result from the material presented herein. All instructions should be carefully studied and clearly understood before beginning a project.

The author and editors at Rodale Press hope you will join with us in preserving nature's beauty so that others may share in the enjoyment of nature crafting. Unless you are certain that the plants or plant materials you are collecting—including leaves, stems, bark, flowers, fruits, seeds, or roots—are very common in your area, or over a wide geographic area, please do not collect them. Do not disturb or collect any plants or plant materials from parks, natural areas, or private lands without the permission of the owner.

To the best of our knowledge, the plants and plant materials recommended in this book are common natural materials that can be grown and collected without harm to the environment.

Printed in the United States of America on acid-free ∞, recycled ♻ paper

Props provided by:

The Cranberry Moose
232 South Washington Street
Naperville, IL 60540

The Olive Branch
322 West State Street
Sycamore, IL 60178

Sue Cooley Designs
5992 West Clare Road
Clare, IL 60111

On the cover: Jinny is shown in the library of her home in Great Falls, Virginia. She is wearing her Holiday Skirt (page 240). The Christmas Star Quilt (page 32) is on the chair and the Boxing Day Charm Quilt (page 12) is above the mantel. The Patchwork Christmas Stockings are on page 233.

Christmas with Jinny Beyer Editorial Staff

Editor: Cheryl Winters Tetreau
Interior Book Designer: Sandy Freeman
Interior Illustrators: Mario Ferro, Barbara Field, Sandy Freeman, Sue Gettlin, Jane Hallman, Robin Hepler, Dan Ramsey
Interior Photographers: Mitch Mandel, Bob Gerheart (pages 99, 105, 113), Kurt Wilson (page 122)
Interior Photo Stylist: Dee Schlagel
Cover Designer: Patricia Field
Cover Photographer: Mitch Mandel
Cover Photo Stylist: Marianne Laubach
Studio Manager: Leslie Keefe
Copy Editor: Sarah Dunn
Manufacturing Coordinator: Patrick Smith
Indexer: Nanette Bendyna
Administrative Assistance: Stephanie Wenner, Amy DiGiovanni

Rodale Home and Garden Books

Vice President and Editorial Director: Margaret Lydic Balitas
Managing Editor, Craft Books: Cheryl Winters Tetreau
Copy Director: Dolores Plikaitis
Office Manager: Karen Earl-Braymer

If you have any questions or comments concerning the editorial content of this book, please write to:

Rodale Press, Inc.
Book Readers' Service
33 East Minor Street
Emmaus, PA 18098

Library of Congress Cataloging-in-Publication Data

Beyer, Jinny.
  Christmas with Jinny Beyer : decorate your home for the holidays with beautiful quilts, wreaths, arrangements, ornaments, and more / by Jinny Beyer.
    p. cm.
  Includes index.
  ISBN 0–87596–716–7 (hardcover alk. paper)
  1. Christmas decorations. 2. Patchwork quilts. 3. Wreaths. I. Title.
TT900.C4B5 1996
745.594' 12—dc20   96–6166

Distributed in the book trade by St. Martin's Press

2 4 6 8 10 9 7 5 3 1 hardcover

To my parents, Polly and Doug Kahle,

who created a wonderful home atmosphere and by their example

instilled in me the importance of family,

the love of creativity, and the nostalgia of family traditions.

$\mathcal{C}$ontents

Acknowledgments viii

Introduction ix

The Colors of Christmas 1

Quilts 11

Boxing Day Charm Quilt 12

Attic Windows Quilt 22

Yuletide Medallion Quilt 26

Christmas Star Quilt 32

Enchanted Forest Quilt 46

Pineapple Quilt 54

Odd Fellows Quilt 62

Quilting Tips and Techniques 72

Knitting 95

Patchwork Squares Tunic Sweater 98

Enchanted Forest Sweater 104

Boxing Day Sweater 112

Wreaths 119

Basic Boxwood Wreath 122

Apple and Holly Boxwood Wreath 126

Boxwood Wreath with Mixed Fruit 128

Basic Evergreen Wreath 130

Juniper Wreath with Woodland Materials 131

Grapevine Wreath with Lotus Pods,
     Rose Hips, and Pomegranate 134

Grapevine Wreath with Ivy and Holly 137

Outside Decorations 139

Pine Roping 140

Over-Doorway Apple Plaque with Pine Roping Trim . . 142

Apple Plaque with Double Swag 145

The Christmas Tree 151
   Miniature Cat Ornaments 152
   Miniature Stocking Ornaments 158
   Miniature Boxwood Tree 162
   Miniature Tree Skirt 164
   Flying Geese Border Print Tree Skirt 168
   Christmas Tree Border Print Tree Skirt 174

Inside Decorations 179
   Apple and Grape Table Tree 180
   Mantel Decoration with Greens and Mixed Fruit 184
   Kissing Ball 187
   Stairway Roping 189
   Border Print Mantel Trim 197

Quick & Easy Patchwork 201
   Border Print Place Mats and Table Runner 202
   Full-Skirted Hostess Apron and Matching Potholder . . 207
   Border Print Throw Pillows 213
   Baker's Apron 218
   Flying Geese Place Mats, Table Runner,
      and Potholder 222
   Cat Doorstop 228
   Patchwork Christmas Stockings 233
   Holiday Skirt 240

   Index 244

$\mathscr{A}$cknowledgments

A book such as this one involves many people, and I am grateful for all the help I received from family and friends. The support of my husband John is most important to me, and he has had to live through a lot of chaos (so what's new?) while I worked on this book. I am particularly grateful to my mother, Polly Kahle, who sewed the Border Print Mantel Trim on page 197 and the Baker's Apron on page 218, and who acted as general all-around consultant. A special thank-you goes to my friends Robin and Dave Morrison. Robin worked with me on several marathon sewing sprees, helping me to finish many of the projects. She made the Christmas Tree Border Print Tree Skirt on page 174 and was always there when I needed extra help. Dave cut the wood bases for the outside decorations, helped me hang the wreaths and plaques, and was always available to lend a hand.

I also want to thank Carole Nicholas for sewing the Holiday Skirt on page 240

and for quilting the Pineapple Quilt on page 54. Thanks to Barb Celio and Sharon Kimmich for sewing the Pineapple Quilt and to Terri Willett for decorating the hat shown on page 240. Thanks to Karen Washburn for her knitting advice and for making the Enchanted Forest sweater variation on page 110. Thanks to Wendy Watson for her gardening expertise, and to Rick Cohan, Jill Johnson, Andrea Perkins, Linda Pool, Bonnie Stratton, and Bev Young for their help and advice.

I also want to thank RJR Fashion Fabrics for the fabrics used in the projects, Mathilda's for their flowers and props, and Krop's Crops for their Christmas trees.

It has been a pleasure to work with the wonderful staff at Rodale Press and I want to give a special thanks to my editor, Cheryl Winters Tetreau, and to the others who worked so hard to produce a quality book: Diana Carswell, Trish Field, Sandy Freeman, Mike Mandarano, Mitch Mandel, Dee Schlagel, and Janet Wickell.

Introduction

Christmas has always been a special time of year for me. From the time I was a small child, my mother helped my sisters and me make gifts, bake cookies, and plan special Christmas projects. The excitement of making something to give away cannot be equaled, and this is part of what Christmas means to me.

Probably one of the most satisfying times for me before Christmas is going for a walk with my basket and clippers to collect pods, berries, hips, and greens for decorating and for gift-giving. Every year there is something different to be found. I have been doing this since 1984 when my husband John and I found and moved into an eighteenth-century farmhouse, complete with an original log cabin in the backyard. Prior to 1984, various owners had added on to the house and its surroundings, including gardens, trees, and shrubs. By the time we moved in, everything had been neglected for several years, and we spent the first five years digging out from under wild grapevines, honeysuckle, and poison ivy.

The more we cleared, the more we uncovered magnificent magnolia, dogwood, and holly trees; a wide variety of pine and fir; wild roses; blackberries; and numerous fruit trees. The more I discovered, the more I experimented with decorating projects, particularly at Christmastime—when I decorate with items I have on hand, with handmade crafts, and with materials I can find in our yard. It is a delightful challenge and has caused me to open my eyes and look at nature's bounty with a newfound appreciation.

I classify my Christmas projects into long-term, short-term, and "getting desperate." Long-term projects include making quilts, knitting sweaters, and planting fruits and vegetables for canning. Short-term projects include making pillows, aprons, skirts, ornaments, and place mats.

Some of the "desperate" projects include quick strip-quilted ornaments, stockings, and potholders. Other quick and easy projects are those made from natural materials, which I can put together in a surprisingly short time. I share many of my Christmastime projects with you in this book, and I hope you will get as much pleasure from making them as I have.

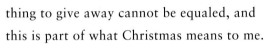

The Colors of Christmas

Red and green, with the addition of perhaps white and gold, are the colors one most readily associates with Christmas. Yet people tell me that the colors in the Boxing Day Quilt (shown on the opposite page and on page 12) give them more of a warm holiday feeling than do the colors of a more traditional red, green, and white Christmas quilt. It is not the individual Christmas colors themselves but what was added to those colors that makes one quilt exude more warmth than the other.

Many years ago, as I was becoming more and more interested in quilting, I realized that the quilts I liked contained many colors and many shades of each color. Slowly I began developing a system of working with colors in quilts. Soon I realized that the system works when planning colors not only for quilts but also for home decorating, knitting, flower arranging, or any other project you might tackle. If you study the ideas in this chapter and work with them for the projects in this book, you should gain a newfound awareness of working not only with the colors of Christmas but also with colors in anything else you do.

My system follows three basic principles: Use several shades of each of the colors you select, plan to have a color just a little darker than the general range of colors you are using, and plan to have a color just a little brighter than all the others.

Several years ago, after continually adding these "transition" colors, I suddenly realized that those "transitions" that had become such an important part of my palettes were actually "blender" colors, ones that were often halfway between two of the distinctly different colors I was using. This discovery made me realize that what I was actually doing while arranging a palette was subtly shading from one color to another. Think of all the colors in a rainbow. There are many distinct and varied colors, yet when you look at a rainbow, it is very difficult to tell where one color ends and the next begins. The colors gradually shade from one to the other, creating a breathtaking effect. This is the same effect I try to achieve with color shading.

It is not the individual colors in a given project that make a beautiful palette but what is added to them. The key to my system is this: No matter what colors you choose, if you can subtly shade them together—just as occurs in a rainbow, adding whatever colors are necessary to get from one to the other—you will have a beautiful palette every time. It works. Furthermore, in the process of shading, you automatically add the darker, the brighter, and the various shades of each of the colors, fulfilling the three basic principles I discussed above.

This concept works for any color planning you do. If you are redecorating a room and want to coordinate the colors around an oriental carpet, select the individual colors in the carpet, add whatever colors are necessary to shade those together, and you will have a palette to work with for the room decor. The following pages show the color palettes I have used in most of the projects in this book.

Diagram 1

There are many different ways colors can be shaded together, and there is no right or wrong way. One possibility is to darken two colors until you finally end up linking them through black. Another possibility is to lighten them until they link through white. Colors can also shade similarly through medium tones.

For the Enchanted Forest Quilt (page 46), I began with lime green, bright green, blue, and purple. All of the other colors were added to shade and blend those original ones together and to form the palette, as shown in **Diagram 1**.

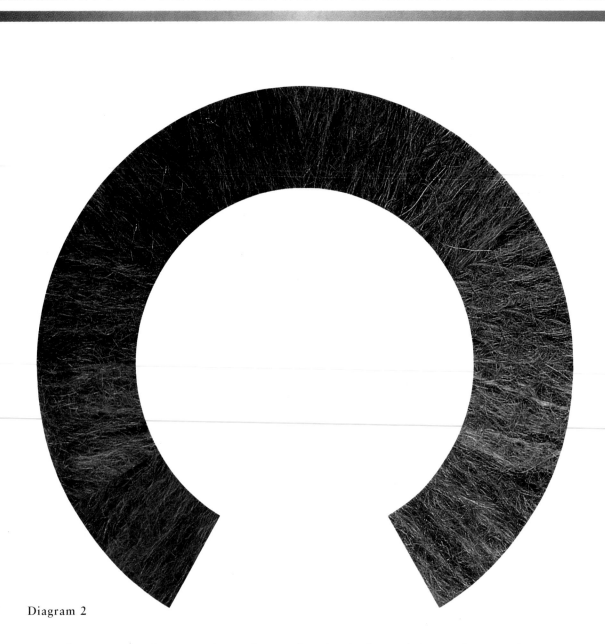

Diagram 2

I began with olive, purple, and navy for the Enchanted Forest Sweater (page 104). I added shades of teal varying from medium to dark for the transition from olive to black, and then shaded from navy to purple-blue and finally into the brighter purples, as you can see in **Diagram 2.**

Diagram 3

    For the Boxing Day Sweater (page 112), I began with the main colors of taupe, red, and brown. I added black and additional shades of the three main colors to link those colors together and complete the palette, as shown in **Diagram 3.**

Diagram 4

So what about the colors of Christmas? How does my color system apply to red, green, and gold? Once again, there are many different ways those colors can be shaded together. To begin, bear in mind that any color can be shaded to white or to black. Let's look at those three original Christmas colors. **Diagram 4** shows one way each of them can be shaded from one side to white and the other side to black. Bear in mind, however, that there are many ways to shade to white or black with an individual color. For instance, the red could shade to white through coral and peach or through rose and pink. Red could shade to black through brick and burgundy or through fuchsia and wine.

Diagram 5

When you create palettes, keep all the shading possibilities in mind. You could join red, green, and gold by shading them all to black, but you may not want so many colors. **Diagram 5** shows one way I shade the three colors through medium tones.

For my palette of Christmas colors, I began with gold and blended into medium brown, terra-cotta, and brick, which lead to red. Then I shaded the red to dark red, burgundy, and finally to black. Next I went into dark green, bright green, and light green until I arrived at white. This is the basic palette I used for the Boxing Day and Pineapple Quilts (pages 12 and 54), the patchwork stockings and ornaments (pages 233 and 158), and the cat doorstop and ornaments (pages 228 and 152).

Diagram 6

Diagram 6 shows the individual colors and the completed palette. An important consideration when working with the completed palette is the amount of each color you want to use. When looking at the palette you are seeing equal amounts of each color—that does not mean that equal amounts of each color will be used in the project. In general, decide which colors you want to be most prominent. Use more of those than the others, and use small amounts of the darkest and brightest colors. If you want a light quilt, use more of the lighter colors; if you want a darker quilt, use more of the darker ones. I use a majority of medium, muted colors and then use the brightest, darkest, and lightest ones to give the project its sparkle.

The concept of creating a palette of colors by shading the original choices together is certainly not new. All you have to do is look at the colors in nature to see that this concept is all around us. Look at a beautiful sunset. On the western horizon you might see bright gold and orange; in the east the sky is almost black. In between, there is a subtle blending of colors that shade all the way from bright gold to black. Depending on the cloud cover, the atmospheric conditions, and the time of year, there may be a different blend of colors between the gold and black, but each blend will be beautiful.

If you look at the boxwood wreath decorated with holly berries and apples shown on this page, what colors do you see? Not just one color of red and one color of green—there are many different shades of each color that make up the image, as well as colors you may not have realized were there. But it is the wide variety of the different shades that make the image visually appealing. If you were to re-create the image of the wreath in paint or patchwork using only two shades each of green and red, the completed color impact would not be nearly as interesting as if you used many shades of red and green.

What draws our attention to a beautiful wreath or quilt made up of materials or fabrics containing the colors of Christmas is not the individual colors themselves but all the others that go with those colors to make up the image. Practice looking at images around you and try to isolate all of the individual colors in that image. You will find that before long you will be looking at colors in an entirely new light—and you will become braver about adding more colors to your projects.

Since my early childhood, I have loved staying busy and have always worked on various embroidery, knitting, and sewing projects in my spare time. But it was not until the early 1970s, while living in India with my husband and children, that I began my first quilt. Having run out of yarn and being unable to acquire more until our next trip to the States, I needed a project and had become intrigued with the hand-printed, richly colored Indian cottons. Armed with leftover scraps from sewing projects, I scoured the marketplace, looking for additional colors and prints. I then began cutting hexagons for my first quilt, little realizing how dramatically that quilt would change my life.

Handwork has always been something I do in the evening or in other quiet moments when I want to relax, so it is natural for me to piece and quilt by hand. People often ask me how I can possibly have time to sew all my quilts by hand, but it would be more difficult for me to find blocks of time to sit and sew at the machine. With hand piecing, I can find little bits and pieces of time in odd moments. The secret is to take advantage of those moments, and to do that you must be organized, with pieces always cut out and ready to sew.

$\mathcal{B}$oxing Day Charm Quilt

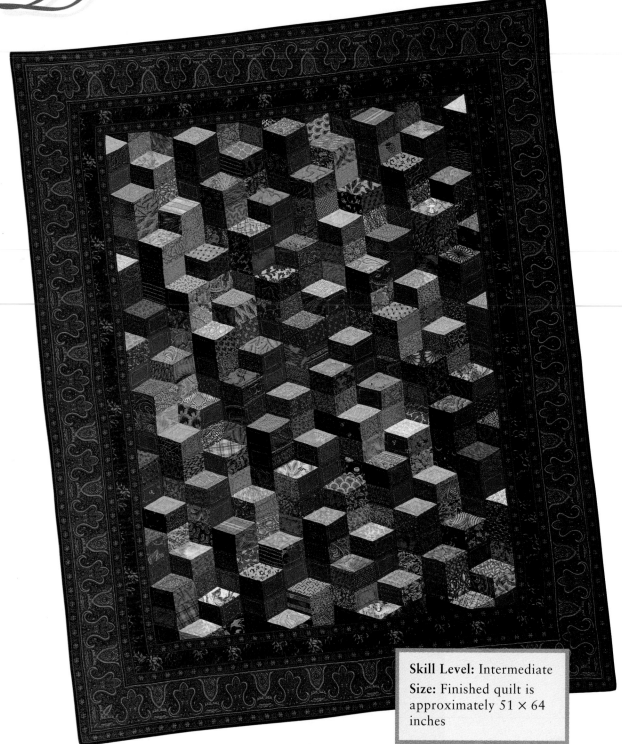

Skill Level: Intermediate
Size: Finished quilt is approximately 51 × 64 inches

Many years ago, we lived in Sarawak on the island of Borneo, when it was still a British Colony. That is where we learned about Boxing Day, a holiday celebrated primarily by the British on the day after Christmas. It is traditionally the day when tips and thank-you gifts are given to people who have served you throughout the year—household help, the postman, delivery people, and so forth. These gifts were originally presented in boxes, which led to the name "Boxing Day." Since this quilt resembles boxes stacked on top of each other, Boxing Day seemed an appropriate name for it. And the design made it a good choice for a charm quilt.

Color and Fabrics

In "The Colors of Christmas" on page 1, I talk about creating a palette of colors for your projects and show you how the Christmas colors can be shaded together to create a palette for the holiday season. I chose the same Christmas palette for this Boxing Day charm quilt. If you would like to make a similar quilt, try to find fabrics to match the palette's color range. As long as the prints fit within the general range of colors, anything will work.

The design for this Boxing Day quilt is derived from the traditional tumbling blocks (or baby blocks) pattern, in

The Story of the Charm Quilt

Charm quilts are usually made with a single template, such as a diamond, triangle, hexagon, or square, where every piece is cut from a different fabric. Even though most charm quilts are made with only one template, you sometimes see examples that contain multiple shapes. The concept for the original charm quilts  called for quilters to collect fabric swatches from family and friends and to put them together into a memory or "charm" quilt. Charm quilts gained popularity in the latter part of the 1800s, and many fine examples from that era have survived to this day.

There are various legends and superstitions about charm quilts. One superstition states that when you finally collect 999 different patches you will meet your true love and live happily ever after. (Only two of all the charm quilts I have seen contain 999 different fabrics. One that I own has 888 and I wonder if there is a story there.) Another tale suggests that the maker should deliberately repeat a fabric and then see how long it takes for people to find the two matching patches. Yet another story says that when the charm quilt is finished and slept under for the first time, whatever the person dreams that night will come true.

In recent years, charm quilts have once again increased in popularity, in part due to the sheer joy quilters get from collecting and working with so many different prints. Those of us who have been collecting fabrics for many years find that making a charm quilt is an easy way to use at least a little piece of all of our fabrics.

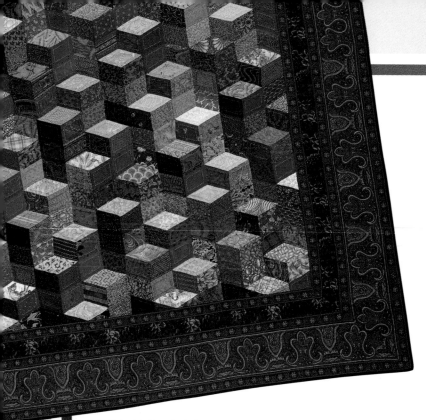

which light, medium, and dark diamonds are always used in the same position to create a three-dimensional block-like effect. The original tumbling blocks pattern uses a single diamond template, but in my Boxing Day design the diamonds have been flattened somewhat, making the finished units resemble short boxes rather than square blocks. Therefore, instead of one single pattern piece there are three: the flattened diamond (top of the box), and two mirror-image parallelograms (left and right sides of the box). The boxes are also arranged so there are both tall and short stacks.

No matter what height the stacks are, the placement of dark, medium, and light patches remains the same throughout the quilt. The top of a box is always light, the left side is dark, and the right side is medium.

To make a quilt the same size as the one shown in the photograph on page 12, you will need 441 different fabrics. It is best to try to collect all the fabrics before you begin cutting. With the basic tumbling blocks pattern you can cut diamonds and sort them later, but since the light, medium, and dark pieces for Boxing Day will each be cut from a different template, it is best to sort the color values first. For ease in sorting, cut a 3 × 5-inch piece of each fabric you intend to use. The actual shapes can be cut after you know whether the fabric will be used as a dark, medium, or light piece.

When sorting into dark, medium, and light piles, keep in mind that the lights do not all have to be very light, and the darks do not all have to be very dark. Study my quilt, shown on page 12. A "light" fabric only has to be lighter than the medium and dark fabrics next to it in order to still read as "light." Likewise a "dark" only has to be darker than the medium and light fabrics next to it.

The one drawback to working with a pattern for a charm quilt that has more than one template is that you have to decide in advance into which category to put each of the fabrics. While making this quilt, there were several times that I recut a piece so that I could use the fabric in a different position than I had originally intended. To save yourself some time, read through the complete instructions for this quilt before purchasing your fabrics.

You Will Need

89 3 × 5-inch rectangles of light prints

176 3 × 5-inch rectangles of dark prints

176 3 × 5-inch rectangles of medium prints

2 yards of border print fabric containing at least four repeats of a 5½-inch (finished width) stripe (outer border) and at least four repeats of a 1-inch (finished width) stripe (inner border)

2 yards of dark green print (middle border; if you don't mind putting a seam in the middle of the strip, you will need only 1 yard)

1 yard of coordinating fabric for binding

60 × 70-inch piece of batting

4 yards of fabric for backing

Template plastic

Permanent marker

Making Templates

Refer to "Making and Using Templates" on page 74. Using the template plastic, make templates by tracing the full-size pattern pieces on pages 20–21. Note that templates with an "R" designation are reversed for some cuts to create a mirror image of the original piece. Piece A is the dark (left) side of a box; piece A Reverse (AR) is the medium (right) side; piece B is the light (top). Templates C, CR, D, DR, and E are partial pieces used to fill in at the edges of the quilt.

Cutting

Sort the fabric squares into dark, medium, and light piles. You will need 89 light pieces, 176 medium pieces, and 176 dark pieces. If you have too many mediums and not enough lights, move your lightest "medium" pieces into the light pile. If there are too many darks and not enough mediums, move the lighter "dark" pieces into the medium pile. Keep shifting the fabrics in this manner until you have the amount you need for each pile.

From the dark fabrics, cut:
160 A pieces
4 D pieces
12 CR pieces

From the medium fabrics, cut:
160 AR pieces
4 DR pieces
12 C pieces

From the light fabrics, cut:
79 B pieces
10 E pieces

Piecing a Boxing Day Unit

When making a quilt where the same shapes are repeated over and over, I like to create a "unit" for sewing. When complete, the units fit together to form the entire quilt. Within each unit, I try to achieve a balance not only of all the colors that will be in the quilt, but also of the wide variety of sizes and types of prints that I have selected. I always try to include one fabric that is a little darker than all the others, and one that is a little brighter. When completed, each unit should reflect a good balance between strong and muted, and grayed and bold colors. If you have a good balance between all of these elements within the individual units, then there should be an overall balance when the units are fitted together to create the finished quilt.

Refer to the **Full Unit** diagram while assembling the unit. Note the placement of the dark, medium, and light pieces and follow that same value placement as you lay out your units.

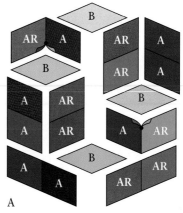

A

Diagram 1

Step 1: Arrange 8 dark A patches, 8 medium AR patches, and 4 light B patches, as shown.

Step 2: Using a ¼-inch seam allowance, sew groups of patches together, as shown in **Diagram 1A.** Always leave ¼ inch of the seam unsewn where indicated by the dots. This allows you to set in the B patches. (For more information about setting in patches, see pages 83–84.) Press.

Step 3: Join the groups into larger units, as shown in **Diagrams 1B** through **1D,** until you have a finished Full Unit.

Step 4: Repeat Steps 1 through 3 to make a total of 18 Full Units.

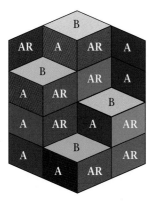

Full Unit

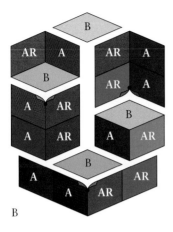

B

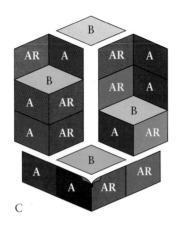

C

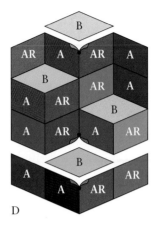

D

Making A Right-Side Fill Unit

Step 1: To make a right-side fill unit, arrange 5 dark A patches, 3 medium AR patches, 1 light B patch, and 2 light E patches, as shown in the **Right-Side Fill Unit** diagram.

Step 2: Sew the patches together as you did for the Full Unit, referring to **Diagrams 2A** and **2B.** Press.

Step 3: Repeat, making a total of 2 Right-Side Units.

Making A Left-Side Fill Unit

Step 1: To make a left-side fill unit, arrange 3 dark A patches, 5 medium AR patches, 1 light B patch, and 2 light E patches as shown in the **Left-Side Fill Unit** diagram.

Step 2: Sew the patches together as you did for the the right half of the full unit, referring to **Diagrams 3A** and **3B.** Press.

Step 3: Repeat, making a total of 2 Left-Side Units.

Make 2

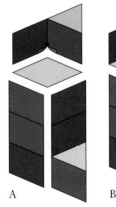

Right-Side Fill Unit

Diagram 2

A

B

Make 2

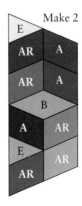

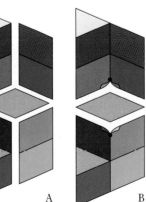

Left-Side Fill Unit

Diagram 3

A

B

Making the Corner Units

Step 1: Refer to the **Corner Units** diagram to assemble the quilt's corner units. Make 1 of each. Pieces required are as follows:

Top left corner: 1 medium DR and 1 medium C

Top right corner: 1 dark D and 1 dark CR

Bottom left corner: 1 light E, 1 medium C, and 1 dark CR

Bottom right corner: 1 light E, 1 medium C, and 1 dark CR

Top Left Corner	Top Right Corner

Make 1 of each

Bottom Left Corner	Bottom Right Corner

Corner Units

Quilt on the Go

Whenever I'm working on a quilt, I like to lay out several units at a time, pinning the pieces in each unit together so they can easily be laid out again. Then I keep the units, along with scissors, needle, thread, and a thimble, in a bag or small box and take it with me wherever I go. That way, I can take advantage of odd moments of time here and there to piece some of the units together.

Making the Top and Bottom Fill Units

Step 1: Refer to the **Top and Bottom Fill Units** diagram to assemble the units required to fill in the gaps at the top and bottom of the quilt. Make 3 of each unit type. Patches required are as follows:

Top: 1 dark D, 1 medium DR, 1 dark CR, and 1 medium C

Bottom: 1 light B, 2 dark CR, and 2 medium C

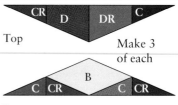

Top   Make 3 of each

Bottom

Top and Bottom Fill Units

Assembling the Quilt Top

Step 1: When all of the units are complete, arrange them on the floor or a design wall, making sure that there is a good balance of color, texture, dark, medium, bright, and light throughout the quilt top. Refer to the **Quilt Layout** for unit placement.

Step 2: Sew the Fill Units and Side Fill Units together in horizontal rows, beginning and ending all seams ¼ inch from either end to allow for setting in adjoining units. Sew the rows together, pivoting to set in pieces where required.

Quilt Layout

S t e p   3 : Sew the Top and Bottom Fill Units to the quilt, pivoting to set in where required. Sew the Corner Units to the quilt. Press.

Adding the Borders

The border for the Boxing Day quilt is made up of three different fabrics—a 1-inch-wide strip of border print (inner border), a 1½-inch-wide strip of dark green print (middle border), and a 5½-inch-wide strip of border print (outer border). Refer to the photograph on page 12 and the **Quilt Layout** on page 19. These are all *finished* measurements; each piece must be cut with a ¼-inch seam allowance on each side. The width of the total finished border in the quilt shown is 8 inches. I add a darker piece of fabric between the two borders because I feel it adds dimension to the overall quilt design, but if you find a one-piece border print that you like, you won't need to piece three strips together. See "Working with Border Prints" on page 77 for complete information on cutting and sewing borders to the quilt top.

Quilting and Finishing

S t e p   1 : Prepare the quilt back and baste the quilt layers together according to the directions in "Quilt Backings" and "Layering and Basting" on page 88. Quilt as desired. I outline quilted each patch ¼ inch in from the seam. In the wide outer border, I fol-

lowed the design on the print. In the green middle border, I used ¼-inch masking tape as a guide and quilted parallel lines ½ inch apart, running perpendicular to the strip.

S t e p   2 : Cut bias binding and sew it to the quilt according to the directions in "Bias Binding" on page 91.

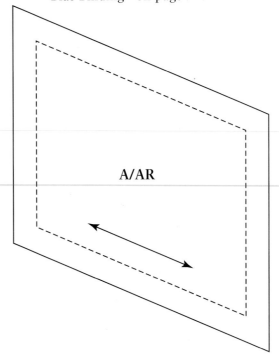

A/AR

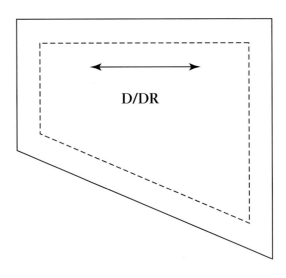

D/DR

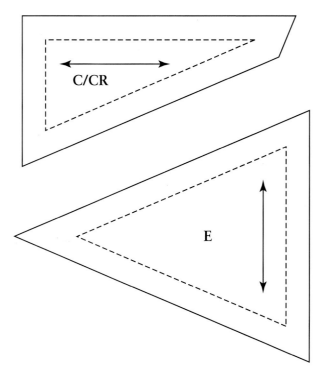

Boxing Day Quilt Variation

Not everyone will want to collect 441 different fabrics for a charm quilt. If you like the Boxing Day design but would prefer to use fewer fabrics, try this variation. It contains only 20 different prints—8 darks, 8 mediums, and 4 lights. You will need ¼ yard each of the 20 prints.

This quilt is made in exactly the same way as the charm version, with one exception—each unit uses identical fabrics. If you have a good balance between the colors and prints within the unit, you will achieve good color balance throughout the quilt. Refer to the Boxing Day Charm Quilt instructions for all assembly procedures and for value placement instructions.

C/CR

E

B

$\mathcal{A}$ttic Windows Quilt

Skill Level: Intermediate

Size: Finished quilt is approximately 36 × 42 inches; finished block is 6 inches square

The Attic Windows Quilt shown here is quite easy to piece, yet it is a design that has great visual impact because of its three-dimensional effect. These instructions are for a small crib or wall quilt, but this block would also be lovely in a larger bed-size quilt.

Color and Fabrics

This quilt requires four fabrics: three for the Attic Windows block, and a border print for the border. To achieve a three-dimensional look in the blocks, select one dark, one medium, and one light fabric. For the A squares in my quilt, I chose a light holiday print with scenic motifs and centered a different design in each square. Although any light fabric will work well for the A squares, multicolored specialty prints can often create visual interest and texture. For the B and B Reverse (BR) pieces, I used one dark green and one medium red fabric. If you'd like to create a scrap look in your quilt, try experimenting with a variety of dark and medium greens and reds. Have fun putting different fabrics together, remembering to place the dark and medium fabrics in the same positions for each block.

You'll want to review "Making and Using Templates" on page 74 and "Working with Border Prints" on page 77 before beginning this quilt.

You Will Need

½ yard of light fabric for the A squares (increase to ¾ or 1 yard for holiday or specialty prints)

⅝ yard of medium red fabric for the B pieces and binding

⅓ yard of dark green fabric for the BR pieces

1¼ yards of a border print fabric with at least four repeats of a 6-inch (finished width) stripe

Crib-size (45 × 60-inch) batting

1¼ yards of fabric for backing

Template plastic

Permanent marker

Making Templates

Using the template plastic, make Template A by drawing a 4-inch square. Add a ¼-inch seam allowance to each side. Make Template B by tracing the full-size pattern piece on page 25.

Cutting

To make sure that the B and BR pieces are exact mirror images of each other, place the red and green fabrics wrong sides together and press them with an iron to make them "stick." Then use template B to cut out the B and BR pieces at the same time.

From the light fabric, cut:
20 A squares

From the red fabric, cut:
20 B pieces

From the green fabric, cut:
20 BR pieces

Piecing the Attic Window Blocks

Step 1: Sew a red B piece to the left side of a light A square, ending the seam ¼ inch in from the edge of the fabric, as indicated by the dot in **Diagram 1.**

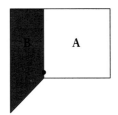

Diagram 1

Step 2: Sew a green BR piece to the bottom of the A square, beginning this seam where the previous seam ended and sewing to the edge of the A square, as indicated in **Diagram 2.**

Step 3: To complete the Attic Window block, sew the corner seam from the point where the B and BR pieces meet the A square out to the corner, referring to **Diagram 2.** Press this corner seam to one side. Press the other two seams away from the A square.

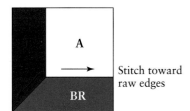

Stitch toward
raw edges

Diagram 2

Step 4: Repeat Steps 1 through 3 to make a total of 20 Attic Window blocks.

Assembling the Quilt Top

Step 1: Sew four Attic Window blocks together into a horizontal row, referring to the **Quilt Assembly Diagram.** Press these seams toward the left side of the row. Repeat to make five of these rows.

Step 2: Sew the five rows of blocks together, as shown in the **Quilt Assembly Diagram.** Press these seams toward the bottom of the quilt.

Adding the Borders

The border for the Attic Windows quilt is made up of 1 fabric—a 6-inch (finished width) strip of border print.

Quilt Assembly Diagram

See "Working with Border Prints" on page 77 for complete information on cutting strips for borders and sewing them to the quilt top.

Quilting and Finishing

Step 1: Prepare the quilt back and baste the quilt layers together according to the directions in "Quilt Backings" and "Layering and Basting" on page 88. Quilt as desired. The blocks in my quilt are quilted ¼ inch inside each seam and around some of the holiday motifs. The border quilting lines follow the designs in the border print.

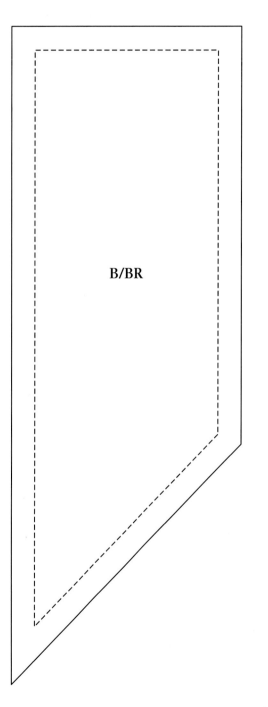

B/BR

Step 2: Cut the bias binding and sew it to the quilt according to the directions in "Bias Binding" on page 91.

Yuletide Medallion Quilt

The medallion quilt pictured here is not difficult to make, since it is composed of large pieces of print and border print fabrics. If you are unable to find a Christmas fabric with scenes on it, substitute a favorite patchwork block of the same size, or create border print squares for the K pieces. You'll want to review "Working with Border Prints" on page 77 and "Making and Using Templates" on page 74 before beginning this quilt.

Color and Fabrics

The quilt shown contains only four different fabrics—a print with holiday scenes, a border print, a dark green holly print, and a light beige fabric.

You Will Need

1 yard of a holiday scene print

1 yard of a dark green, medium-scale print

⅝ yard of a light beige print

Enough border print fabric to yield the following:

1-yard strip of 1½-inch (finished width) stripe for pieces B1 and B2

7 yards of a 3-inch (finished width) stripe for pieces E, I, and IR

11 yards of a 5-inch (finished width) stripe for pieces G and M

5½ yards of a ¾-inch (finished width) stripe for piece L

⅔ yard of coordinating dark fabric for binding

Twin-size (63 × 99-inch) batting

3¾ yards of fabric for backing

Template plastic

Permanent marker

Graph paper

Making Templates

Since large pieces are required for this quilt, it is impossible to put the templates in the book. To make patterns, refer to the measurements on page 29. Draft the patterns onto graph paper, then add a ¼-inch seam allowance to each side and make templates from the template plastic.

Customizing the Pattern

If you are unable to find a border print with the dimensions given, use the measurements from the border print you have and make adjustments to the pattern as necessary. With a few alterations, the large square (outlined in green in the **Quilt Diagram** on page 28) can still be 32½ inches. For example, if your G border is narrower, piece F will be larger. If your G border is wider, piece F will be smaller. Similarly, the diagonally placed square

(continued on page 30)

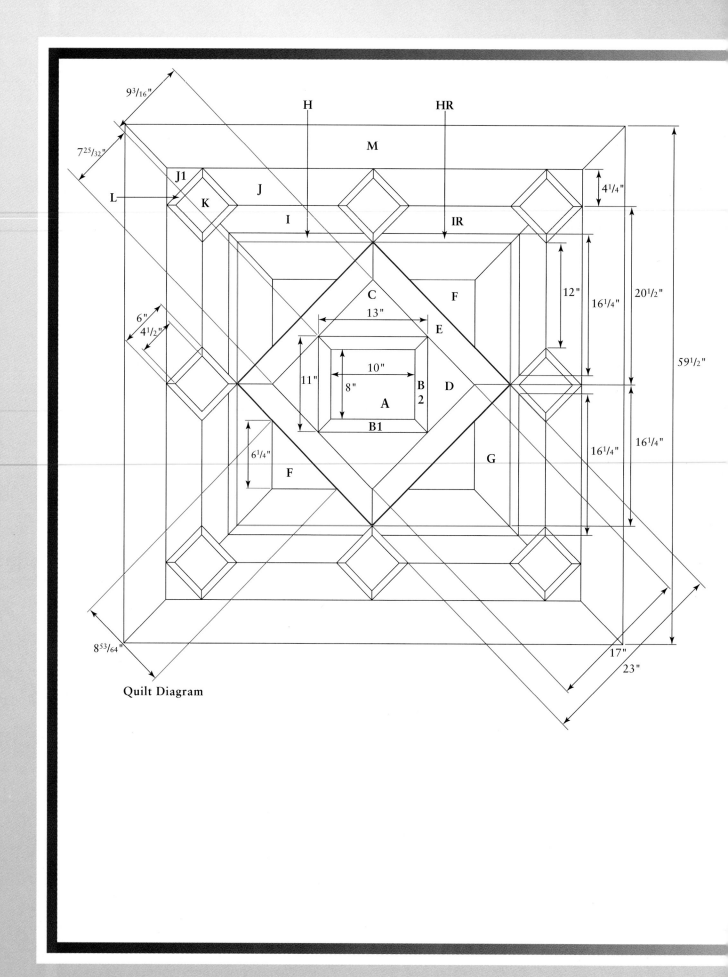

Quilt Diagram

Template Chart for Yuletide Medallion Quilt

Piece	Template Dimensions*	Comments
A	8" × 10"	
B1	1½" × 13"	Inner long side measures 10"
B2	1½" × 11"	Inner long side measures 8"
C	9¼" × 9¼"	Cut in half diagonally, then add seam allowances
D	7¾" × 7¾"	Cut in half diagonally, then add seam allowances
E	3" × 23"	Inner long side measures 17"
F	6¼" × 6¼"	Cut in half diagonally, then add seam allowances
G	5" × 16¼"	Inner long side measures 6¼"
H/HR	1¼" × 17½"	Each long side measures 16¼"
I/IR	3" × 17½"	Inner long side measures 16¼"; outer long side measures 12"
J	4¼" × 20½"	Inner long side measures 12"
J1	4¼" × 4¼"	Cut in half diagonally, then add seam allowances
K	4½" × 4½"	
L	¾" × 6"	Inner long side measures 4½"
M	5" × 59½"	Inner long side measures 49½"; adjust as needed to fit

*Add ¼" seam allowances to *all* sides of *all* templates.

(outlined in purple in the diagram) can still be 23 inches. However, you will need to adjust the pieces inside border E if that border is larger or smaller than 3 inches.

If the border you have chosen for piece I is wider, piece H will be narrower. If I is narrower, H will be wider. The same holds true with the small border L. If yours is a little wider, square K will be smaller. If yours is narrower, square K will be larger. If your outer border M is narrower or wider, the finished quilt will be slightly smaller or larger.

Make all of the necessary adjustments directly on the graph paper as you take the measurements of your own border print pieces. If you mark carefully, the patterns will provide an accurate guide for your own unique quilt top.

Cutting

Cut each of the pieces to correspond with the letters and measurements on the chart, or on your drawing if adjustments were made. Refer to the **Quilt Diagram** for pattern pieces (marked with an R) that must be positioned face down for cutting. Cut the pieces so that the fabric's straight-of-grain will be positioned around the outer perimeter of each section. Make sure to include a ¼-inch seam allowance around all sides of all pieces before cutting out the fabric.

From the holiday scene print, cut:
1 A piece
4 F pieces
8 K pieces (orient all pieces so the scenes are right side up when sewn)

From the green print, cut:
2 C pieces
2 D pieces
8 J pieces
4 J1 pieces

From the beige print, cut:
4 H pieces
4 HR pieces

From the 1½-inch border print, cut:
2 B1 pieces
2 B2 pieces

From the 3-inch border print, cut:
4 E pieces
4 I pieces
4 IR pieces

From the 5-inch border print, cut:
8 G pieces
(M pieces will be cut after the quilt is assembled)

From the ¾-inch border print, cut:
32 L pieces

Piecing the Quilt Top

Refer to the **Quilt Diagram** on page 28 as you assemble the quilt. When adding borders around a square or triangle, stop sewing ¼ inch before the end. Sew up the miters after all the borders have been added.

Step 1: Sew the B1 and B2 border strips to the sides of the A rectangle. Press.

Step 2: Sew the green C triangles to the top and bottom of the rectangle. Add the D triangles to the sides. Press.

Step 3: Add the E border strips to the outside of the square. Press.

Step 4: Making sure to orient each scene in the right direction, sew a G border to each short side of an F triangle. Press. Repeat for the remaining three F triangles. Press.

Step 5: Sew the four large triangles from Step 4 to the medallion square, making sure scenes are positioned correctly. Press.

Step 6: Leaving ¼ inch unsewn at the beginning and end of each seam, sew an I border to an H piece. Repeat three times. Sew an IR border to an HR piece. Repeat three times. Press.

Step 7: Sew four L strips around each K square. Press.

Step 8: Lay the quilt on the floor and position the HI strips along with the KL squares in the way in which they will be pieced. Make sure to orient the scenes so they are upright.

Step 9: Set aside the corner KL squares for now. Sew the HI borders to the four sides of the center side KL squares, beginning and ending each seam ¼ inch from the edge.

Step 10: Sew the Step 9 units to the sides of the quilt.

Step 11: Sew a KL square to each corner.

Step 12: Add the green J pieces to the spaces between the squares, pivoting to set in the strips at the corners. Press.

Step 13: Sew the four J1 pieces to the quilt corners. Press.

Adding the Borders

The border for the Yuletide Medallion Quilt is made up of 5-inch-wide strips of border print (piece M). Measure, cut, and miter the M border strips according to the directions in "Working with Border Prints" on page 77. Do not rely on your drawing measurements since the size of your quilt may have changed slightly. Sew the final borders to the quilt. Press.

Quilting and Finishing

Step 1: Prepare the quilt back and baste the quilt layers together according to the directions in "Quilt Backing" and "Layering and Basting" on page 88. Quilt as desired. I emphasized the scenes and border prints by quilting around important elements. I quilted the dark green holly print with a grid of parallel lines, spaced 1 inch apart. The light beige pieces were quilted with a crosshatch design of double lines ¼ inch apart. Those double lines were then spaced 1 inch apart.

Step 2: Cut bias binding and sew it to the quilt according to the directions in "Bias Binding" on page 91.

Christmas Star Quilt

Skill Level: Advanced
Size: Finished quilt is approximately 79 × 92 inches; finished block is 11 inches across when measured from parallel side to parallel side, or 13¼ inches after adding the 1⅛-inch border

The Christmas Star quilt looks much more complicated and time-consuming than it really is. There are only 14 fabrics and 9 blocks in the quilt, and each block contains just 24 pieces. Small diamonds and triangles are used to link rectangular segments of the large print that surrounds each block, but the remainder of the quilt is made up of fairly large pieces of fabric—resulting in less sewing than in most quilts of a comparable size.

The blocks in this quilt are made using a technique called soft-edge piecing, which is a combination of piecing and appliqué. (For a complete explanation of this technique, see *Soft-Edge Piecing* by Jinny Beyer.) In the original Christmas Star block, illustrated in **Diagram 1A,** the C points were cut and pieced in the traditional manner. In the soft-edge version, shown in **1B,** the points are "soft," meaning they are shapes cut from a fabric, then appliquéd to the background before the block is pieced.

Before beginning this quilt, it will be helpful for you to read "Working with Border Prints" on page 77, "Making and Using Templates" on page 74, and "Setting In Pieces" on pages 83 and 84. I also suggest that you read through this pattern a few times before beginning to familiarize yourself with the techniques used.

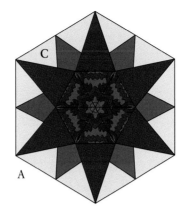

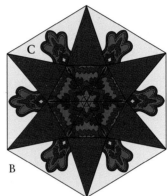

Diagram 1

You Will Need

⅛ yard each of nine different red prints (or ⅔ yard total if you use one red print; piece B)

1 yard of light beige print (piece C)

2½ yards of large-print multicolor fabric (pieces E, F, and G). To center a motif, purchase additional yardage to cut 48 full pieces and 12 partial pieces for the sides.*

(continued)

You Will Need—Continued

1 yard of large floral print (piece I). To center a motif within each diamond, count the number of times the motif repeats in your fabric, make sure there will be enough room to cut the diamonds, and adjust yardage accordingly. You will need 16 repeats to center a motif.

3¼ yards of dark purple fabric (pieces L, N, K, and middle border). If you do not mind having a seam in the border, 2⅛ yards will be sufficient.

Enough of a border print to yield the following (add ¼-inch seam allowances when cutting out your pieces):

16 yards of a ¾-inch (finished width) stripe (pieces M and O)

36 yards of a 1⅛-inch (finished width) stripe (pieces D, I, K, and inner border)

10½ yards of an 8-inch (finished width) stripe (outer border)

8 yards of a 4-inch (finished width) stripe (piece A)

1 queen-size (90 × 108-inch) quilt batting

5½ yards of fabric for backing

Approximately 2 yards of a fabric suitable for the "soft-edge" points in the star block—the fabric should have mirror-image motifs with relatively smooth edges that would be easy to appliqué (a Persian or paisley-type print would be suitable)

Template plastic

Permanent marker

*The quilt shown has these pieces centered. Even though centering uses more fabric, the centered motif creates a secondary design that adds to the complex look of the quilt.

Making Templates

Using the template plastic, make templates for pieces A through R as follows:

▲ A: Trace the full-size pattern on page 42.

▲ B: Trace the full-size pattern on page 43.

▲ C: Trace the full-size pattern on page 42.

▲ D: Trace the full-size pattern on page 42. Note that the pattern is only one-half of the template; flip your template plastic across the dashed line to complete an entire D piece.

▲ E: Trace the full-size pattern on page 44, following the instructions for piece E. Note that this template is reversed (ER) for some cuts.

▲ F: Draw a 4 × 7⅝-inch rectangle. Add a ¼-inch seam allowance to each side.

▲ G: Trace the full-size pattern on page 44, following the instructions for piece G. Note that this template is reversed (GR) for some cuts.

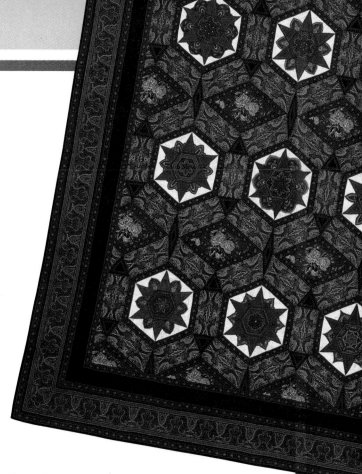

▲ H: Trace the full-size pattern on page 45, following the instructions for piece H. Note that the pattern is only one-half of the template; flip your template plastic to complete an entire H piece.

▲ I: Trace the full-size pattern on page 43. Note that this template is reversed (IR) for some cuts.

▲ J: Trace the full-size pattern on page 45, following the instructions for piece J. Note that this template is reversed (JR) for some cuts.

▲ K: Trace the full-size pattern on page 42. Note that this template is reversed (KR) for some cuts.

▲ L: Trace the full-size pattern on page 42, following the instructions for piece L.

▲ M: Trace the full-size pattern on page 43. Note that this template is reversed (MR) for some cuts.

▲ N: Trace the full-size pattern on page 43.

▲ O: Trace the full-size pattern on page 42.

▲ P: Trace the full-size pattern on page 45, following the instructions for piece P. Note that the pattern is only one-half of the template; flip your template plastic to complete an entire P piece.

▲ Q: Trace the full-size pattern on page 45, following the instructions for piece Q. Note that this template is reversed (QR) for some cuts.

▲ R: Trace the full-size pattern on page 42, following the instructions for piece R.

Cutting

From each of the nine red prints, cut:
6 B triangles

From the light beige print, cut:
54 C pieces

From the multicolored fabric, cut:
12 F rectangles (if you plan to center a portion of the design in the middle of each piece, center the design in the middle of template F, then match the right angle corners of templates E and F and mark the same design onto templates E and G)
18 E pieces
18 ER pieces
6 G pieces
6 GR pieces

From the large floral print, cut:

4 H diamonds (if you plan to center a portion of the design in the middle of each diamond, mark the design directly onto the template to use as a guide and be sure to mark the same design on the partial diamonds)

4 P half-diamonds

2 J partial diamonds

2 JR partial diamonds

2 Q pieces

2 QR pieces

From the dark purple fabric, cut:

1 yard (reserve for bias binding)

4 3-inch-wide strips (reserve for middle border)

6 L diamonds

6 R half-diamonds

24 N triangles

From the 4-inch-wide border print strip, cut:

9 sets of 6 identical A pieces. You will need a total of 54 triangles.

From the ³/₄-inch-wide border print strip, cut:

18 M pieces

18 MR pieces

72 O pieces

From the 1¹/₈-inch-wide border print strip, cut:

54 D pieces

18 I pieces

18 IR pieces

6 K pieces

6 KR pieces

From the fabric to be used for the soft-edge points, cut:

9 sets of 6 identical C pieces (blocks can be identical or varied). Follow the steps below for cutting the soft-edge points:

▲ Place template C on the soft-edge fabric and move it around until you find a pleasing motif to center within the template, as shown in **Diagram 2.**

▲ When you are satisfied with your selection, mark a portion of your design directly onto the template so that you will have a guide for positioning and cutting identical pieces. Cut along sides a and b, which represent the cutting lines for the "pieced" sides of the patch.

▲ Cut out the soft edge by following the design on the fabric, leaving approximately ⅛ inch of fabric past the design to allow a seam allowance for appliquéing, as shown in **Diagram 3.**

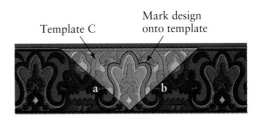

Diagram 2

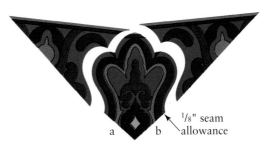

Diagram 3

▲ Repeat, cutting a total of six identical pieces per block. They will be appliquéd onto the beige print background pieces (C) before the block is pieced.

Piecing the Christmas Star Blocks

Step 1: Sew together three A triangles, as shown in **Diagram 4.** Repeat with three more identical triangles. Matching center points, sew both units together, as shown, to assemble the block's center hexagon.

Step 2: Sew a red B piece to an A triangle in the hexagon, beginning and ending the seam ¼ inch from each end, as indicated by the dots in **Diagram 5.** Sew with the border print facing you if there is a printed line on the piece that

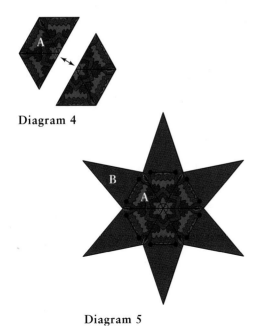

Diagram 4

Diagram 5

Making an Appliqué Stitch

To appliqué the soft-edge pieces, follow this technique. Use a standard-weight 100 percent cotton sewing thread and a thin needle. Try to make the stitches as invisible as possible. Using a single strand of thread cut no longer than 18 inches, bring the needle up from underneath, through the backing fabric, and right at the edge of the soft-edge piece. Next, put the needle down into the background piece directly below where the thread came out of the top of the piece. Bring the needle underneath and over approximately ¹⁄₁₆ inch, and come up through both layers into the edge of the top piece. Once again, go down into the background piece directly below the point where you came out into the top piece. Continue until the entire piece is appliquéd. Make sure as you sew that the stitch is on the *back* of the work and that only a small thread, if any, is visible on top.

will help guide your seam. Continue adding points until all six are joined to the center hexagon.

Step 3: Clip any inward curves or points on the soft-edge C pieces.

Step 4: Carefully turn under ⅛ inch around the soft-edge side of the piece (the part that will be appliquéd). Baste the edge under, leaving the knot on the right side. Do not make a knot at the end of the basting. Repeat, basting all six pieces.

Step 5: Place a soft-edge piece right-side-up on the right side of a beige C piece, aligning its a and b edges (see **Diagram 3** on the opposite page) with the corresponding edges on the beige piece. Pin in place, then baste the two together about ¼ inch from the edge. Leave the beginning knot on top and do not make a knot at the end of the basting. See **Diagram 6.**

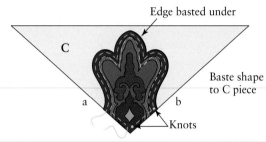

Diagram 6

Step 6: Appliqué the soft-edge piece to the beige piece, using a thread color that matches the color on the edge of the soft-edge fabric, as shown in **Diagram 7.** Take hold of the knots and pull out the basting threads.

Diagram 7

Step 7: Cut away the excess beige fabric from behind the appliqué piece to reduce bulk, leaving about ¼ inch inside the appliqué stitches.

Step 8: Sew the C triangles into the block, pivoting to set in the seam where each piece meets the center hexagon, as shown in **Diagram 8.**

Diagram 8

Step 9: Sew six D border strips around the outer edge of the star block, leaving ¼ inch of the long seams open on each end. Sew up the miters.

Step 10: Repeat Steps 1 through 9 to make a total of nine Christmas Star blocks.

Piecing the Large Diamonds

Step 1: Sew two I and two IR strips around each large H diamond, as shown in **Diagram 9,** beginning and ending each seam ¼ in from the end. Sew up the miters.

Step 2: Sew one I and one IR strip along the two short edges of each P half-diamond, ending each seam ¼ inch from the end where the two borders will meet. Sew up the miters. See **Diagram 10.**

Step 3: Sew I, IR, K, and KR strips around each J partial diamond used on the sides of the quilt, leaving ends free as before to allow miters to be joined. See **Diagram 11.**

Step 4: Sew KR and I strips to the Q corner pieces, as shown in **Diagram 12.** Sew K and IR strips to the QR corner pieces.

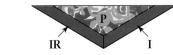

Diagram 9

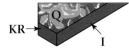

Diagram 10

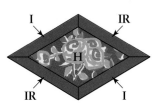

Diagram 11

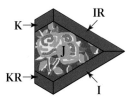

Diagram 12

Piecing the Small Triangles and Small Diamonds

Step 1: Sew three O strips around each N triangle, leaving ¼ inch unsewn at each seam end. Sew up the miters. See **Diagram 13.**

Step 2: Sew two M and two MR strips around each L diamond, leaving ¼ inch unsewn at each seam end. Sew up the miters. See **Diagram 14.**

Step 3: Sew one M and one MR strip onto the long edges of each of the six R half-diamonds, leaving ¼ inch unsewn at each seam end. Sew up the miters. See **Diagram 15.**

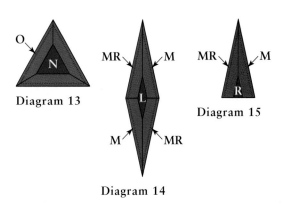

Diagram 13

Diagram 15

Diagram 14

Assembling the Quilt Top

There is no particularly easy way to assemble the top because there are a lot of set-in pieces that require pivoting. The method that requires the least amount of pivoting and has gentler angles is shown in the **Quilt Layout** on page 40.

Step 1: Lay all of the pieces out on the floor. If your components vary, rearrange the units until you are pleased with the balance.

Step 2: Sew the individual pieces together in diagonal "rows," as shown in the **Quilt Layout.** Leave ¼ inch unsewn at the end of each seam where

Quilt Layout

another unit of the quilt will be set in later. Sew all rows together, pivoting as necessary to set in seams.

Adding the Borders

The border for the Christmas Star quilt is made up of three different fabrics—a 1⅛-inch-wide border print, a 2½-inch-wide strip of dark purple, and an 8-inch-wide border print. These are all finished measurements. The width of the total finished border is 11⅝ inches. See "Working with Border Prints" on page 77 for complete information about sewing border strips to the quilt top.

Quilting and Finishing

Step 1: Prepare the quilt back and baste the quilt layers together according to the directions in "Quilt Backings" and "Layering and Basting" on page 88. Quilt as described below, referring to **Diagram 16.**

Step 2: To emphasize the kaleidoscope-like motifs that are formed where triangles meet, follow the fabric's design when quilting the hexagon centers of the stars. Outline quilt ¼ inch in from the edge around the red points of the stars.

Step 3: Quilt very close to the appliquéd edges of the soft-edge pieces, then in parallel lines ¼ inch apart in the beige areas. You may even want to quilt along some part of the fabric design within the soft-edge pieces.

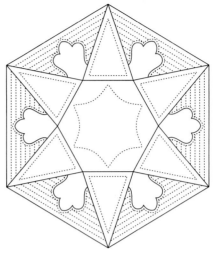

Diagram 16

Step 4: Quilt following the fabric's design in the large triangles, the borders, and the large rectangular pieces. Quilt in the ditch around the small borders.

Step 5: Quilt the purple border with parallel lines ½ inch apart, placed at the same angle as the N triangles.

Step 6: Cut bias binding and sew it to the quilt according to the directions in "Bias Binding" on page 91.

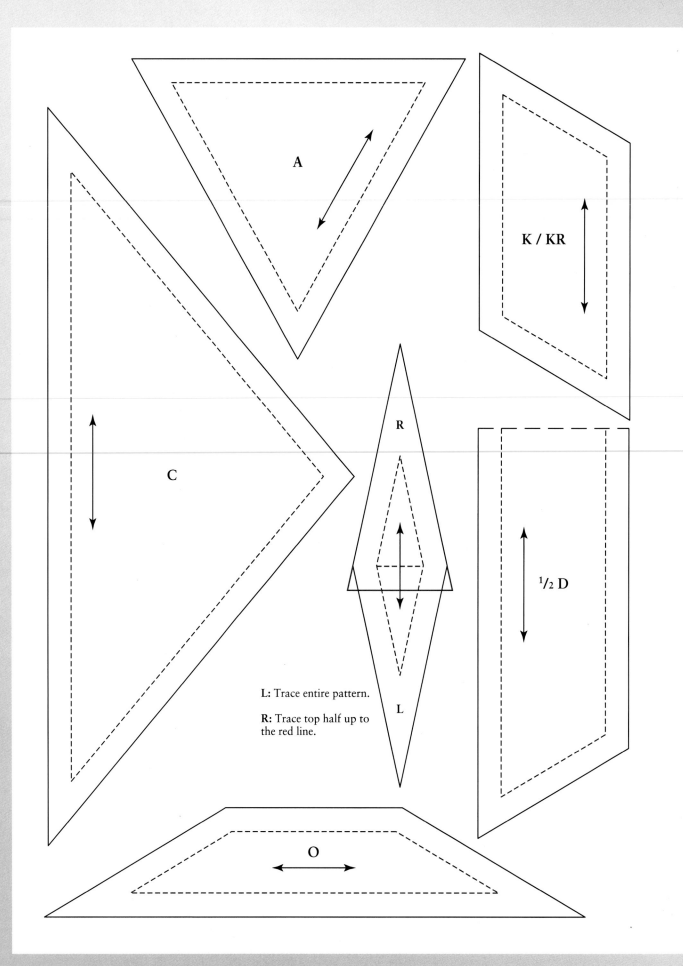

A

K / KR

C

R

½ D

L

L: Trace entire pattern.

R: Trace top half up to the red line.

O

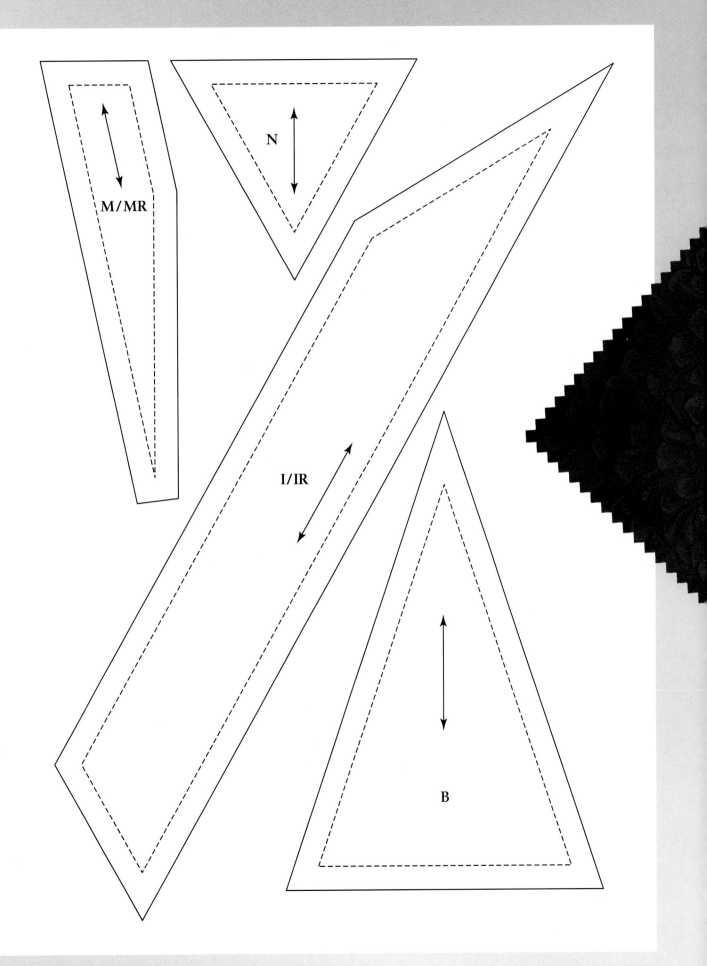

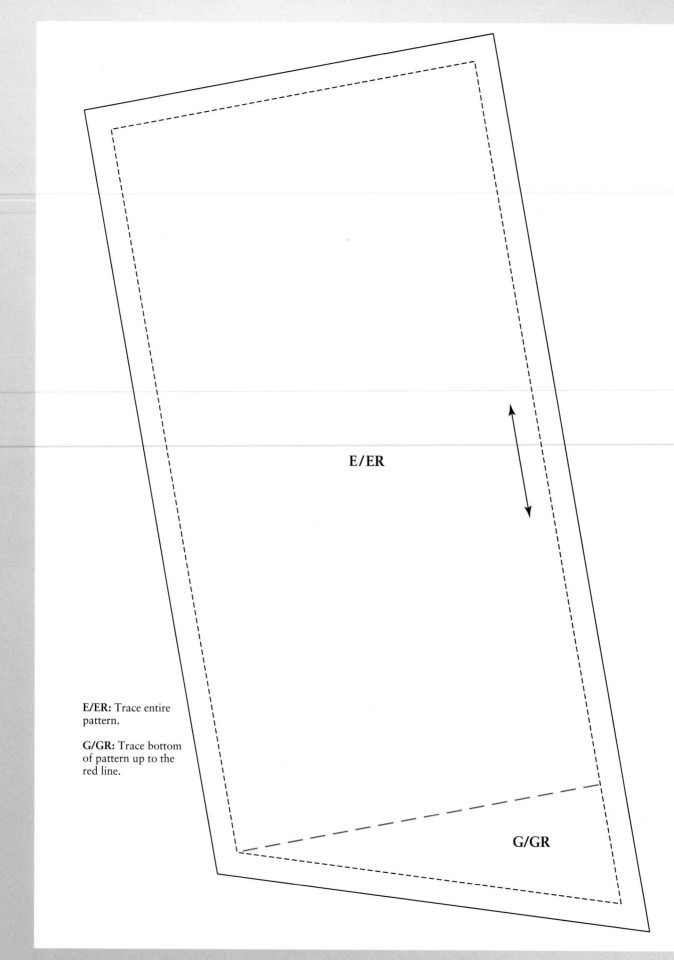

E/ER

E/ER: Trace entire pattern.

G/GR: Trace bottom of pattern up to the red line.

G/GR

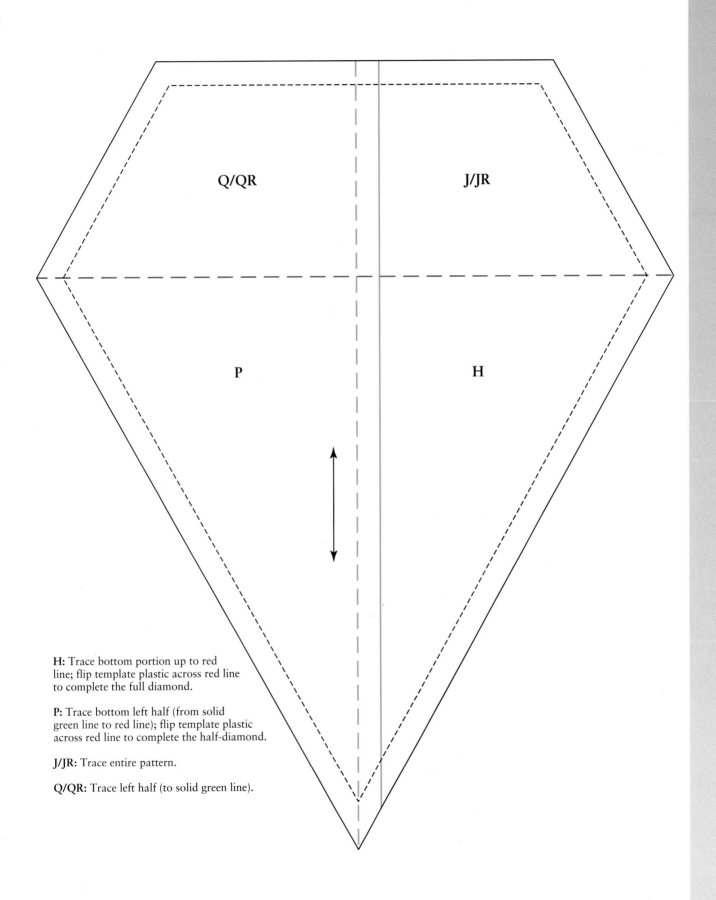

Q/QR

J/JR

P

H

H: Trace bottom portion up to red line; flip template plastic across red line to complete the full diamond.

P: Trace bottom left half (from solid green line to red line); flip template plastic across red line to complete the half-diamond.

J/JR: Trace entire pattern.

Q/QR: Trace left half (to solid green line).

$\mathcal{E}$nchanted Forest Quilt

Skill Level: Intermediate to Advanced

Size: Finished quilt is approximately 58 × 67 inches; finished tree is approximately $5\frac{1}{8} \times 7\frac{3}{4}$ inches

The design for this quilt developed when I was experimenting with tessellated, or interlocking, patterns. Each tree fits like a puzzle piece into the trees adjacent to it. The same basic design was used for the Enchanted Forest sweater on page 104. Each tree is made up of four different fabrics of the same color family, which are subtly shaded from dark to light from the bottom of the tree to the top. Overall, some trees are darker than others. Trees made up of green and teal fabrics form the "forest" and are all pointing upward. Trees made up of blues and purples form the "sky" and are all pointing downward.

You'll want to review "Making and Using Templates" on page 74 and "Working with Border Prints" on page 77 before beginning this quilt.

Color and Fabrics

The color palette for Enchanted Forest includes lime green, bright green, blue, and purple. Other colors were added as needed to shade those colors together. The final palette is illustrated on page 3. To accumulate fabrics, I searched through scraps I had on hand, then purchased a few more that fit within the palette. More than 60 different prints were used in the quilt. If you find at least 40 different fabrics, ⅛ yard of each will be more than enough to make the trees.

You Will Need

⅛ yard each of at least 40 different fabrics for the trees

Enough of a border print to yield the following:

   5½ yards of a 1-inch-wide (finished width) stripe (inner border)

   8 yards of a 7-inch-wide (finished width) stripe (outer border)

1½ yards of dark print (middle border)

1 yard of coordinating fabric for binding

62 × 72-inch piece of batting

4 yards of fabric for backing

Template plastic

Permanent marker

Making Templates

Using the template plastic, make Templates A through D from the full-size patterns on page 53. Also make Templates ½B, ½C, and ½D, which are used to make the half-trees on the edges of the quilt. (These templates are reversed to cut pieces for half-trees on the right edge of the quilt.) The half-division mark is a dashed red line running vertically through each pattern piece. Add a ¼-inch seam allowance around all sides of the half pieces. For the ½ templates, add the seam allowance on the *right* side of the red dashed sewing line; for the ½R templates, add it on the *left* side of the red dashed sewing line.

Cutting

To make a quilt similar to the one shown on page 46, you will need the following pieces:

▲ 36 complete green trees (A, AR, B, C, and D)

▲ 6 green trees with the top (D) left off

▲ 6 green tops (D)

▲ 30 complete blue trees (A, AR, B, C, and D)

▲ 5 blue trees with the top (D) left off

▲ 5 blue tops (D)

▲ 6 blue half-trees (A, ½B, ½C, and ½D)

▲ 6 blue half-trees Reverse (AR, ½BR, ½CR, and ½DR)

▲ 1 blue half-tree with the top (½D) left off

▲ 1 blue half-tree Reverse with the top (½DR) left off

▲ 1 blue half-tree top (½D)

▲ 1 blue half-tree top Reverse (½DR)

I suggest you cut out only half of the trees at this time. When these trees are complete, lay them all out on the floor to check color balance and contrast. You may find that everything is too light or too dark, or that you need more contrast between the green and blue trees. If so, adjust the problems when you select fabrics for the remaining trees.

Step 1: Sort your fabrics into two piles: one pile of green and teal prints, and the other of blue and purple prints.

Step 2: From the green pile, select four fabrics to make a tree. The fabrics should shade subtly from dark to light.

Step 3: To make one tree, cut an A and an AR from the darkest fabric. From the next darkest fabric cut a B piece, and from the next cut a C piece. Cut a D piece from the lightest fabric. If you like the combination of fabrics, repeat, cutting enough pieces to make two to four identical trees.

Step 4: Continue selecting fabrics for the trees and cutting them out, making some of the trees darker than others. Plan a few trees with your brightest fabric at the top, and one or two others with black at the bottom. Use very bright and very dark fabrics sparingly.

Step 5: Cut out pieces for the blue trees in the same manner.

Step 6: Use the ½ templates to cut out pieces for the half-trees on the left side of the quilt. Reverse the ½ templates to cut out pieces for the half-trees on the right side of the quilt.

Piecing the Trees

Step 1: Sew an A piece to an AR piece, stopping ¼ inch before the end of the seam, as indicated by the dot in **Diagram 1.**

Step 2: Fold piece B in half to find the center point along its wide base. Finger press or mark the center with a pin.

Step 3: With right sides together, pin and sew the base of the B piece to the sewn A unit, aligning the midpoint of the base with the seamline. The ends of piece B will extend past the sides of the A unit. Begin and end the seam ¼ inch from each edge of the A unit, as indicated by the dots in **Diagram 2.**

Step 4: Find the midpoint on the top of piece B and the bottom of piece C. Pin and sew the pieces together as in Step 3, beginning and ending the seam ¼ inch from each edge of the B unit, as indicated by the dots in **Diagram 3.**

Step 5: Find the midpoints of the top of piece C and the bottom of piece D and pin and sew them together, leaving the

ends of the seam unsewn as before, as shown in **Diagram 4.** Your finished unit should look like the one in **Diagram 5.**

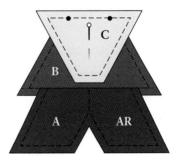

Diagram 3

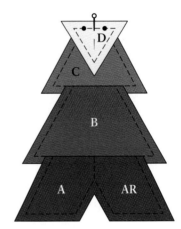

Diagram 4

Diagram 1

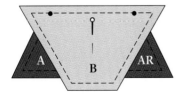

Diagram 2

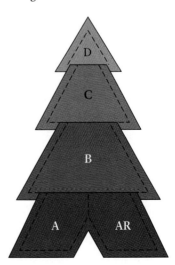

Diagram 5

Enchanted Forest Variation

If the thought of setting in all these trees has you a little nervous, try this easier-to-piece variation. Refer to the instructions for the quilt, making the changes described here.

Instead of using and shading 40 different fabrics, use only 3—a red print, a green print, and a coordinating large-scale paisley print. You will need 1½ yards each of the green and paisley fabrics and 2½ yards of the red. The borders, binding, and backing are the same as for the original quilt; choose fabrics that coordinate with your tree colors.

Cut out all your pieces—you will need 22 whole green trees, 6 green trees without tops, 2 each green ½ tree and ½ tree Reverse, 5 green tops, and 1 each green ½D and ½DR; 22 paisley whole trees, 2 each paisley ½ tree and ½ tree Reverse, 1 each paisley ½ tree and ½ tree Reverse without tops, and 6 paisley tops; 22 whole red trees, and 2 each red ½ tree and ½ tree Reverse.

Lay out the quilt pieces as follows. Bottom row: Green trees point up and paisley trees point down. Second row: Red trees point up and green trees point down. Third row: Paisley trees point up and red trees point down. Repeat the rows in this order for a total of 7 rows. Fill in the bottom row with the paisley tree tops and the top row with the green tree tops.

Sew the quilt top together in rows. This saves you from having to set in all the pieces; the only pieces you will need to set in are the tree tops between the A and AR pieces. Set these in before joining the A/AR pieces into rows.

Step 6: Sew the remaining trees in the same manner.

Step 7: Sew together half-trees by aligning their straight edges, using pieces A, ½B, ½C, and ½D for six trees for the left side of the quilt, and pieces AR, ½BR, ½CR, and ½DR for six trees on the right side. Make one more blue half tree for each side, omitting the D top. End all seams ¼ inch from the edge of the lower piece, as indicated by the dots in **Diagram 6.**

Step 8: Press the seams in each tree toward its base.

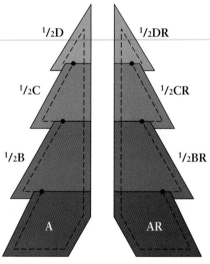

Diagram 6

Assembling the Quilt Top

Step 1: Use the floor or a design wall to arrange the completed trees, with the green and teal trees pointing up and the blue and purple ones pointing down. Fill in the sides, top, and bottom with the half-trees and topless trees.

Step 2: Place the six green D tree tops across the bottom row to fill in the gaps between the A/AR bases of the green trees, making sure there is enough contrast between the bottom of the tree and the top you are fitting into it.

Step 3: Place the five blue D tree tops across the top row to fill in the gaps between the A/AR bases of the blue trees, making sure there is enough contrast between the bottom of the tree and the top you are fitting into it.

Step 4: Place a blue ½D at the top left corner of the quilt, and a blue ½DR at the top right corner.

Step 5: When you are satisfied with the layout of the trees, pick them up in horizontal rows, as illustrated in the **Quilt Layout.** To retain their position in the quilt, stack trees in each row one on top of the other from the left to the right, then pin each group together. Write "Row 1," "Row 2," "Row 3," and so forth on seven scraps of paper

and attach one of these labels to each row. This step will help keep the trees organized as you are sewing them together.

Step 6: Piece the trees in each row together, then join the rows. As you are sewing, pivot the edges of the trees to fit them together. This may sound difficult, but as long as you left ¼ inch free at the seam ends, there should be no problem in joining them.

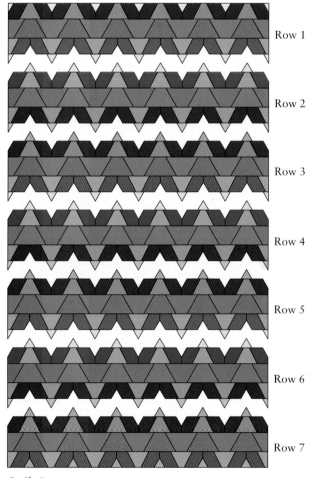

Row 1

Row 2

Row 3

Row 4

Row 5

Row 6

Row 7

Quilt Layout

Adding the Borders

The border for the Enchanted Forest quilt is made up of three different fabrics—a 1-inch-wide strip of border print, a 1¾-inch-wide strip of dark purple, and a 7-inch-wide strip of border print. These are all *finished* measurements; a ¼-inch seam allowance must be added to each side when you cut them out. The width of the total finished border is 9¾ inches.

If you find a border print that looks good all in one piece, you won't necessarily need to sew three different strips together. Don't worry if the border prints you find for your quilt are not exactly the same widths as the ones I used. The main consideration is to have a nice balance between the total width of the border in comparison to the size of the quilt. As long as the fabrics you choose produce a finished border width of 9 to 10 inches, you will have a well-proportioned border. See "Working with Border Prints" on page 77 for complete information on cutting strips for borders and sewing them to the quilt top.

Quilting and Finishing

Step 1: Prepare the backing and baste the quilt layers together according to the directions in "Quilt Backings" and "Layering and Basting" on page 88. Quilt as desired. I outline quilted each tree piece ¼ inch in from the seamline, and followed the design on the border

fabric. The 1¾-inch-wide dark purple strip was quilted using the **Border Quilting Template** on this page. Position the template within the strip, as shown in **Diagram 7,** and mark around it with tailor's chalk. Move approximately ½ inch down the strip, reverse the position of the template, and mark again. Continue marking in this manner until you have surrounded the strip with the motif.

Step 2: Cut the bias binding and sew it to the quilt according to the directions in "Bias Binding" on page 91.

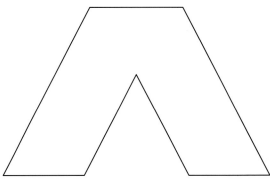

Border Quilting Template

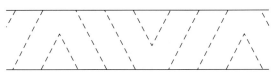

Diagram 7

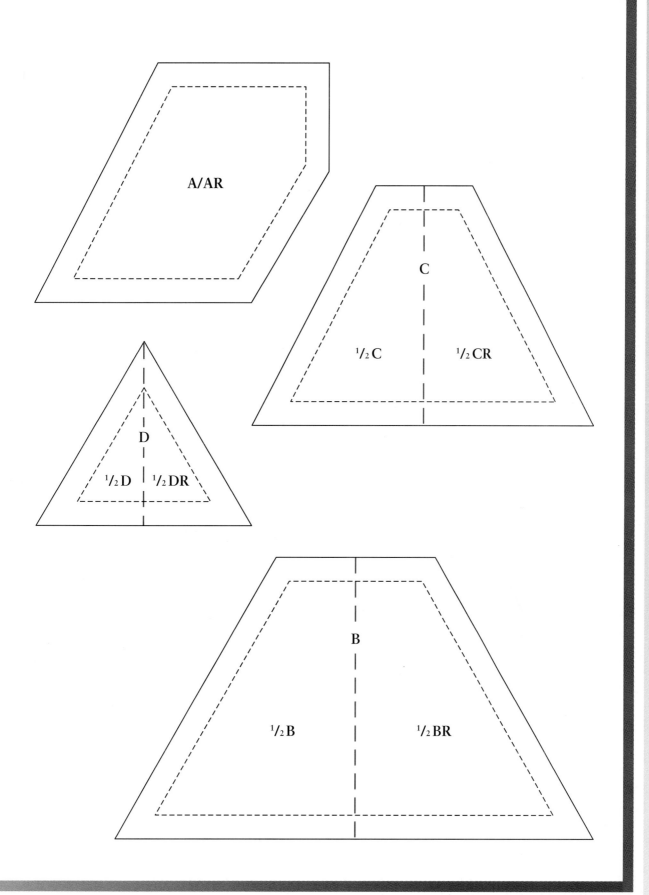

A/AR

C

½ C   ½ CR

D

½ D | ½ DR

B

½ B   ½ BR

$\mathcal{P}$ineapple Quilt

Skill Level: Intermediate to Advanced

Size: Finished quilt is approximately 71 inches square; finished block is 11¼ inches

The pineapple has long been a symbol of friendship and welcome, so it seems fitting to make a Pineapple Quilt from Christmas colors to use during the holidays. This is a perfect quilt to make if you want to experiment with using many different fabrics. The glow that can be achieved by subtly shading patches from light to dark, bright to dull, and medium to dark is very exciting.

While my preference is to piece by hand, pineapple blocks can be pieced quickly and accurately with the foundation piecing method described here. For general information about this technique, and for help in choosing the foundation material best suited for your project, be sure to read "Foundation Basics" on page 75 and "Making and Using Templates" on page 74.

Color and Fabrics

The fabrics for this quilt were selected from the same palette of Christmas colors described on page 6, with the exception of the addition of darker browns. There are eight groups of fabric in the pineapple block, each containing eight different subtly shaded fabrics. **Diagram 1** on page 56 shows the patch positions and the placement of the various groups.

A total of 66 different fabrics were used in the quilt—64 for the narrow strips in the block, a bright red for the center square, and a border print for the outer block triangles and the inner and outer borders. The green print used in the middle border is a repeat of one of the fabrics in the block. For more flexibility in fabric placement, purchase ¼ yard of each of the 64 fabrics required for block strips.

The following list explains how each group is blended. Group A is at the top center of the block, with Groups B through H following in a clockwise direction (when you sew on the reverse side of the foundation).

▲ Group A: shades from medium green to dark green to black

▲ Group B: shades from dark fuchsia to red to brown to gold

▲ Group C: shades from light green to very dark green

▲ Group D: shades from dark eggplant to fuchsia to red

▲ Group E: shades from teal to dark green to black

▲ Group F: shades from dark brown to burgundy to tan

▲ Group G: shades from light green to medium green to dark green

▲ Group H: shades from dark brown to rust to red

You Will Need

¼ yard each of fabrics for patches 1 through 64

⅛ yard of bright red fabric for center squares

2½ yards of a border print fabric that contains at least four repeats of both a 3¾-inch (finished width) stripe (outer border) and a 2-inch (finished width) stripe (inner border)

3¾ yards of border print fabric for block corner triangles

2 yards of dark green print for the middle border*

1 yard of dark red, green, or black fabric for binding (select a fabric that blends with the final stripe on the border print)

79-inch square piece of batting

4½ yards of fabric for backing

Template plastic

Permanent marker

*This can be a repeat of one of the fabrics used in the block. If you don't mind having a seam in the middle of border strips, 1 yard will be sufficient.

Making the Foundations and Templates

S t e p   1 : Trace the **Pineapple Foundation Template** on page 60 four times and carefully join the pieces to make the whole-block pattern. Transfer the

group and piece numbers, shown in **Diagram 1**, to your complete template. Repeat for a total of 25 foundation templates. If you prefer to hand piece, make templates by adding ¼-inch seam allowances to each numbered piece.

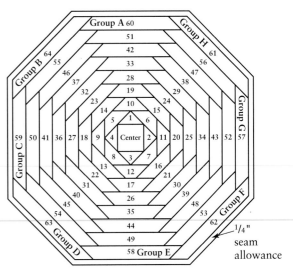

Diagram 1

S t e p   2 : For Template A, draft a 3-inch square. Cut the square in half diagonally. Add a ¼-inch seam allowance to each side of the resulting triangle.

Cutting

S t e p   1 : Arrange the fabrics in each of the eight shaded groups in the order in which they appear in the block, shading each group from the center of the block outward. Line up the groups by group name. Cut a 1¼-inch-wide strip from each fabric, across the width of the yardage.

S t e p   2 : Cut 25 1¾-inch center squares from the bright red fabric.

Step 3: From the border print, cut 100 corner triangles using Template A. Align the template so that the design in all the triangles is exactly the same. See "Working with Border Prints" on page 77 for more information.

Piecing a Block

This block is pieced in a circular direction, from the center outward. As you sew, remember that the printed side of the foundation is a *mirror image* of the finished block. Since each narrow strip in this block is different, it would be helpful to use a piecing system to ensure that all strips are sewn in the correct position. One way to do this is to use an adhesive label to mark each long strip of fabric with its corresponding foundation number. That way, there will be no question as to where each strip should be sewn. To mark your strips, refer to the foundation for the strip numbers within each group. If you've arranged and cut your fabrics in order, it should be easy to mark the strips.

It would be difficult to organize 64 long strips next to your sewing machine. Instead, select strips for positions 1 through 6, and lay them out in order, along with the 1¼-inch red center squares. Although the instructions given here instruct you to add strips to one block at a time, you can use assembly-line piecing to sew a center square and strip 1 to all 25 foundations, then add all strip 2s, followed by all strip 3s, and so on.

Add the remaining strips in the same manner, working with just the number of strips at your sewing table that you are comfortable with. Cut additional strips as necessary, adjusting their width to suit your sewing style, as discussed in "Foundation Basics" on page 75.

Step 1: Place a 1¾-inch red square *right side up* on the reverse (unprinted) side of a foundation, completely covering the center square, as shown in **Diagram 2.** Hold the patch in place with a straight pin, a piece of tape, or a dab of glue stick. Check the square's placement by holding the foundation up to the light, printed side facing you. The shadow of the fabric square should overlap the printed square by approximately ¼ inch on each side. **Note:** This is the only piece in the block that is placed right side up. All remaining pieces are positioned right side down for sewing.

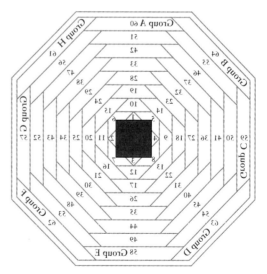

Diagram 2

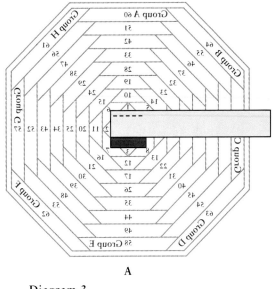

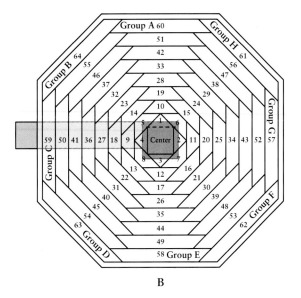

A   B

Diagram 3

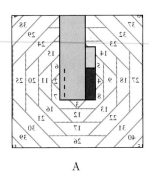

Trim away "ear"

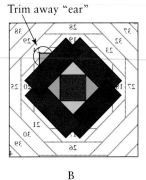

A   B   A   B

Diagram 4   **Diagram 5**

S t e p 2 : Place one end of strip 1 (from Group A) right side down on top of the red fabric square, matching the cut edges, as shown in **Diagram 3A.** Holding the strip in place, flip the foundation over and stitch directly on the line separating strip 1 from the center square, beginning and ending the seam approximately ⅛ inch past either side of the line, as shown in **3B.**

S t e p 3 : Turn the template over and cut off the excess tail of fabric, just past the line of stitching. Trim the seam allowance if necessary to reduce bulk.

Flip strip 1 right side up and finger press firmly in place. Check the strip's alignment. All edges of the piece should overlap the unsewn printed lines that surround strip 1 by approximately ¼ inch so that a stable seam allowance will be formed when adjoining pieces are added.

S t e p 4 : Place one end of strip 2 (from Group G) right side down on top of the square and strip 1, as shown in **Diagram 4A.** Holding the strip in place, flip the foundation over and sew on the line that separates strip 2 from the center square, beginning and ending stitching approximately ⅛ inch past the printed line as before. Repeat Step 3 above. Your unit should resemble **Diagram 4B.**

Step 5: Add strip 3 (from Group E) and strip 4 (from Group C) in the same manner.

Step 6: Sew strips 5 through 8 to the foundation in exactly the same way, but aligned at a 45 degree angle to the first row, as shown in **Diagram 5A.** After sewing each piece, trim away excess seam allowance and the "ears" created by the seam allowances in the previous row. If you do not trim the excess fabric each time, your quilt will become very bulky and virtually impossible to quilt.

After adding, trimming, and finger-pressing strips 5 through 8, the reverse side of your foundation should resemble **Diagram 5B.**

Step 7: Continue adding strips in numerical order, taking care to match each strip to its correct position on the foundation. Always trim excess seam allowances, flip each piece right side up, and finger press firmly in place before adding the next piece. When the block is complete, press it lightly and remove excess fabric by cutting directly on the outermost line of the foundation. This line includes a ¼-inch seam allowance.

Step 8: Sew an A border print triangle to the angled strip at each of the block's four corners, as shown in **Diagram 6.** Press the block. Do not remove the foundation.

Diagram 6

Assembling the Quilt Top

Step 1: Stack five pineapple blocks on top of each other, matching the color groupings and orienting them all so that Group A is at the top. Retaining their matched positions, sew the five blocks together to create the first row (see the **Quilt Layout** on page 61).

Step 2: Match the color groups in five more blocks, and stack them with Group E at the top. Retaining their matched positions, sew the five blocks together to create the second row. Sew rows 1 and 2 together, making sure they are oriented correctly.

Step 3: Assemble Row 3 in the same manner as you assembled Row 1. Assemble Row 4 in the same manner as you assembled Row 2. Join the two new rows.

Step 4: Assemble Row 5 as you did Row 1. Join all the rows together to complete the quilt top.

Adding the Borders

The border for the Pineapple Quilt is made up of two different fabrics—a 2-inch (finished width) border print stripe for the inner border, a 1¾-inch (finished width) dark green fabric for the middle border, and a 3¾-inch (finished width) border print stripe for the outer border. Add ¼-inch seam allowances to each long edge of each border when cutting. I prefer to add a darker piece of fabric between the two border strips because I feel it adds dimension to the overall quilt design, but if you find a wide enough border print that looks good with the quilt, you won't need to piece three strips together. See "Working with Border Prints" on page 77 for complete directions for cutting strips for borders and sewing them to the quilt top. If you are using removable foundations, tear them away after adding the border.

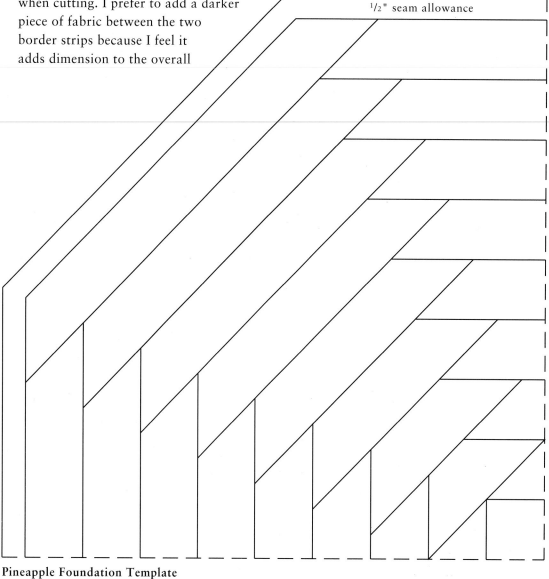

½" seam allowance

Pineapple Foundation Template

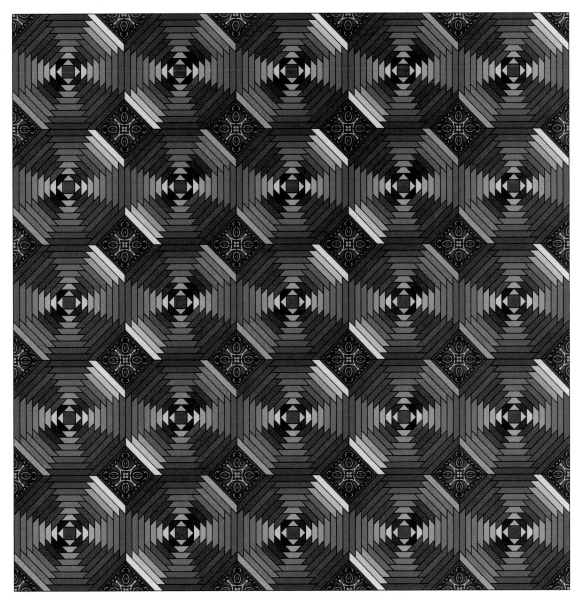

Quilt Layout

Quilting and Finishing

Step 1: Prepare the quilt back and baste the quilt layers together according to the directions in "Quilt Backings" and "Layering and Basting" on page 88. Quilt as desired. For the pineapple it is often easiest to quilt down the middle of each strip of fabric, or "in the ditch" at either side of each strip. For the border print, I like to follow the design on the fabric. The dark green border strip could be quilted with parallel lines spaced ½ to 1 inch apart, running perpendicular to the strip.

Step 2: Cut bias binding and sew it to the quilt according to the directions in "Bias Binding" on page 91.

Odd Fellows Quilt

Amish quilts always radiate a simple elegance, and this one is no exception. The stark green and black fabrics create a wonderful backdrop for any holiday decor. I always bring this quilt out at Christmas to display with our other holiday decorations.

I prefer hand piecing (and I don't use a rotary cutter), but rotary cutting techniques combined with foundation piecing methods will help you assemble this quilt quickly and accurately. For more information about both methods, see "Foundation Basics" on page 75 and "Rotary Cutter and Cutting Mat" on page 72.

Color and Fabrics

This antique Amish quilt is made from black and gray-green cotton sateen. If you cannot locate sateens, try one of the many marble-like fabrics, which will add a subtle sheen to the quilt and provide more texture than solid colors.

You Will Need

3½ yards of green fabric (including 1 yard for binding)

11 yards of black fabric (including fabric for backing)

77 × 90-inch piece of batting

Making the Foundations

Use the **Flying Geese Foundation Template** on page 69 to prepare 80 foundations. For help in choosing foundation material, see "Foundation Basics" on page 75.

Cutting

Before cutting fabric, reserve 1 yard of green for the bias binding and 5¼ yards of black for the backing. If you are hand piecing the quilt, make templates by adding ¼-inch seam allowances to pieces 1 and 3 on page 69.

From the green fabric, cut:

2 3 × 60-inch top and bottom inner border strips

2 3 × 72-inch side inner border strips

20 2⅜-inch-wide strips across the remaining width of yardage, which should be about 30 inches wide. Use your rotary cutter and ruler to cut 12 2⅜-inch squares from each strip. Cut each square in half once diagonally to make a total of 480 triangles.

4 2⅞-inch-wide strips across the width the remaining yardage. Cut 10 2⅞-inch squares from each strip. Cut each square in half once diagonally to make a total of 80 triangles.

From the black fabric, cut:

2 8½ × 81-inch top and bottom outer border strips

2 8½ × 90-inch side outer border strips

20 3-inch squares. Cut these from the narrow fabric that is left after cutting the border strips.

9 2⅞-inch-wide strips of fabric across the full width of your yardage. Cut 14 2⅞-inch squares from each strip. Cut each square in half once diagonally to make a total of 252 triangles. You will use 240 of these triangles in the quilt.

4 6⅝-inch strips. Cut 20 6⅝-inch squares from these strips. Cut each square in half *twice* diagonally to make a total of 80 triangles.

1 7¾-inch strip. Cut 2 7¾-inch squares from this strip. Cut each square in half once diagonally to make a total of 4 corner triangles.

2 13⅝-inch strips. Cut 4 13⅝-inch squares from these strips. Cut each square in half *twice* diagonally to make a total of 16 triangles. You will use 14 of these setting triangles in the quilt.

3 9¼-inch strips. Cut 12 9¼-inch filler squares from these strips.

Piecing the Odd Fellows Blocks

The four Flying Geese bands in each block are pieced on separate foundations. The center square and side triangles, which were quick-cut with your rotary equipment, are added to the geese bands to complete the block.

S t e p   1 : Place a 2⅞-inch green triangle and a 2⅞-inch black triangle right sides together on the reverse (unprinted) side of a foundation with the green on the underside, as shown in **Diagram 1**. Make sure the triangles cover the piece 1 space entirely, then hold them in place with a straight pin. Check for correct placement by holding the foundation up to the light with the printed side facing you. The shadow of the triangles should overlap the seam between pieces 1 and 2 by approximately ¼ inch, and should be beyond the outermost lines of the foundation.

S t e p   2 : Turn the foundation over and stitch directly on the line separating pieces 1 and 2, beginning and ending approximately ⅛ inch past the ends of the line, as shown in **Diagram 2**. Turn the foundation over, trim excess bulk from seam, then flip the black triangle right side up. Finger press the black triangle to hold it in place. Hold the front of the foundation up to the light to make sure the black triangle extends past the lines separating piece 2 from pieces 3 and 4. The back side of your foundation should resemble **Diagram 3**.

S t e p   3 : To add piece 3, center the long edge of a 2⅜-inch green triangle right side down along the right edge of the black triangle, as shown in **Diagram 4**. (If your black triangle overlaps the line between the two pieces by more than ¼ inch, back the green triangle away from the edge a bit.) Hold the triangles together and turn to the right side of the foundation. Sew on the line separating pieces 2 and 3, again beginning and ending your seam approximately

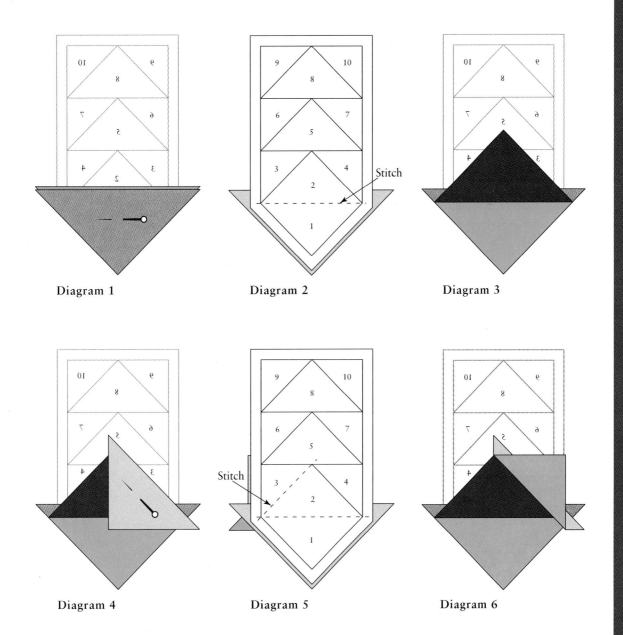

Diagram 1

Diagram 2

Stitch

Diagram 3

Diagram 4

Stitch

Diagram 5

Diagram 6

⅛ inch beyond the ends of the line. The printed side of your foundation should look like **Diagram 5.**

Step 4: Turn to the back side of your foundation and trim excess seam allowance in the new seam. Flip the green triangle right side up. Hold the unit up to the light to make sure the triangle's top edge overlaps the line

separating it from piece 5 by approximately ¼ inch. The triangle's right edge should extend beyond the outer drawn line on the foundation. Do not trim excess fabric from the outer edges of the foundation. The edges will be trimmed to size later. Finger press in place. The reverse side of your foundation should resemble **Diagram 6.**

Step 5: Add piece 4 in the same manner, centering the green triangle's long edge along the unsewn edge of piece 2, as shown in **Diagram 7.** Check the seam position again (the line between pieces 2 and 4), and adjust the green triangle's long edge if necessary to avoid sewing a too-large seam. Pin the pieces in place and sew on the line separating pieces 2 and 4. Turn to the reverse side of the foundation, trim the

seam allowance, and finger press the green triangle in place. Your Flying Geese unit should now resemble **Diagram 8.**

Step 6: To add piece 5, align a 2⅞-inch black triangle to the patches, as shown in **Diagram 9.** The triangle's long edge should overlap the horizontal line dividing piece 5 from pieces 2, 3, and 4 by approximately ¼ inch. Sew on the line in the same manner as for all other

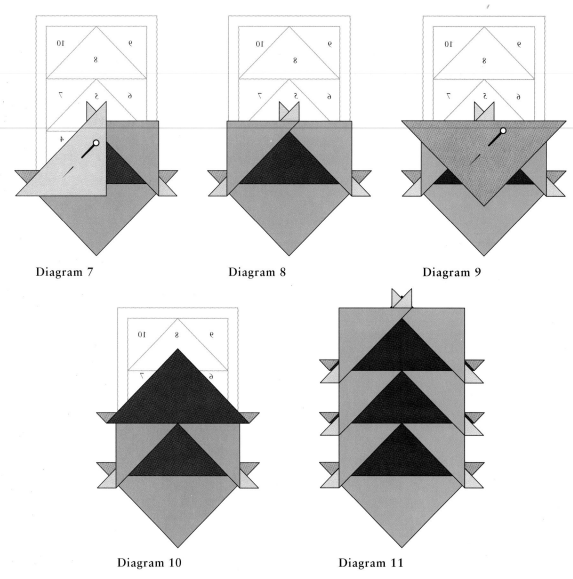

Diagram 7 Diagram 8 Diagram 9

Diagram 10 Diagram 11

lines. Turn to the back side of the foundation, trim excess seam allowance, and finger press piece 5 in place. The reverse side of your foundation should resemble **Diagram 10.**

S t e p 7 : Continue adding the remaining triangles to the foundation in the same manner. When all pieces are in place, as shown in **Diagram 11,** press the unit lightly; do not use steam if you are using paper foundations (the paper will curl). Use a scissors or rotary cutter to trim the excess fabric from the unit. Cut directly on the outermost line of the foundation, which includes ¼-inch seam allowances on all sides. Leave removable foundations in place for now.

S t e p 8 : Repeat Steps 1 through 7 to make a total of 80 Flying Geese units (four per block).

S t e p 9 : Gather four Flying Geese units, four black triangles cut from 6½-inch squares, and one 3-inch black square. Sew the block together, as shown in the **Block Assembly Diagram.** Press seam allowances toward the solid black areas.

S t e p 1 0 : Repeat Step 9 to assemble all 20 Odd Fellows blocks.

Block Assembly Diagram

Assembling the Quilt Top

S t e p 1 : Lay out the 20 quilt blocks, 12 filler squares, 14 setting triangles, and 4 corner triangles in diagonal rows, as shown in the **Quilt Assembly Diagram** on page 68.

S t e p 2 : Sew the pieces in each row together, pressing seam allowances toward the black filler units.

S t e p 3 : Sew the rows together, matching seam intersections carefully. Press.

Adding the Borders

The border for the Odd Fellows quilt is made up of two different fabrics, 2½-inch-wide green strips and 8-inch-wide black strips, making the width of the total finished border 11½ inches. Use the precut 3-inch-wide green strips to make the inner border, and the 8½-inch-wide black strips to make the outer border. See "Border Prints

Quilt Assembly Diagram

Framing a Square Block or Quilt" on page 78 for complete information about cutting, mitering, and sewing border strips to the quilt top. If you are using removable foundations, tear them away after adding the borders.

You will notice in the photograph on page 62 that the border pieces are not mitered. Most Amish quilts do not have mitered corners, so if you want your quilt to be "authentic," you may want to attach the border strips the way they are in the photo. My preference is to miter the corners of borders.

Quilting and Finishing

Step 1: Prepare the quilt back and baste the quilt layers together according to the directions in "Quilt Backings" and "Layering and Basting" on page 88. Quilt as desired. A feathered wreath was quilted in the large black squares, a curved design was quilted in the green inner border, and a feathered plume appears in the black outer border. Diagonal lines were quilted across the Odd Fellows block. Another option for quilting the block would be to outline quilt each patch ¼ inch inside the seamline.

Step 2: Cut the bias binding and sew it to the quilt according to the directions in "Bias Binding" on page 91.

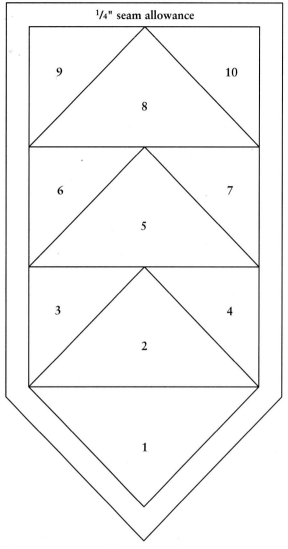

Flying Geese Foundation Template

Odd Fellows Variation

One of the most exciting aspects of quiltmaking is that two people can begin a project using the same pattern but end up with two completely different-looking quilts. My variation of the Odd Fellows quilt, which makes use of border prints, looks very different from the Amish version on page 62 made from the same pattern. This variation finishes at approximately 67½ × 80 inches. Before beginning this quilt, be sure to read "Working with Border Prints" on page 77 and "Foundation Basics" on page 75.

Making Templates

Make the following templates:

▲ A: Draft a 2½-inch square. Cut the square in half *twice* diagonally. Add a ¼-inch seam allowance to each side of one triangle.

▲ B: Draft a 6¾-inch square. Add a ¼-inch seam allowance to each side.

▲ C: Draft a 1¾ × 9¼-inch rectangle. Fold the ends up to meet the sides and form the 45 degree miters. Do *not* add seam allowances to this template.

▲ D: Draft a 6¾-inch square. Cut the square in half diagonally. Add a ¼-inch seam allowance to each side of one triangle.

▲ E: Draft a 6¾-inch square. Cut the square in half *twice* diagonally. Add a ¼-inch seam allowance to each side of one triangle.

Piecing the Quilt

Step 1: Refer to the Fabric and Cutting Chart on the opposite page and cut the pieces for the quilt.

Step 2: Refer to "Foundation Basics" on page 75 and use the **Flying Geese Foundation Template** on page 69 to prepare a total of 80 foundations.

Step 3: Follow Steps 1 through 10 under "Piecing the Odd Fellows Blocks" on page 64, making the following changes:

▲ Substitute a border print A and a red triangle in Step 1. In all subsequent Flying Geese piecing, substitute red for black; green remains green. Refer to the **Finished Block** diagram.

▲ Substitute green 6½-inch triangles for black in Step 9. Substitute a pieced square for the 3-inch black square; make the square from four border print As. Refer to the **Piecing Diagram.**

▲ Assemble 12 Setting Blocks, 14 Setting Triangles, and 4 Corner Triangles, referring to the diagrams on the opposite page.

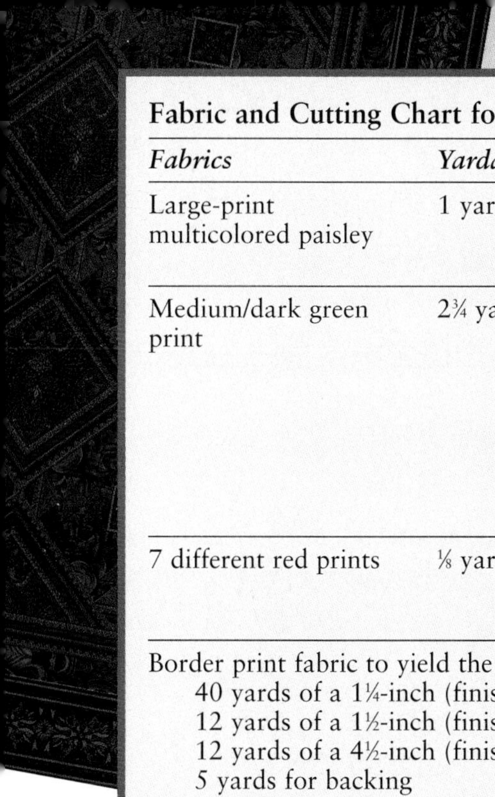

Fabric and Cutting Chart for Odd Fellows Variation Quilt

Fabrics	Yardage	Pieces	Quantity	Comments
Large-print multicolored paisley	1 yard	B	12	If you plan to center a motif in each block, you may need more yardage.
		D	14	
		E	4	
Medium/dark green print	2¾ yards	2½" × 80"	4	Middle border; do not add seam allowances
		2⅜" × 2⅜"	240	Flying Geese; cut each square in half diagonally for a total of 480 triangles
		6⅝" × 6⅝"	40	Block setting triangles; cut each square in half diagonally for a total of 80 triangles
7 different red prints	⅛ yard each	2⅞" × 2⅞"	120	Flying Geese; cut each square in half diagonally for a total of 240 triangles

Border print fabric to yield the following:
    40 yards of a 1¼-inch (finished width) stripe for Piece C and inner border
    12 yards of a 1½-inch (finished width) stripe for Piece A; cut 2 sets of 80 matching As
    12 yards of a 4½-inch (finished width) stripe for outer border
    5 yards for backing
    1 yard of coordinating fabric for binding

Supplies

▲ Foundation material   ▲ 76 × 88-inch piece of batting   ▲ Template plastic   ▲ Permanent marker

Finished Block

Finished Setting Block

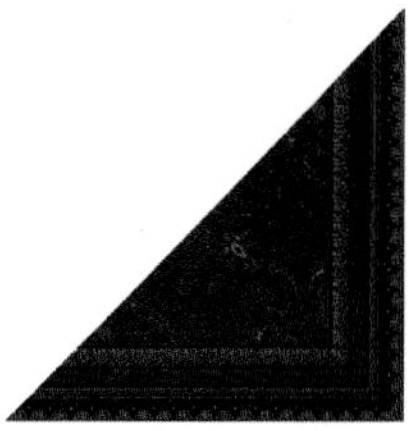

Finished Setting Triangle

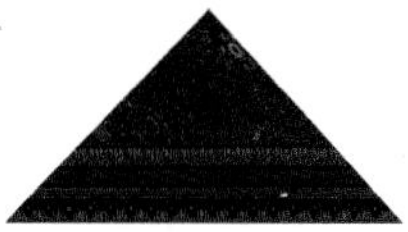

Finished Corner Triangle

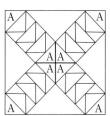

Piecing Diagram

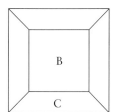

Piecing Diagram

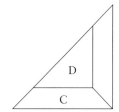

Piecing Diagram

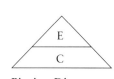

Piecing Diagram

Step 4: Follow Steps 1 through 3 in "Assembling the Quilt Top" on page 67.

Step 5: Add the inner, middle, and outer borders to your quilt, mitering the corners as you go. Refer to "Working with Border Prints" on page 77 for more information.

Step 6: Follow the directions in "Quilt Backings" and "Layering and Basting" on page 88. Quilt as desired.

Step 7: Prepare and attach bias binding, following the directions in "Bias Binding" on page 91.

Quilting Tips and Techniques

Use this section as a refresher course in basic quiltmaking.

Quiltmaker's Basic Supply List

Here are the items you should have on hand before beginning a quilting project.

Iron and Ironing Board: Careful pressing is essential for accurate cutting and piecing. To save steps and increase efficiency, keep your ironing board and iron close to your sewing area. See "Pressing Basics" on page 85 for more information.

Mirrors: A pair of small mirrors (approximately 4 × 4 inches) is useful for working with border prints (see page 81). Mirror pairs are available at quilt shops, or look for mirrored bathroom tiles at the hardware store.

Needles: Quiltmakers generally use three types of needles—sharps, betweens, and darners. **Sharps** are long, thin needles that many quiltmakers use for hand piecing and appliqué. **Betweens** are short, sturdy needles that

most people use for quilting; I also use these needles for piecing. **Darners** are long, thicker needles that make it easier to baste the layers of the quilt together. Hand sewing needles come in a variety of sizes—the higher the number, the smaller the needle. Experiment with different sizes and types of needles to see which feel most comfortable in your hand and which are the easiest to manipulate through the fabric.

Rotary Cutter and Cutting Mat: Many quiltmakers have found the rotary cutter and mat to be invaluable tools for providing greater speed and accuracy in cutting fabric. There are a variety of cutters available, all with slightly different handle styles and safety latches. Always use a special mat with a rotary cutter. The mat protects the work surface and helps grip the fabric, helping to keep it from shifting as you cut. An all-purpose size is 18 × 24 inches, but purchase the largest mat practical for your sewing area.

Rulers and Right Angles: Rigid, see-through plastic rulers are used with rotary cutters. A 6 × 24-inch ruler is

a good, standard size. For the most versatility, be sure it has 45 and 60 degree angle markings. For general patchwork and quilting, it is helpful to have a variety of sizes of rulers and right angles on hand. A 6-inch see-through ruler and a small right triangle are invaluable when working with small projects. A 12- or 14-inch square ruler is helpful for making sure blocks are square.

Scissors: When cutting fabric with scissors, use a sharp pair of dressmaker's shears that you reserve only for fabric. You should also have a pair of small, sharp embroidery scissors for trimming threads and seam allowances, and a pair of general scissors for cutting paper and template plastic.

Sewing Machine: Keep your machine clean and in good working order. Always have extra needles on hand.

Straight Pins: Do not use pins that have become burred or rusted; they may leave marks in your fabric. Long (1½-inch) pins with glass or plastic heads are easy to work with, especially when pinning through layers.

Template Material:
Templates are rigid master patterns used to mark patchwork and appliqué shapes on fabric. Some people use cardboard, but since I like to work with border prints and other printed fabrics and often center motifs in the middle of a piece, I prefer using thin, semi-transparent plastic, available in sheets at quilt and craft shops.

Thimbles: I use a thimble for both piecing and quilting, but find I need a different type of thimble for each of those activities. For hand piecing, my preference is to use a thimble with a flat rim. For quilting, I use a rolled-rim thimble. Look for a thimble that fits the finger you use to push the needle.

Thread: I prefer to use only 100 percent cotton thread for both patchwork and quilting. As a rule, your thread type should be compatible with the type of fabric you are using. I like to use a heavy-duty thread for hand piecing, a 50-weight thread for hand appliqué, and a quilting thread for quilting.

When sewing a dark fabric to a light one, the stitches will be less noticeable if you match the thread color to the darker fabric. When making a multicolor scrap quilt, I like to use two or three different medium colored "blender" threads that go with most of the fabrics I am using. For machine quilting, some quilters use a very fine, clear or smoke nylon thread through the needle, and cotton thread in the bobbin.

Selecting and Preparing Fabrics

The traditional fabric choice for quilts is 100 percent cotton. It handles well, is easy to care for, presses easily, and frays less than synthetic blends. The yardages in this book are generous estimates based on 44- to 45-inch-wide fabrics. It's a good idea to always purchase a bit more fabric than necessary to compensate for occasional cutting errors.

To preserve color and avoid bleeding, always wash your fabrics and quilts in *cold* water. If you have purchased a dark or bright colored fabric that you suspect might bleed, "set" the color by soaking it for about an hour in very cold water (ice cubes added to the water will

help.) If a lot of dye bleeds into the water, wash the fabric with detergent in cold water and put a scrap of white fabric in with it to see if it becomes contaminated with any of the dye. If no dye bleeds onto the white, it should be safe to use the fabric in your quilt. If the white fabric becomes discolored, then you will have to be careful where you use the fabric.

After washing, put your fabric in a dryer on a medium setting. To keep wrinkles under control, remove the fabric from the dryer while it is still slightly damp and press it immediately. *Never* use a very hot iron on your fabrics. The dye in the majority of today's printed fabrics has a latex base, just like paint. If the dye gets too hot it can actually melt, making the colors appear to bleed onto adjacent areas.

Washing and Drying the Finished Quilt

The most common causes for fabric bleeding are washing the quilt in warm or hot water, using detergents with phosphates, and allowing excess water to remain in the quilt. The safest way to launder a quilt is to place it in the washing machine and soak it for about 10 minutes in cold water. Add a phosphate-free detergent and allow the machine to agitate on the gentle cycle for about 5 minutes. Spin, rinse with cold water, and spin again to remove all excess water from the quilt. To dry the quilt, lay it flat on several layers of towels. *Do not put the quilt in the dryer.*

Making and Using Templates

To make templates, place semi-transparent template plastic directly over the book page, carefully trace the patterns onto the plastic, and cut them out with scissors. Most patterns have a dashed line to indicate the sewing line and a solid line (¼ inch outside the sewing line) to indicate the cutting line. Use a permanent marker to record all identification letters and lines that appear on each template, as well as the size and name of the block and the number of pieces needed. Always check your templates against the printed pattern for accuracy.

Using templates with the seam allowance added is the method I prefer, as it allows

me to make a block very quickly—I can cut two or three pieces at a time (unless I am centering a motif from the print). Pinning the pieces together is also faster and easier, since it is simply a matter of lining up the raw edges. Sewing pieces together is faster, too, because it is not necessary to constantly check the back of the work to see if you are sewing on the line.

Eventually, you will learn to eyeball the ¼-inch seam allowance, but if you need a guide for sewing, try this technique.

Trace the dashed sewing line onto the template, then put small holes in the template at intervals along the sewing line, as shown in **Diagram 1.** Make holes where seam allowances intersect at corners, then add as many to each side as you think are necessary to provide a good sewing guide. To

make the holes, use a ⅛-inch hole punch, a #1 knitting needle, or a tapestry needle (for the latter two, place the template onto a folded washcloth or towel and poke through the plastic).

Marking and Sewing

Most patterns in this book have an arrow indicating where the template should be placed in regard to the grain line of the fabric. Wherever possible, place the arrow along the lengthwise or crosswise grain of the fabric. In general, when making a patchwork block, try to place the fabric's straight-of-grain along the outer edges of the block, as shown in **Diagram 2.** Note that even though the two triangles marked A and B are the same size and will use the same template, they are cut differently so the grain will fall on the outside edges of the block. Template C will have

Diagram 1

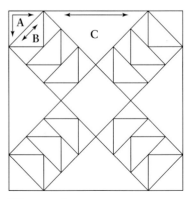

Diagram 2

the straight-of-grain along the long side of the triangle.

There are a variety of markers suitable for transferring a template's shape onto fabric. For light fabric, use a pencil. For dark prints, tailor's chalk works well. Many people are shocked to learn that I use a good-quality ballpoint pen to mark around templates, but let me clarify my method. My templates *always* include a seam allowance. After marking around the template, I cut the fabric just within the marked line, so the pen line is actually cut away from each piece. I like to use a pen because its mark is visible on most fabrics and it glides easily, without tugging or distorting. I would never use a ballpoint pen to mark the sewing line because the pen line would remain on the patch and would be stitched into the quilt.

Since I often center motifs within a piece and need to see the right side of my fabric, I place the template right side *up* on the front of the fabric for marking. If you mark on the wrong side of fabric, place the template right side *down* to mark around it.

To sew two pieces together, pin them, aligning their edges. Place the corresponding template on top of the piece facing you and, if you need a sewing guide, put small pencil dots directly through the holes. Sew dot-to-dot. This method will save a lot of time because you do not have to mark the sewing line on each piece, only on the piece facing you as you sew. If pieces have been cut with the exact ¼ inch added, you can get very accurate seam allowances with this method.

Most of the patterns in this book are printed full-size so no drafting is required. Some patterns that contain larger templates, equilateral triangles, or simple geometric shapes have instructions for drafting.

Foundation Basics

Nineteenth-century quilters often relied on foundation piecing to accurately assemble their pineapple and log cabin blocks.

With this technique, a block is drawn full-size on a foundation material. It can be a permanent foundation, such as muslin, which remains in the quilt forever, or a removable foundation, such as paper, which is pulled away from the block after the quilt top is assembled. There are advantages and disadvantages to each type of foundation.

Permanent Foundations

Muslin is the most commonly used permanent foundation, but sheer interfacing and flannel are two alternatives. A permanent foundation will add another layer to the quilt and may make it more difficult to needle. Using sheer interfacing will lessen the problem.

A permanent foundation often eliminates the need for batting. It also stabilizes patches permanently, making careful placement of fabric grain less important.

Permanent foundations made of woven fabrics, such as muslin, sometimes become distorted as you work, both from handling and from the loft that is created as seams are sewn. Using a tightly woven fabric often helps correct the problem.

Removable Foundations

Paper is the most commonly used removable foundation. Blank newsprint is a good choice. It is sturdy enough to remain intact while handling, but pulls away easily when the quilt is complete. It is also available in pads from 9 × 12 inches up to poster size, so it works well for blocks that are too

large to draft onto a piece of standard 8½ × 11-inch paper. For smaller blocks, try inexpensive copier paper, onionskin, or tracing paper. Keep in mind that it can be time-consuming to remove paper foundations, especially if pieces are very small.

Other removable foundation options include vanishing muslin—a loosely woven fabric that deteriorates and falls away when ironed—and the tear-away material designed to be used as a stabilizer for machine embroidery.

Since it will be pulled away, a removable foundation does not add an extra layer of fabric to your quilt. And papers remain rigid as you work, so they are unlikely to distort the block. But because the foundations will not remain in place to permanently stabilize fabric, you must be careful about cutting and positioning patches on grain.

Duplicating Foundations

You must make an exact copy of the foundation template for each individual block (or partial block if a combination of techniques is used, as in the Odd Fellows projects). Photocopies are fine, but make sure they are accurate reproductions before using them. An alternative is to use a hot-iron transfer pen to draw the full-size block onto tracing paper. The image can usually be ironed onto foundation material five or six times. Retrace over the original transfer for additional ironings, being careful to mark exactly on the existing lines. A transfer pen can be used on both fabric and paper foundations, but do a test first to be sure it will work on your chosen material.

If the printed lines are not visible from the back side of your foundation, place it against a window or light box and lightly pencil in the lines to make fabric placement easier. Be sure to use a permanent marker on permanent foundations.

Sewing Fabric to the Foundations

The only seam allowance included on a foundation template is the one around the outer perimeter of the design. **Diagram 3** illustrates the foundation used for the pineapple block in the quilt on page 54. Position fabric on the back side of the foundation, and sew on the printed side. The numbers indicate the order in which you sew patches to the foundation. The lines separating patches are seamlines. You create seam allowances when you overlap patches on the back side of the foundation.

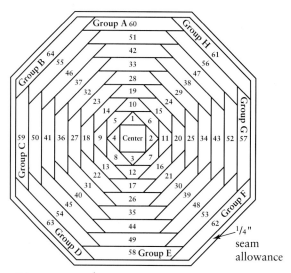

Diagram 3

The strip widths and triangle sizes given within each pattern are recommendations. Most piece sizes given are slightly larger than you will actually need. It is usually easier for a beginner to use slightly oversize pieces but, if you like, you can scale back the strip width once you are familiar with the foundation piecing method.

Since the fabric will be sewn to the *back* of the foundation, the finished block will always be a *mirror image* of the template. Jotting color names or codes for your fabrics onto the foundation before sewing will help you keep track of their position in the block. For blocks that use many types of fabrics, such as the pineapple project, a mock-up is helpful. A simple mock-up can be made by gluing a small strip of the correct fabric within each patch area on the reverse side of the foundation. Keep the example next to you as you sew for quick reference and to ensure accuracy.

For maximum strength and stability and minimum distortion, fabric strips should be cut along the crosswise or lengthwise grain. Ideally, the straight-of-grain should be parallel with the outer perimeter of your block.

Although preparing foundations requires additional time as well as added materials, there are also important benefits. You save cutting time by not having to cut individual pieces to exact sizes and, in many cases, you will work with strips that are simply trimmed as you go, which means the quilt construction moves along quickly.

Working with Border Prints

Border prints are fabrics that have repeated, decorative stripes printed lengthwise on the cloth. Most of the sewing projects in this book contain border prints somewhere in the design.

Buying Border Prints

Border print fabrics usually have two to four different decorative stripes repeated across the width of the cloth. If a pattern calls for 5 yards of a 4-inch stripe from a border print, you do *not* need to buy 5 yards of fabric. Count how many times the stripe you want to use repeats, and buy enough fabric to give you 5 yards of that particular stripe. For instance, if the stripe repeats

five times across the width, you only need to buy 1 yard of fabric. If the stripe repeats three times, 1¾ yards would be enough.

When using a border print in the border of your quilt, avoid the need to piece the border by purchasing enough yardage to run the length of the quilt. If you have extra fabric left over, use it in other projects.

Border Print Borders

When using border prints to frame a block or quilt, in order to have a balanced design, you must always center a motif from the border print in the middle of the side of the block or quilt. If two pieces will join together at an angle, such as the ends of a mitered border, the two must

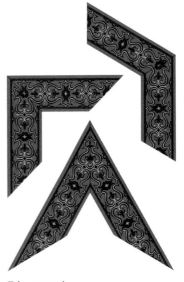

Diagram 4

be cut so that the design on one of the pieces is a mirror image of the design on the other piece. Note the three angles in **Diagram 4** on page 77, all cut from border prints, and how the designs "match" because a motif is centered in the middle of each piece, and because one of the pieces is the exact mirror image of the other.

Border Prints Framing a Square Block or Quilt

When I surround a block or quilt with a border print, I usually cut the strips and miter their edges *before* sewing them to the unit. Two things are essential—a proper fit, and cutting the design on each strip so that it matches at all four corners. To achieve a match, you must center the same motif in the border print at the midpoint of each side of the quilt. If the strip is centered, the design will stop at the same point on both ends; if all four borders are identical, the design will flow around the corners. Here is how to get a perfect match.

Note: The instructions given here for adding border prints to quilts are the same ones you would use for adding strips of regular fabrics. For fabric designs with large, bold prints, such as paisleys and florals with symmetrical designs, you would still want to center motifs so the corners match. With small-print fabric designs, matching is unnecessary, but mitering and sewing procedures are the same.

Step 1: Measure accurately for a proper fit. The best place to measure is across the *center* of the piece, rather than at its edge, since seam joints and bias can cause the edge to stretch. If you measure across the quilt edge, you will invariably cut the border too long, causing the quilt to "ruffle" at the edge.

Step 2: Place the quilt or block on a table or the floor. I like to put it on a carpet to keep it from shifting around. Cut a length of border print, making sure it is long enough to accommodate the corner miters and any adjustment you may need for centering the design.

To determine how much extra fabric you need for mi-

tering, measure the width of the border strip you are using. Add twice that width to the length of the strip required. Then measure the distance of the design repeat in the border and add that amount to the strip to allow for centering (this is usually between 1 and 8 inches, depending on the design).

Once your strip of border print is cut, lay it across the center of the block or quilt, centering a motif from the border at the center of the quilt, as shown in **Diagram 5.**

Step 3: Place a 45 degree triangle along the border print, at the edge of the block or quilt (this will allow for a seam allowance on the border print), and cut the miter, as shown in **Diagram 6A.**

Step 4: Carefully lift the end you just cut and fold it exactly at the center of the unit being framed, laying it

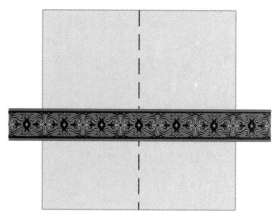

Diagram 5

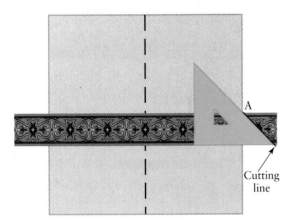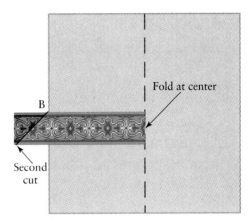

A   Cutting line

B   Second cut

Fold at center

Diagram 6

face down on top of the un-mitered end, as shown in **Diagram 6B.** Be sure you don't disturb the strip's alignment with the quilt or block center. Use the first miter as a guide to cut the second miter, making sure the design at the new cut is an exact mirror image of the first cut. Do not be tempted to use your triangle to make the second cut. Since the outer edges may be slightly stretched or distorted, simply cutting a miter at the oppo-site edge may not result in a mirror image of the first cut.

S t e p   5 : Use the first mitered border strip as a cut-ting guide for the others, laying it along the remaining lengths of border print. Cut three more identical pieces. Match the design carefully at all miters.

S t e p   6 : With right sides together, pin the center of a border strip to the center of one side of the block or quilt, then match and pin the ends. Find the midway points be-tween the pins and pin again. Continue pinning evenly across the width of the block or quilt, easing in any full-ness that may occur at the edge. Sew the border to the block or quilt, beginning and ending the seam ¼ inch from either end. Repeat with the remaining border strips.

S t e p   7 : Sew the miters with a ¼-inch seam al-lowance. Press. Repeat all steps to sew additional bor-ders to the quilt.

Border Prints Framing a Rectangular Quilt

Many quilts are longer than they are wide, and most motifs will not match at the corners of a rectangular quilt using the previous method.

Instead, two border strips are pieced together on each long side of the quilt to make the match possible.

S t e p   1 : Follow steps 1 through 5 on the opposite page for cutting borders, but measure and cut borders for the two short sides of the quilt only.

S t e p   2 : Lay one of the mitered pieces on top of a strip of border print that is more than half the length of the long side of the quilt. Use the mitered piece as a guide to cut a miter near one end of the strip, matching designs exactly at the miter. Lay the newly mitered strip along the length of the quilt, across the center, with the miter posi-tioned at the edge. Smooth out the strip and cut it off straight across, ¼ inch be-yond the center of the quilt, as shown in **Diagram 7** on page 80.

Border Tricks

When you're making a quilt with more than one border, try this: Measure and cut each set of strips. Place them around the quilt as they will be positioned. Matching center points, sew together the border strips for each side of the quilt, then add them as units to the quilt sides. Sew up the miters last, carefully matching any patterns.

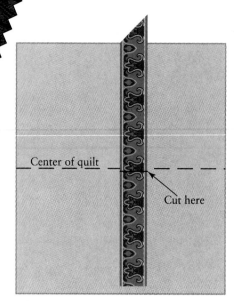
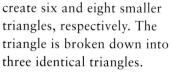

Center of quilt

Cut here

Diagram 7

Step 3: Cut a second strip identical to the strip cut in Step 2, then cut two more strips that are mirror images of those strips. Position one of each strip type along each longer side of the quilt.

Step 4: With right sides facing, sew the strips together across the unmitered edge to make one long border. Sew the borders to the quilt using the same method described in Step 6 on page 79. Repeat all steps to sew additional borders to the quilt.

Using Border Prints within Shapes or Blocks

Border shapes can be used in squares, hexagons, octagons, and triangles. To use a border print, I break each of those shapes down into smaller, equal-sized triangles and then cut the number of triangles I need from the border print to recreate the original size of the piece.

Look at the shapes in **Diagram 8.** The square is divided diagonally from corner to corner to create four smaller triangles. Straight lines connect all the angles of the hexagon and octagon to create six and eight smaller triangles, respectively. The triangle is broken down into three identical triangles.

Follow these steps to use a border print within one of the shapes in **Diagram 8.** The following example illustrates the hexagon.

Step 1: Make a template of the small triangle within the hexagon. Add a ¼-inch seam allowance to all sides.

Step 2: To help you center your design within the template, draw a line on the template that divides it in half from the center peak to the base.

Step 3: Center the template on a symmetrical motif in the border print. Position the template on the fabric so that a line from the border print falls on what will be the outside edge of the shape, indicated with an

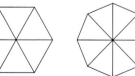

Diagram 8

arrow in **Diagram 9.** This line will then act as a frame for the finished shape. Cut out the first triangle.

Diagram 9

Step 4: Using a permanent marker, draw a portion of the design from the fabric directly onto the template. This mark will act as a guide for the remaining pieces, which must be exactly the same as the first one.

Step 5: Reposition the template on the border print until you match the design you marked on the template. Cut five more identical pieces for the hexagon and sew them together, as shown in **Diagram 8.**

Piecing Basics

The standard seam allowance for piecing is ¼ inch. For precise patchwork where the pieces always meet exactly where they should, you must be vigilant about accurate seam allowances.

When hand sewing, you may want to mark the sewing line on the piece facing you as you sew (see "Making and Using Templates" on page 74). When machine piecing, use a ¼-inch foot, or mark a guide on the throat plate of your machine.

When assembling pieced blocks, keep in mind these basic rules: Combine smaller pieces to make larger units, join larger units into rows or sections, and join sections to complete blocks. If you follow these rules, you should be able to build most blocks using only straight seams. Setting-in pieces at an angle should only be done when necessary. (See "Setting in Pieces by Hand" on page 83 and "Setting In Pieces by Machine" on page 84 for more information.)

Whether you are sewing by hand or machine, begin by laying out the pieces for the block right side up, as shown in the project diagrams. For quilts with multiple blocks, cut out and piece a sample block first to make sure your fabrics work well together and that you have cut the pieces accurately.

Hand Piecing

Be sure to add an exact ¼-inch seam allowance around all sides of your template

It's All Done with Mirrors

No matter where you place your template on the border print fabric, you will have an interesting kaleidoscopic effect as long as each triangle in the shape is centered on a motif in the fabric. But you may want to know exactly what the finished shape will look like before you cut the pieces from your fabric. This is where a pair of square mirrors will come in handy. Center the triangle template on some motif in the fabric, with the edge of the triangle that will eventually form the outer edge of the complete shape on the straight grain of the print. (I like to have a straight line from the border print design fall just within the seamline on that edge.) Place the two mirrors along the sewing lines of the template on the two sides of the shape that will be pieced together to re-form the shape. Gently remove the template without disturbing the placement of the mirrors. The image in the mirrors will show what the complete shape will look like.

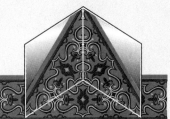

(unless otherwise indicated, seam allowances have been added to templates in this book), and to mark and cut the pieces accurately. Join the pieces by placing them right sides together, matching the raw edges, and securing them with pins. If you need a guide for your sewing line, place your cutting template on top of the piece facing you and mark dots through the small holes you punched in the sewing line. Use a single thread approximately 18 inches long, in a neutral color to blend with both pieces, or in a color to match the darker of the two pieces. Sew with a running stitch from dot to dot, using an accurate ¼-inch seam allowance, as shown in **Diagram 10.** Sew edge to edge, unless you are sewing together pieces that will require another piece to be set in later. For those, end your seam where it intersects another seamline. (See "Setting In Pieces by Hand" on the opposite page .) Take a backstitch every four or five

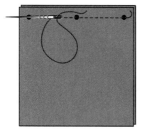

Diagram 10

stitches to reinforce and strengthen the seam. Secure the corners with an extra backstitch.

When you cross the seam allowances of previously joined units, leave the allowances free rather than stitching them down. Make a backstitch just before you cross, slip the needle through the seam allowance at the base of the seam, make a backstitch just after you cross, and then resume stitching the seam, as shown in **Diagram 11.** When your block is finished, press the seam allowances toward the darker fabric.

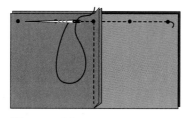

Diagram 11

Getting four points to meet: When sewing four pieces together, such as four squares, first sew them together in pairs of two. Press the seams in opposite directions, as shown in **Diagram 12,** so that when the two are positioned to be sewn together with right sides facing each other, their seam allowances will abut. Put a pin directly through the seam allowances and begin sewing

from one side. As you approach the center seam, carefully pull the pin out and make sure that the two seams are still butted next to each other.

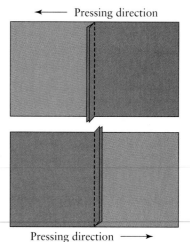

← Pressing direction

Pressing direction →

Diagram 12

Continue sewing, leaving the seam allowances free, as shown in **Diagram 11.**

Getting six points to meet: When sewing six points together, such as the six triangles at the center of the Christmas Star Quilt on page 32, sew straight lines whenever possible.

To make the first half, lay out three of the pieces. With right sides together, place and pin Piece A on top of piece B. Starting at the outside edge and sewing toward the center, sew just to the point where the seam allowance would cross, and take a small backstitch. Do not break the thread. Take the pin out, open up the seam, and gently finger press the seam toward the right, as shown in **Diagram 13.**

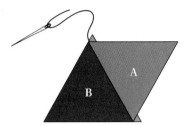

Diagram 13

Place piece C on top of piece B with right sides together. You should be able to feel the ridge from the seam allowance with your thumbnail. Carefully bring the needle directly through the end of the last stitch you made and through the base of the seam allowance. Do a backstitch along the ridge, then continue sewing this last piece to the edge. Check to make sure that the point on piece B is securely bounded by pieces A and C, as shown in **Diagram 14.** If this point is not neat and sharp at this stage, it will not be neat and sharp when the

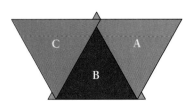

Diagram 14

two halves are sewn together.

Sew the remaining three pieces in the same manner to make the second half. Place the two halves together with right sides facing each other, making sure that the points of the B pieces in each half meet exactly. Place a pin through the points. Sew from the edge toward the center. As you reach the center, carefully pull out the pin and move the seam allowances away from the needle's path. Sew up to the seamline, making sure you do not catch any of the seams in the stitches. Backstitch at the center, then pass the needle through the base of the seam. Pull the seams out of the way again, do another backstitch right next to the seam, and continue sewing across.

Getting eight points to meet: Sewing eight points together is exactly like sewing six, with the exception that there is one more piece per side. Lay out four pieces and sew the first three together exactly as described in the previous section. Make a knot and cut the thread. Open the first three pieces out, right sides up, and finger press the seams toward the right. Pin piece D on top of piece C. Using a new thread, bring the needle

all the way from piece A, at the exact point where the first seam ended at the center, through the bases of the seams, and onto piece D, as shown in **Diagram 15.**

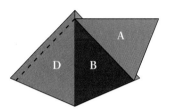

Diagram 15

Do a backstitch along the edge of the seams and continue sewing the last piece, working from the center toward the edge. Sew the remaining four triangles together the same way, then sew the halves together using the same technique as for matching six points.

Setting In Pieces by Hand

Not all patchwork patterns can be assembled with continuous straight seams. Examples in this book include the Boxing Day Quilt on page 12 and the Christmas Star Quilt on page 32. Setting-in calls for precise stitching as you insert pieces into angles, as shown on page 84.

Step 1: Place the template on the piece to be set in. Make holes at the intersections of seam allowances and mark through the holes onto the fabric. Do the same on the adjacent pieces.

Step 2: Pin the piece to be set in right sides together on one of the pieces adjacent to it. Beginning at the outside mark you made and working toward the set-in corner, stitch along the seamline, as shown in **Diagram 16**. Remove pins as you sew, stopping at your second mark. Backstitch, but do not cut the thread.

Step 3: Pivot the other adjacent piece and pin it to the other side of the set-in piece, as shown in **Diagram 17**. Continue sewing the

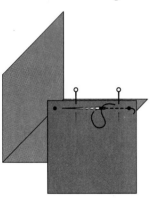

Diagram 16

Diagram 17

seam from the corner out, stopping at the mark along this sewing line.

Machine Piecing

For machine piecing, cut pieces with seam allowances included. Before sewing a block, sew a test seam to make sure you are taking accurate ¼-inch seams, since even ¹⁄₁₆ inch of inaccuracy can result in a block that is not the right size, especially when it is compounded over many seams. Adjust your machine to sew 10 to 12 stitches per inch. Select a neutral-color thread that blends well with the fabrics you are using.

Join the pieces by sewing from raw edge to raw edge (unless pieces will be set in). Press the seams before crossing them with other seams. Since seam allowances will be stitched down when crossed with another seam, you will need to think about the direction in which you want them to lie. Whenever possible, press seam allowances toward the darker of the two fabrics to prevent them from shadowing through lighter ones. See "Pressing Basics" on the opposite page.

Setting In Pieces by Machine

Step 1: Mark seam intersections at the corners of all pieces involved in the setting-in process. Pin the piece to

be set in to one of the adjacent pieces with right sides together, matching the dots. Beginning and ending the seam with a backstitch, sew from the raw edge toward the set-in corner, and stop stitching exactly on the marked corner dot, as shown in **Diagram 18** on the opposite page. Don't allow any stitching to extend into the set-in seam allowance.

Step 2: Remove the work from the sewing machine and realign the pieces to sew the set-in piece to the other adjacent piece, matching the dots and pinning the pieces together.

Step 3: Sew from the corner dot to the outside edge to complete the seam, as shown in **Diagram 19** on the opposite page. Backstitch at the beginning and end. Press seams toward the set-in piece.

Assembly-Line Piecing

For many quilts, you will sew a large number of the same size or shape pieces together to create units. For a bed-size quilt, this can mean 100 or more shapes that need to be stitched together. The method known as assembly-line piecing can reduce the drudgery.

Run pairs of pieces or units through the sewing machine one after another without cutting the thread,

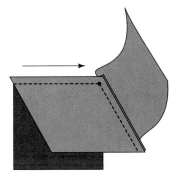

Diagram 18

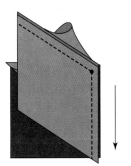

Diagram 19

Diagram 20

as shown in **Diagram 20.** After all the units have been sewn, snip them apart and press. Continue to add more pieces to these units in the same fashion until the sections are the size you need.

Pressing Basics

Proper pressing can make a big difference in the appearance of a finished block or quilt top. A large fluffy towel folded two or three times and placed on the ironing board allows you to get a smoother finish on the piece and eliminates little puckers that sometimes ap-

pear when pressing on a harder surface. You will also find that pieced and appliqué work will be more rounded, and not pressed into hard, flat lines. Review these general pressing techniques.

▲ Press, don't iron. Bring the iron down gently and firmly on the fabric from above, rather than rubbing the iron over the surface of the fabric.

▲ When machine stitching, press a seam before crossing it with another seam.

▲ Press seam allowances to one side, not open, unless instructed otherwise.

▲ Press seams of adjacent rows of blocks, or rows within blocks, in opposite directions. The pressed seams will fit together snugly, producing precise intersections.

▲ To press appliqués, place the piece right side down on the towel and press very gently on the back side.

I usually do not press a hand-pieced block until it is complete. I place it on the ironing board, right side up, and press it from the top, letting the seams go where they want. This method is usually better than trying to force the seams to go in a direction that might cause bulk or puckers. The exception is when light and dark fabrics are used side by side. In that case, I press the seams toward the darker fabric so the dark fabric doesn't show through the light one.

Quilt-As-You-Go Techniques

For some quick-and-easy projects, quilt-as-you-go techniques work very well. You simply layer the batting onto a backing and then sew strips or fabric pieces directly to the layers. This method has you sewing the pieces together and quilting them at the same time.

Strip Quilting

Strip quilting involves sewing together fabric strips of either random or consistent widths. Any shape—a square, patchwork stocking, cat shape, or triangle—can be strip quilted using this technique.

Step 1: Cut a piece of backing and a piece of batting to match the shape you intend to strip quilt (make sure you have included a seam allowance around all sides). Baste the backing and batting securely together.

Step 2: Cut strips of fabric about 2 inches longer than the pattern shape. These can be cut in random or even widths of approximately 1 to 2 inches.

Step 3: Place the batting and backing unit on your sewing machine with the batting side up. Beginning at the center of the unit, lay the first strip right side up across the batting at the angle you want the strips to run.

Step 4: Place a second strip on top of the first one, with right sides together and raw edges even. Pin in place and machine stitch ¼ inch from the edge, as shown in **Diagram 21.** Flip this second strip right side up and press. **Note:** If you are using a polyester batting, set your iron to a medium setting.

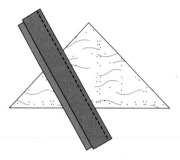

Diagram 21

Step 5: Continue adding strips until the piece is entirely covered. Then turn the unit wrong side up and trim off the excess ends of strips so they are flush with the batting and backing.

To save time, I like to sew strips in pairs before I iron. After machine sewing a strip to one side of the first strip, I turn the piece and machine sew another strip to the opposite side of the first one. I continue adding strips in this flip-flop order, pressing after each pair.

If I am making several strip-quilted pieces at a time, I speed up the process by adding strips to all of the pieces in assembly-line fashion. Then I press all the pieces during one trip to the iron.

Crazy-Patch Quilting

Quilt-as-you-go crazy-patch quilting is done in the same way as strip quilting, but instead of working with strips, you sew on odd-size patches of fabric.

Step 1: Cut a piece of backing and a piece of batting to match the shape you intend to crazy quilt (make sure you have included a seam allowance around all sides). Baste the backing and batting securely together.

Step 2: Gather a stack of scrap fabrics to use for the crazy patches. With batting side up, place the first piece of fabric right side up somewhere on the batting and pin it in place.

Step 3: Take another piece of fabric and place it right side down, aligning one of its edges along an edge of the first piece. Sew a ¼-inch seam through all layers. Turn the new piece right side up and press.

Step 4: Place another piece of fabric right side down on top of one or both sewn pieces, bringing its edge as close to the edges of the other pieces as possible. Sew, then flip right side up and press. The unit will now look like **Diagram 22.** Continue adding fabric pieces until all the space is covered.

You will likely sew over odd edges of fabric as you add pieces, but the goal is to cover the entire unit, leaving no batting visible. I occasionally place a long strip of fabric (such as a border print) across the entire unit to even out the patches.

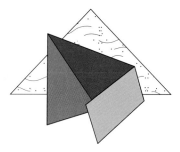

Diagram 22

Assembling Quilt Tops

Lay out all the blocks for your quilt top using the quilt diagram or photograph as a placement guide. Pin and sew the blocks together in vertical or horizontal rows for straight-set quilts, or in diagonal rows for diagonally set quilts. Press the seam allowances in opposite directions from row to row so that the seams will fit together snugly when rows are joined.

To keep a large quilt top manageable, join rows into pairs first and then join the pairs. When pressing a completed quilt top, press on the back side first, carefully clipping and removing hanging threads. Press the front last.

The Quilting Design

Most quilts in this book have a quilting design that follows the shape of the patchwork pieces, ¼ inch in from the seam. I do as little marking as possible on the quilt top and I usually eyeball the ¼-inch line. If you prefer more of a guide, lay a piece of ¼-inch masking tape along the seamline and quilt next to the tape.

For border prints and other areas that are filled with large-print fabrics, I often quilt following the fabric's design. When I do mark quilting designs, such as in solid areas of the border, it is usually after the quilt is basted and in the frame. I make plastic templates of the quilting design, lay them on top of the quilt, and draw around them. On dark fabrics, I mark very lightly with a white or silver pencil or a sharp tailor's chalk. On light fabrics, I mark very lightly with a .5mm lead pencil. Place a

book underneath the quilt to provide a hard surface for marking.

Thread color is a matter of personal preference. I often use off-white thread throughout the quilt, but sometimes when I am using a dark fabric—particularly in the border—I like to use dark thread.

Quilt Batting

I have experimented with all types of quilt batting and use many different kinds, depending on the project. If you want a puffy look, choose a thick batting. For a flatter, more antique look, choose a thinner batting. When hand quilting, a thinner batting is much easier to quilt. When machine quilting, a cotton or cotton/polyester batting works best because these types do not slip as readily as 100 percent polyester battings do. Always use a 100 percent cotton batting for potholders because polyester will conduct heat and burn your hands.

When purchasing batting, take time to read the manufacturer's literature. Experiment with different batts to find which type works best for you in different situations.

Polyester: Batting made of 100 percent polyester launders without shrinking and needles easily for hand quilting. One disadvantage of polyester batting is the "bearding" that often occurs when fibers migrate through the fabric, creating a fuzzy, or bearded, look on the surface of your quilt. This is particularly noticeable on quilts made with dark fabrics. Many polyester batts are bonded, or coated, to reduce bearding, but it does not totally eliminate the problem. Polyester batting comes in many different lofts, which makes it suitable for everything from quilted clothing and home accessories to puffy, tied comforters.

Cotton: All-cotton batting is the best choice for potholders because the cotton will not conduct heat. For quilts, this natural fiber is the warmest in winter and the coolest in summer. Most cotton batts are more difficult to needle than polyester or poly-cotton ones. Be sure to consider this trait if you are hand quilting—it is necessary to quilt cotton batts more closely since they tend to disintegrate a bit when washed. Cotton batting does not beard, and if you want to create an antique look, cotton is the best choice.

Cotton-Polyester Blends: Batting made from a blend of cotton and polyester combines the low-loft, sculpted look of cotton with the stability of polyester. This is one of my favorite types of batting for quilts. I presoak the batting to soften the fibers and make it easier to quilt. To do this, soak the batting in lukewarm water in the washing machine for about 10 minutes. Do not agitate. Spin and then dry it in the dryer. (Do *not* presoak 100 percent cotton batting— it could disintegrate.)

Wool: Wool batting is generally very easy to needle, very warm, and quite soft. I stay away from wool batting, however, because in our home we have problems with moths in wool garments, and I would not want them to get into my quilts! Wool batting tends to beard to the same extent as polyester batting.

Quilt Backings

For each of the quilting projects in this book, the materials list includes yardage for the quilt backing. For small quilts, simply use a full width of yardage if it is wide enough. For large quilts, check at your quilt shop for extra-wide fabric. If none is available, piece the backing in two or three panels with the seams running parallel to the long side of the quilt. For these quilts, divide the yardage in half crosswise. Then, to avoid having a seam down the center of the quilt back, divide one of the pieces in half lengthwise. Sew a narrow panel to each side of a full-width central panel, as shown in **Diagram 23**. Be sure to trim the selvage from the fabric before joining the panels. Press the seams away from the center of the quilt.

Diagram 23

Layering and Basting

Some people lay their quilt out on a large table or smooth floor to baste it. I find that when I do this the back tends to pucker, so I prefer to baste on a carpet, using the following technique.

Step 1: Make sure the batting and backing are at least 4 inches larger than the quilt top on all sides. Press all seams in the backing to one side.

Step 2: Lay the backing on the carpet, wrong side up. Using long, glass-head pins, stretch and pin the backing directly into the carpeting, inserting the pins into the carpeting at an angle. It is helpful to have two people for this task. Start at the center of opposite sides of the quilt and stretch and pin, then go to the center of the other sides and stretch and pin. Continue pinning, alternating sides until the entire back is pinned to the carpet.

Step 3: Carefully lay the batting on top of the backing, smoothing out any lumps and making sure the two are aligned.

Step 4: Carefully center the quilt top on top of the batting and backing. Smooth it out and pin it directly into the carpeting in the same way you pinned the backing.

Step 5: Check to make sure the quilt top is square. Measure it in several places across its width and length to see if dimensions are the same. If not, unpin the uneven area and pull or push slightly to square it up.

Step 6: Using a long darning needle and lightweight (or special basting) thread, begin basting the layers together. Start at the center of the quilt and baste toward each of the four corners, then toward each side. After this preliminary basting is complete, baste in a grid. I usually do one-quarter of the quilt at a time, leaving no more than a 5-inch section unbasted. To avoid sewing the quilt to the carpet, lift up slightly with each stitch to make sure you have not caught any of the carpet fibers with the needle.

Step 7: If you plan to machine quilt, lay out the layers in the same manner as above, but baste with safety pins. Thread basting does not hold the layers securely enough during machine quilting, and the thread is more difficult to remove when quilting is completed. Use rustproof, nickel-plated brass safety pins, starting in the center of the quilt and pinning approximately every 3 inches.

Hand Quilting

I have always loved the look of hand quilting and enjoy the actual quilting process. All of the quilts I have made, including the ones you see in this book, are hand quilted.

For best results, use a hoop or a frame to hold the quilt layers taut and smooth during quilting. This is as important for creating a smooth, finished quilt as an embroidery hoop is for creating smooth embroidery stitches. Work with one hand on top of the quilt (most quilters will use a thimble on the middle finger of this hand) and the other hand underneath, guiding the needle.

Don't worry about the size of your stitches in the beginning; concentrate on making them even, and they will get smaller over time. Since the quilting stitch is a completely foreign process to the new quilter, I have found that many people can learn to quilt with either hand, particularly left-handed people. Being able to quilt with both hands is a great advantage, particularly when working on a large frame. You might try it and see if it works for you.

Getting Started: Thread a 9, 10, or 12 "between" needle with quilting thread and knot the end. The thread should be no longer than about 18 inches because longer pieces tend to knot and fray. Insert the needle through the quilt top and batting about 1 inch away from where you will begin stitching. Bring the needle to the surface in position to make the first stitch. Gently tug on the thread to pop the knot through the quilt top and bury it in the batting.

Taking the Stitches: Insert the needle straight down through the three layers of the quilt. When you feel the tip of the needle with your underneath finger, gently guide it back up through the quilt. When the needle comes through the top of the quilt, press your thimble against the eye and guide it down again through the quilt layers. Continue to quilt in this manner, taking two or three small running stitches at a time. Most new quilters find that the first stitch is larger than the next ones. Don't worry, with practice they will soon be all the same size.

Ending a Line of Stitching: Some people make a knot at the end of the line of quilting and pop it through to the middle of the quilt. I prefer to take a small backstitch, work my needle through the layers about an inch, come up, take another tiny backstitch, work the needle through the layers again for about an inch, and then cut the thread. I cut the thread close to the quilt so the thread end will be lost between the layers.

Machine Quilting

Many people prefer to quilt by machine. While my preference is hand quilting, there are many small projects, such as place mats, potholders, and throw pillows, where machine quilting makes more sense.

For best results when doing machine-guided quilting, use a walking foot (also called an even-feed foot) on your sewing machine. For free-motion quilting, use a darning or machine-embroidery foot. Use thread to match the fabric colors, or use clear nylon thread in the top of the machine and a white or colored thread in the bobbin. To secure the thread at the beginning of a line of stitches, adjust the stitch length on your machine to make several very short stitches, then gradually increase to the regular stitch length. As you near the end of the line, gradually reduce the stitch length so that the last few stitches are very short.

For machine-guided quilting, keep the feed dogs up and move all three layers as smoothly as you can under the needle. To turn a corner in a design, stop with the needle still inserted in the fabric. Raise the foot, pivot the quilt, lower the foot, and continue stitching.

For free-motion quilting, disengage the feed dogs so you can manipulate the quilt freely as you stitch. Use both hands to guide the quilt under the needle, coordinating the speed of the needle with the movement of the quilt to create stitches of consistent length.

Making Binding

Double-fold binding, which is also called French-fold binding, can be made from either straight-grain or bias strips. I prefer bias binding because I feel it provides a smoother finished edge. It is also more durable because straight-grain binding is folded along one continuous thread, creating a weakness that can cause it to wear and fray much more quickly. To make double-fold binding, cut strips of fabric four times the finished width of the binding, plus the seam allowance. I usually work with 2-inch-wide strips.

Straight-Grain Binding

To make straight-grain binding, cut lengthwise strips from the binding fabric in the desired width. Sew them together by placing two strips perpendicular to each other, right sides together, so that the edges overlap each other by ¼ inch, as shown in **Diagram 24**. Sew a diagonal seam and trim the excess fabric, leaving a ¼-inch seam allowance.

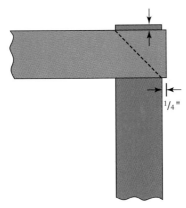

Diagram 24

Bias Binding

When binding a quilt, I prefer to piece together long strips of binding, so there will be fewer seams. Seams create excess bulk, which can cause problems, especially if they fall at the corners. The method described here results in leftover fabric, but I put the excess with my scraps and use it for other projects. The shorter pieces of bias are handy for binding small projects, such as potholders and place mats.

S t e p 1: Begin with a large square of fabric—a good size is about 45 inches. Remove the selvage from both sides, fold it in half on the diagonal, and press.

S t e p 2: Cut along the fold, but leave the two pieces aligned. Using a see-through ruler and a pencil or tailor's chalk, mark cutting lines along the diagonal on the top piece of fabric, as shown in **Diagram 25**. Cut through both layers.

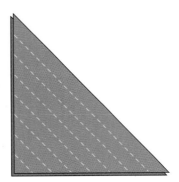

Diagram 25

S t e p 3: With right sides facing, use a ¼-inch seam allowance to sew the binding strips together at their ends, as shown in **Diagram 26**.

Since you cut the strips all the way to the edge of the fabric, their ends should be at the correct angle.

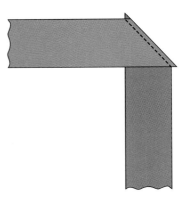

Diagram 26

Continuous Bias Binding

Bias binding can be cut in one long strip from a square of fabric that has been cut apart and resewn into a tube. The disadvantage to this method is that there are many shorter segments and thus more seams. To estimate the number of inches of continuous binding a particular square will produce, use this formula: Multiply the length of one side of the square by itself and divide the result by the width of your binding. For example, cutting 2-inch binding strips from a 30-inch square will yield: $30 \times 30 = 900 \div 2 = 450$ inches of binding.

S t e p 1: Cut a square in half diagonally to get two triangles. Place the two triangles right sides together, positioned as shown in **Diagram 27**, and sew with a ¼-inch seam. Press open.

Diagram 27

S t e p 2 : Using a pencil or tailor's chalk and a see-through ruler, mark cutting lines on the wrong side of the fabric in the desired binding width (including seam allowances). Draw the lines parallel to the bias edges, as shown in **Diagram 28**.

Bias edge

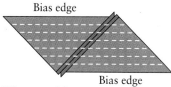

Bias edge

Diagram 28

S t e p 3 : Fold the fabric with right sides facing, bringing the two nonbias edges together and offsetting them by one strip width, as shown in **Diagram 29**. Pin the edges right sides together, creating a tube, and sew with a ¼-inch seam. Press the seam open.

S t e p 4 : Cut on the marked lines, turning the tube as you cut to form one long bias strip.

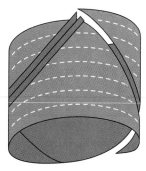

Diagram 29

Attaching Binding

Most projects I make have border prints around their edges. In order for the seam to look even, it is important to sew the binding directly to a line along the border print.

The conventional way of adding binding is to sew it to the front of the project and then bring it to the back and stitch it down. When I use a border print around the edges, I do the opposite, sewing the binding first to the back and then bringing it to the front. I use a small blind stitch to sew it down right alongside the edge of the line on the border print.

Whether sewing by hand or machine, begin by trimming the excess batting and backing to make it even with the quilt top. For double-fold binding, fold the long binding strip in half lengthwise, wrong sides together, and gently press.

Adding Binding by Hand

S t e p 1 : Beginning along one side, not in a corner, align the raw edges of the binding along the edge of the wrong side of the quilt. Pin the binding to the quilt, leaving an approximate 5-inch "tail" of binding hanging (it will be used later to connect the ends of binding). Sew the binding to the quilt, using a ¼-inch seam and stitching through all layers. Check the reverse side of your stitching frequently to make sure you are sewing on a line from the border print.

S t e p 2 : As you approach a corner, stop stitching ¼ inch from the edge and take a backstitch. Fold the binding strip up at a 45 degree angle, as shown in **Diagram 30A**. Fold the strip back down so there is a fold at the upper edge, as shown in **30B**. Insert the needle through the base of the fold and continue sewing to the next corner. Miter all four corners in this manner.

S t e p 3 : When you are approximately 8 inches from your original starting point, pin the 5-inch tail of binding along the edge. Take the piece you are currently sewing and bring it over to meet the 5-inch tail, as shown in **Diagram 31A**. Cut

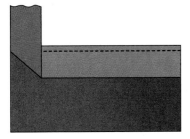

A

B

Diagram 30

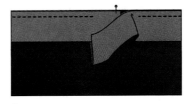

A

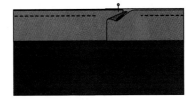

B

Diagram 31

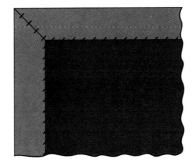

Diagram 32

off the excess binding, allowing enough length to connect the two ends and have a ½-inch overlap (it is better to cut it too long than too short). Cut the binding to match the angle of the original tail. Fold under ¼ inch of the cut-off end and press. Slip the raw edges of the 5-inch tail inside the folded edges. Blindstitch the ends together, as shown in **31B**.

Step 4: Carefully pin and sew this last bit of binding down.

Step 5: Turn the binding to the front of the quilt and blindstitch the folded edge in place along the line of the border print, covering the first set of stitches with the folded edge. At the corners, fold in the adjacent sides to form a miter. Take several stitches in the miter on both sides of the quilt, as shown in **Diagram 32**.

Adding Binding by Machine

Step 1: Working on the front of the quilt, carefully stitch along a line in the border print ¼ inch from the edge.

Step 2: Using the line of stitches as a sewing guide, attach the binding to either the front or the back of the quilt. If you want to attach it to the front first, carefully pin the folded binding to the right side of the quilt, aligning the raw edges.

Step 3: Sew from the wrong side of the quilt, with the binding on the underneath side. Sew directly on the line of stitches you made earlier. As you approach a corner, stop stitching ¼ inch from the edge. Backstitch and remove the quilt from the machine. Fold the binding strip the same as for hand stitching, then return it to the machine and begin sewing ¼ inch from the top edge of the quilt. Finish the binding in the same manner as for hand sewing.

Signing Your Quilt

Be sure to sign and date your quilt. This finishing touch can be a simple signature in permanent ink or an elaborate inked or embroidered label. Add any other pertinent details that will help family members or quilt collectors understand, years from now, just what went into the making of your quilt.

Knitting

For the last 25 years I have considered myself a quiltmaker. The vast majority of my projects have been patchwork oriented, and making quilts has been close to an all-consuming passion. Prior to quilting I considered myself a knitter. Even when knee-deep in many other craft projects, I always had at least one sweater in progress and gave several sweaters as gifts each Christmas.

I was always a very structured person regarding craft projects and, when knitting, not knowing how to be creative, I followed purchased patterns. Once I became interested in quiltmaking, its appeal was that even very traditional patterns could look unique and different simply by changing the placement of the blocks, colors, and fabrics. As the years went by, I became more and more adventuresome regarding quiltmaking and more confident in my approach to design, color, and fabric use, and I discovered the excitement of designing my own patterns for quilts. Quiltmaking allows me the freedom to be creative within the structure that appeals to me.

Even when I had multiple quilt projects in progress, it was still difficult for me to pass a knitting shop without going in, and every now and then I just had to purchase some yarn and begin a new sweater. But one day several years ago when I entered a yarn shop, something different happened. I suddenly realized that sweaters could be

rics. When I see a beautiful colored yarn, I buy two or three balls of it to add to my stash. The fabrics sitting on my shelves in many different colors and prints now share space with a supply of yarns, shaded from one color to another. I love making sweaters with many different yarns just as I love making quilts with many different fabrics.

The nice thing about using many different yarns in a sweater (just as using many different fabrics in a quilt) is that you don't have to worry about running out of anything. If you run out of a particular yarn, just use a different one in a slightly different color and it will add more to the uniqueness of the design.

Three of the patterns for sweaters in this book use mohair yarn. I like using many different types of textured yarns in a single project, but for anyone experimenting for the first time with using multiple yarns in a sweater, mohair is one of the most forgiving in terms of changing colors, blending, and uniformity of design.

The technique for planning colors explained in "The Colors of Christmas" on page 1 is the same whether I am making quilts or making sweaters. For knitting, I still begin with two or three colors of yarn and try to find other colors of yarn that will shade the original ones together.

made the same way as quilts! It wasn't necessary to find a pattern to rigidly copy. As long as there was a basic style—crewneck, cardigan, raglan—and as long as I knew what needles were needed for the size of the yarn, then it was possible to apply all my quiltmaking color and design principles to knitting. All those years of thinking that the only sweaters I could make were from a knitting magazine or book—and my lack of confidence to try something different— were in the past. I began to experiment with different textures of yarns and to chart out on graph paper quilt patterns that could be used for sweater designs. A renewed interest in knitting was kindled.

The confidence I gained in creating quilts now extends to knitting, and I find myself collecting yarns of various colors and textures as fervently as I collect fab-

Using Multiple Yarns

When using many different yarns at one time, there are two techniques to choose from: Fair Isle and intarsia. In the *Fair Isle* technique the various colored yarns are carried across the back of the sweater, and the strands are twisted around the current color every few stitches. *Intarsia* involves letting the color yarn you just finished using remain where it is and picking up the new yarn to begin knitting with it. In order to avoid holes, the new yarn must be twisted once around the old one. My preference is to use the intarsia method because less yarn is used, you do not run the risk of puckering from improper tension while carrying the yarn, and the sweater is not so heavy and bulky.

Any time multiple yarns are used in a sweater, the yarns can become badly tangled. In order to avoid all the tangles, I cut shorter lengths of yarn (approximately 3 to 4 yards long) and knit with these individual strands. As you switch colors, it is very easy just to pull the new strand through all the other threads and keep knitting. When using more than five different yarns at one time, I find this the easiest approach.

To weave in the ends, when you have about 6 inches left of a strand, cut a new piece of yarn. Knit the next two stitches with both the old and the new yarn together, as shown in **Diagram 1**. Then pick up the tail of the new strand of yarn along with the portion of the new strand that knitted the previous two stitches and drop the old yarn. Once again knit two stitches, this time with the two strands of new yarn. Repeat this process, alternating the remaining piece of the old yarn and the tail of the new yarn, until the ends of both yarns have been knitted into the sweater. Connecting yarn in this manner leaves very few loose ends for you to weave into the sweater later.

Since I knit with many different types of textured yarns, the extra thickness that comes from knitting these few stitches double is not apparent. This is also why I like to knit with mohair—by its very nature it is both thick and thin.

If you are working with bulky or very smooth yarn where knitting two stitches together might be apparent, try the following method. When you are ready to end one yarn and begin another, twist the new yarn around the old, and leave about 6 inches of both yarns hanging. When the piece is finished, working from the back, weave in the ends, as shown in **Diagram 2**. Using a yarn needle and working diagonally, carefully weave the strands in through the stitches. For very bulky yarn, split the end into two strands and weave each individually.

Diagram 1

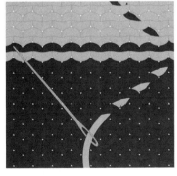

Diagram 2

Patchwork Squares Tunic Sweater

Red and green shade together to create the color palette for this Patchwork Squares Tunic Sweater, which was inspired by an antique quilt with large squares sewn together. The sweater is made by working long strips of reverse stockinette stitch (meaning the purl side is the right side of the piece) and

Skill level: Intermediate

Size: Directions are for size small. Changes for medium, large, and extra-large are given in parentheses.

Finished chest size: 42 (44, 46, 48) inches

Finished length: 29 inches

Sleeve length: 18½ inches

Gauge: With mohair yarn in reverse stockinette stitch, 16 stitches = 4 inches; 22 rows = 4 inches

changing the color every 5½ inches to give the illusion of squares. The strips are then sewn together to form the front, back, and sleeves of the sweater with the purl/seam side as the right side of the sweater. The seams and boundaries of the squares are then finished with a mock blanket stitch.

Before starting this project, I sorted through odd balls of mohair yarn and found some deep teal, burgundy, and red, then supplemented those colors with ones I purchased to complete the palette. You will need approximately 17 skeins of mohair and 1 skein of black worsted-weight yarn to complete the sweater, as listed at right. Most skeins of mohair contain approximately 100 yards of yarn.

You Will Need

1 300-yard skein of black worsted-weight 100 percent wool yarn for the ribbing

50-gram/1¾-ounce skeins of 100 percent mohair, in the colors and quantities listed at right

1 pair of size 9 (5½ mm) straight knitting needles, or size to obtain gauge

1 size G (4.25 mm) crochet hook

Yarn needle

Ring-type stitch marker

T-pins for markers

A
2 skeins of green-and-red multicolor mohair

B
2 skeins of red-and-burgundy multicolor mohair

C
2 skeins of bright red mohair

D
3 skeins of medium red mohair

E
3 skeins of burgundy mohair

F
1 skein of medium green mohair

G
2 skeins of slightly darker green mohair

H
2 skeins of deep teal mohair

For the sweater shown here, I knitted the strips, alternating the yarn colors in a variety of ways on each strip. Then when all the strips were complete I arranged them for the front and back in a way that seemed pleasing.

The arrangement for the sweater shown in the photograph is indicated in the charts on this page, but you may have more or fewer colors and different varieties of yarn in your sweater. It is fun to experiment and make each strip different. This is a great sweater for using up odds and ends of yarn.

Back

Step 1: Following the **Patchwork Squares Back Chart** or adding your own colors as you like, for the first patchwork strip, with size 9 needles, cast on 24 (25, 26, 27) stitches. Beginning with a knit row, work in reverse stockinette stitch for 30 rows, or until the piece measures 5½ inches long. (*Note:* Since the thickness of different brands of mohair may be different, it is best to measure the length of each square rather than just rely on the number of rows.) Check your gauge; the piece should measure 6 (6¼, 6½, 6¾) inches wide.

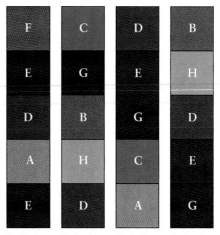

Strip 1   Strip 2   Strip 3   Strip 4

Patchwork Squares Back Chart

Step 2: Leaving about a 6-inch tail to weave in later, cut the first color. Change to the next color and work another 30 rows or 5½ inches. Continue until you have completed five different color blocks. Bind off all stitches.

Step 3: Following the chart for color placement, make three more patchwork strips as for the first.

Front

Step 1: Following the **Patchwork Squares Front Chart**, make strips 1 and 4 in the same manner as for the back.

Step 2: For Strip 3, work this strip the same as for previous strips through completion of the fourth square. For the fifth square,

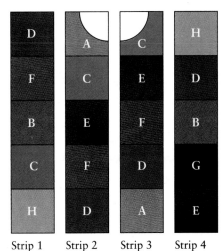

Strip 1   Strip 2   Strip 3   Strip 4

Patchwork Squares Front Chart

change colors and work even for 2 inches, ending with a purl row. The strip should measure 24 inches.

Step 3: Bind off 10 stitches at the beginning of the next row for the neck. Continue in the established pattern, decreasing 1 stitch at the neck edge every row until 10 stitches remain. Work even until the fifth square measures 5½ inches, ending with a purl row. Bind off the remaining 10 stitches.

Step 4: For Strip 2, complete four squares. Change color and work even for 2 inches, ending with a knit row.

Step 5: Bind off 10 stitches at the beginning of the next row for the neck. Continue in the established pattern, decreasing 1 stitch at the neck edge every row until 10 stitches remain. Work even until the square measures 5½ inches. Bind off.

Sleeves

Each sleeve consists of a right strip and a left strip. I made the color placement on each of them different. You can refer to the sleeve charts below, or use your own placement. It mainly depends at this point on which colors of yarn you have left.

Step 1: For the right strip of the left sleeve, cast on 22 (24, 24, 26) stitches. Beginning with a knit row and following the color placement on the chart, work in reverse stockinette stitch, increasing 1 stitch at the right edge every ¾ inch 20 times. Work even

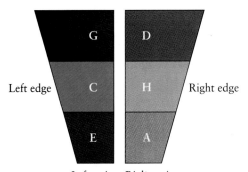

Left edge   Right edge

Left strip   Right strip

Patchwork Squares Left Sleeve Chart

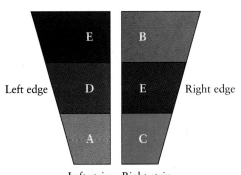

Left edge   Right edge

Left strip   Right strip

Patchwork Squares Right Sleeve Chart

Joining Seams

There are many different ways to join the seams of knitted garments. The method I use is shown in the three diagrams below. Use a color yarn that matches the sweater; in the case of multiple colors, use a yarn that will blend with all the others. If the stitches show, change yarn as the color changes.

Joining two knit edges: This seam is worked row by row from the knit side and produces an invisible seam on the sides and sleeves. The seam will show on the purl, or wrong side, of the work. Find the horizontal bar between the first and second stitches on one of the pieces to be joined and insert the needle under the bar. Find the corresponding horizontal bar on the second piece and insert the needle under that bar. Working back and forth, continue inserting the needle through the bars on both pieces, as shown in **Diagram 1**. Gently pull the yarn so that the seam is not too tight or too loose.

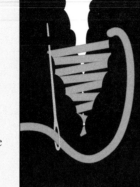

Diagram 1

Joining bound-off shoulder seams: Working from the knit side and with the bound-off stitches next to each other, insert the needle under the first stitch just within the bound-off edge of one of the sides, and then under the corresponding stitch on the other side, as shown in **Diagram 2**. Continue stitch by stitch, pulling the yarn tight enough to hide the bound-off stitches but loose enough so there is some elasticity in the seam.

Diagram 2

Joining sleeves to the sweater body: Working from the knit side, insert the needle under one of the stitches just inside the bound-off edge of the sleeve, then under one of the two horizontal bars between the first and second stitches on the body of the sweater, as shown in **Diagram 3**. Continue alternating, being careful not to pull the stitches too tight.

Sleeve   Body

Diagram 3

on the 42 (44, 44, 46) stitches until the strip measures 16½ inches from the beginning, ending with a purl row. Bind off all stitches loosely.

Step 2: For the left strip of the left sleeve, follow the same instructions as for the right strip, but increase at the left edge only.

Step 3: Using the instructions for the left sleeve, make a right sleeve following the color placement on the chart.

Blocking and Finishing

Step 1: Lay the strips out flat on a towel or pressing board and, without touching the iron to the yarn, steam the strips. Allow them to dry thoroughly.

Step 2: Thread the yarn needle with a long strand of mohair. Beginning with the back, sew strips 1 and 2 together following **Diagram 1** in "Joining Seams" on this page, making sure that the squares match and the seam will protrude on the purl (right) side of the work. Let the seam allowance roll naturally. Join the remaining strips the same way. Join the front and sleeve strips as for the back.

Step 3: For decorative embroidery trim, use the yarn needle and a double strand of the black yarn to embroider a mock blanket stitch over each seam and between squares, making the stitches about ¼ inch apart and ½ inch long, as shown.

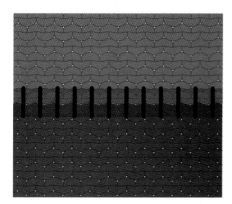

Mock Blanket Stitch

Step 4: Join the shoulder seams, following **Diagram 2** in "Joining Seams" on the opposite page, and embroider the mock blanket stitch on each.

Step 5: For the neck band, with the right side facing, using the crochet hook, join the black yarn (draw up a loop and chain 1) at the left shoulder seam. Mark the beginning of the round. *Round 1:* Work 70 (72, 74, 76) single crochet stitches evenly spaced around the neck edge. *Rounds 2, 3, and 4:* Single crochet in each stitch in the previous round. *Round 5:* Single crochet in each stitch in the previous round. Decrease 10 stitches evenly spaced (draw up a loop in each of the next 2 single crochet, yarn over, and draw through all 3 loops on the hook). *Rounds 6 and 7:* Single crochet in each of the remaining 60 (62, 64, 66) stitches in the previous round. Fasten off by cutting the yarn and drawing it through the loop.

Step 6: Place a marker about 10¼ (10¾, 10¾, 11¼) inches down each side from the shoulder seams. Set in the sleeves between the markers, following **Diagram 3** in "Joining Seams" on the opposite page. Embroider the mock blanket stitch over this seam.

Step 7: Sew the side seams. Still working with the seams on the outside of the sweater, and using a color of mohair that will blend with both patches being sewn, sew the sides and underarms together as for the back strips. Embroider the mock blanket stitch over this seam.

Step 8: For the cuff, with the right side facing, using the crochet hook, join the black yarn as for the neck band. Mark the beginning of the round. *Round 1:* Work 23 (25, 25, 27) single crochet stitches evenly spaced around the lower sleeve edge. *Round 2:* Single crochet in each stitch in the previous round. Continue working rounds until the cuff measures 2 inches. Fasten off. Work a cuff on the second sleeve.

Step 9: For the waistband, with the right side facing, using the crochet hook, join the black yarn as for the neck band. Mark the beginning of the round. *Round 1:* Work 16 (17, 18, 19) single crochet stitches evenly spaced *in each square* around the lower sweater edge for a total of 128 (136, 144, 152) *Round 2:* Single crochet in each stitch in the previous round. Continue working rounds until the waistband measures 1½ inches. Fasten off.

Step 10: Weave in the ends of yarn on the wrong side of the fabric.

Enchanted Forest Sweater

I knitted this sweater with a variety of yarns with subtle differences in color to create dimension and visual interest in the tessellated shapes. The pattern is an adaptation of the design in the Enchanted Forest Quilt on page 46. The trees are shaded from olive green to teal to black, and from navy to dark purple to bright purple. If you like this look, use the same or similar shades. If you prefer working in another color palette, try experimenting with yarns you have on hand and add new ones to them. The

Skill level: Intermediate

Size: Directions are for size extra-small. Changes for small, medium, large, and extra-large are given in parentheses.

Finished chest size: 42½ (44½, 46½, 48½, 50½) inches

Finished length: 26 inches

Sleeve length: 18 inches

Gauge: In stockinette stitch and color pattern, 16 stitches = 4 inches; 22 rows = 4 inches

most important thing to remember is to place contrasting values next to each other to give the trees a defined appearance in the finished sweater. All in all you will need about 12 colors of mohair to complete the sweater. When working with mohair, my preference is to use worsted-weight wool yarn for the ribbing because mohair does not give a firm enough rib stitch.

You Will Need

1 300-yard skein of dark teal worsted-weight 100 percent wool yarn for the ribbing (color A)

50-gram/1¾-ounce skeins of 100 percent mohair, in the colors and quantities listed at right

1 pair of size 9 (5½ mm) straight knitting needles, or size to obtain gauge

1 pair of size 6 (4 mm) straight knitting needles

16-inch size 6 circular knitting needle

2 stitch holders

Yarn needle

Ring-type stitch marker

T-pins for markers

A
1 skein of dark teal wool

B
2 skeins of olive mohair

C
1 skein of khaki mohair

D
1 skein of light turquoise mohair

E
1 skein of medium turquoise mohair

F
1 skein of bright teal mohair

G
1 skein of dark-teal-with-fleck mohair

H
1 skein of dark teal mohair

I
2 skeins of navy mohair

J
2 skeins of black mohair

K
1 skein of deep plum mohair

L
1 skein of soft purple mohair

M
1 skein of bright purple mohair

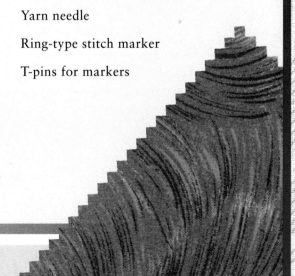

If you cannot find this many colors, you could substitute deep plum for navy, soft purple for bright purple, khaki for olive, light turquoise for medium turquoise, and one teal for all three teals. Each tree in this intarsia pattern requires about 36 yards.

Back

Step 1: With the size 6 needles and color A, cast on 80 (84, 88, 92, 96) stitches.

Step 2: Work in K1, P1 ribbing for 2¾ inches, increasing 5 stitches evenly spaced across the last row for a total of 85 (89, 93, 97, 101) stitches.

Step 3: Change to the larger needles and mohair yarn. Following the **Enchanted Forest Front/Back Chart** on page 108, begin working in stockinette stitch with Row 1 as a knit (right-side) row. Begin and end the chart at the markings for the size you are knitting. Work across the chart from right to left for all knit rows and from left to right for all purl (wrong-side) rows. Twist the strands at each color change to prevent holes. Work even for 4 inches. Check your gauge; the piece should measure 21¼ (22¼, 23¼, 24¼, 25¼) inches wide. Complete the chart, ignoring the indications for neck shaping.

Step 4: In the established color pattern, bind off the first 25 (27, 29, 31, 33) stitches. Work across the next 35 stitches and place them onto a stitch holder for the back neck. Bind off the remaining 25 (27, 29, 31, 33) stitches.

Front

In order for the partial trees on the sides and at the shoulders to match when the sweater is assembled, the coloring on the front must be the mirror image of that on the back. I find it easiest to follow the colors for the front by looking at the wrong side of the back, rather than the color chart. Or, either pencil in the new colors on your chart by reversing their order, or simply work the chart from left to right for knit rows and from right to left for purl rows.

Step 1: Work the same as for the back (except for mirror-imaging the colors) until the neck shaping is indicated on the chart. Your last row before the shaping will be a purl row.

Step 2: To shape the neck, following the chart, knit across the first 32 (34, 36, 38, 40) stitches; place the remaining 53 (55, 57, 59, 61) stitches on a stitch holder to be worked later.

Step 3: Working the left neck/shoulder first, follow the chart and decrease 1 stitch at the neck edge every row until 25 (27, 29, 31, 33) stitches remain. Complete the chart and then bind off the remaining stitches.

Step 4: Return the remaining stitches to the needle. Place the first 21 stitches onto a stitch holder for the front neck and work the remaining stitches to match the left side.

Sleeves

S t e p 1 : With the size 6 needles and color A, cast on 34 (36, 38, 40, 42) stitches. Work in K1, P1 ribbing for 2½ inches, increasing 11 stitches evenly spaced across the last row for a total of 45 (47, 49, 51, 53) stitches. **Note:** For people who need a longer sleeve length, either increase the ribbing or lengthen the sleeves.

S t e p 2 : Change to the larger needles and mohair yarn. Beginning with Row 1, follow the **Enchanted Forest Sleeve Chart** on page 109 and increase 1 stitch each edge every sixth row until there are 71 (73, 75, 77, 79) stitches. Work to the end of the chart. The sleeve should measure 18 inches long. Bind off loosely.

S t e p 3 : Work the second sleeve in the same way as the first.

Blocking

Lay the pieces flat on a towel or pressing board. Without touching the iron to the yarn, steam each piece and let dry thoroughly.

Neck Band

S t e p 1 : Join the shoulder seams, following **Diagram 2** in "Joining Seams" on page 102.

S t e p 2 : With the right side facing, using the circular needle and color A, pick up and knit 16 stitches evenly spaced along the left front neck edge.

S t e p 3 : Knit across the 21 stitches from the front neck holder, pick up and knit 16 stitches evenly spaced along the right front neck edge, then knit the 35 stitches from the back neck holder.

S t e p 4 : Place a marker to indicate the beginning of the round. Work around in K1, P1 ribbing for 3 inches. Bind off loosely in ribbing.

Finishing

S t e p 1 : Fold each sleeve in half and mark the center line of the bound-off edge with a small piece of yarn.

S t e p 2 : Place markers 9¼ (9½, 9¾, 10, 10¼) inches down each side from the shoulder seams. Matching the center sleeve to the shoulder seam, set in the sleeves between the markers. Using color A, join the underarm and side seams, following **Diagram 3** in "Joining Seams" on page 102.

S t e p 3 : Turn the neck band to the inside and loosely slip stitch the bound-off edge to the base of the neck band using color A. Weave in all loose ends on the wrong side of the sweater.

Extra-large
Large
Medium
Small
Extra-small
F I B L J E L
Shaping for front neck
M G D K C F J
K B J H M I B
D C L
Row 1 (right side)
Enchanted Forest Front/Back Chart

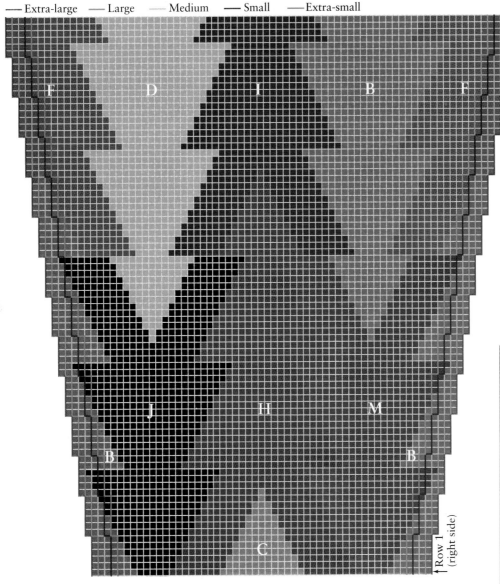

—Extra-large —Large —Medium —Small —Extra-small

F D I B F

J H M

B B

C

↑ Row 1 (right side)

Enchanted Forest Sleeve Chart

Enchanted Forest Color Key

A ■ dark teal wool

B ■ olive

C ■ khaki

D ■ light turquoise

E ■ medium turquoise

F ■ bright teal

G ■ dark-teal-with-fleck

H ■ dark teal

I ■ navy

J ■ black

K ■ deep plum

L ■ soft purple

M ■ bright purple

A Variation on the
Enchanted Forest Sweater

You can make the Enchanted Forest Sweater using any non-mohair yarns that have a gauge of 4 stitches = 1 inch. My friend Karen Washburn made the variation shown here. She used mostly hand-dyed yarns in the colors listed in the color key.

The construction of the sweater is identical to the mohair version. Use the charts at right for placement of the colors. Use Color J, purple, for the ribbing as well as for some of the trees.

H	G		D	B		C	E	I
B	A		E	I		F	J	A
F	C		B	D		G	A	H
		E			F		C	

Enchanted Forest Variation Front/Back Chart

Enchanted Forest Variation Color Key

A ▦ green tweed

B ■ black

C ▦ light purple

D ▦ light green

E ▦ dark green

F ▦ turquoise

G ■ plum

H ▦ raspberry

I ▦ bright
raspberry

J ▦ purple

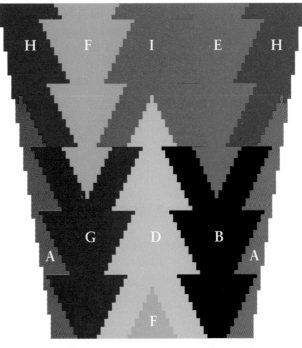

H	F	I	E	H
	G	D	B	
A				A
		F		

Enchanted Forest Variation Sleeve Chart

$\mathscr{B}$oxing Day Sweater

The colors in the Boxing Day sweater are a subtle shading from red to brown to black. The design is an adaptation of the Boxing Day Quilt on page 12, where the dark colors fall on the left side of the boxes, the medium colors are on the right, and the tops of the boxes are light. While a total of 10 different yarns have been used for the boxes, you could make the sweater even more multicolored by using a wider variety of scraps. Another possibility is to use only

Skill level: Intermediate

Size: Directions are for size small. Changes for medium and large are given in parentheses.

Finished chest size: 42 (44, 46) inches

Finished length: 26½ inches

Sleeve length: 18 inches

Gauge: In stockinette stitch and color pattern, 16 stitches = 4 inches; 22 rows = 4 inches

three yarns—dark, medium, and light. If you chose this variation, you would need approximately 800 yards each of the dark and medium yarns and 400 yards of the light yarn. Each small parallelogram in this pattern requires approximately 4¼ yards. The medium parallelograms use 8½ yards, and the largest ones use 12¾ yards.

You Will Need

1 300-yard skein of black worsted-weight 100 percent wool yarn for the ribbing (color Z)

50-gram/1¾-ounce skeins of 100 percent mohair, in the colors and quantities listed at right

1 pair of size 9 (5½ mm) straight knitting needles, or size to obtain gauge

1 pair of size 6 (4 mm) straight knitting needles

16-inch size 6 circular knitting needle

2 stitch holders

Yarn needle

Ring-type stitch marker

T-pins for markers

A
1 skein of tan mohair

B
1 skein of light taupe mohair

C
1 skein of medium taupe mohair

D
2 skeins of dark taupe mohair

E
2 skeins of black mohair

F
2 skeins of burgundy mohair

G
1 skein of rust mohair

H
2 skeins of red mohair

I
2 skeins of medium brown mohair

J
2 skeins of dark brown mohair

A Variation on the Boxing Day Sweater

You can make this sweater with scraps of non-mohair yarn. Hand-dyed wool or other yarns with a gauge of 4 stitches = 1 inch will work. As long as you maintain the placement of dark, medium, and light colors, any variety of scrap yarns can be used.

Back

S t e p 1 : With size 6 needles and color Z, cast on 80 (84, 88) stitches.

S t e p 2 : Work in K1, P1 ribbing for 2¾ inches, increasing 4 stitches evenly spaced across the last row for a total of 84 (88, 92) stitches.

S t e p 3 : Change to the larger needles and mohair yarn. Referring to the **Boxing Day Front/Back Chart** on page 116, begin at your size and with Row 1. Knit across for the first right-side row. Read each knit row from right to left and each purl (wrong-side) row from left to right. Remember to twist the strands at color changes! Work even for 4 inches. Check your gauge; the piece should measure 21 (22, 23) inches wide. Continue following the chart to the end, ignoring the neck shaping and ending with a purl row.

S t e p 4 : To shape the shoulders, working in the established color pattern, bind off the first 25 (27, 29) stitches. Knit the center 34 stitches and place onto a stitch holder for the back neck, then bind off the remaining 25 (27, 29) stitches.

Front

S t e p 1 : Work the sweater front in the same manner as the back until you reach the front neckline.

S t e p 2 : To shape the neck, on the next row, knit the first 32 (34, 36) stitches. Place the remaining stitches on a stitch holder to be worked later.

S t e p 3 : Working the left side first, decrease 1 stitch at the neck edge on every row until 25 (27, 29) stitches remain. Continue until the length of the front matches the back, and bind off the remaining 25 (27, 29) stitches for the left shoulder.

S t e p 4 : Return the remaining stitches to the needle. Place the first 20 stitches onto a stitch holder for the front neck. Continuing in pattern, shape the right side of the neckline to match the left.

Sleeves

S t e p 1 : With size 6 needles and color Z, cast on 36 (38, 40) stitches. Work in K1, P1 ribbing for 2½ inches, increasing 10 stitches evenly spaced across the last row for a total of 46

(48, 50) stitches. **Note:** For people who need a longer sleeve length, either increase the ribbing or lengthen the sleeves.

Step 2: Change to mohair yarn and larger needles. Follow the **Boxing Day Sleeve Chart** on page 117, increase one stitch at each edge on every sixth row until there are 72 (74, 76) stitches. Complete the chart and bind off all stitches loosely.

Step 3: Work the second sleeve in the same way as the first.

Blocking

Lay the pieces out flat on a towel or pressing board. Without touching the iron to the yarn, steam each piece and allow to dry.

Neck Band

Step 1: Sew the shoulder seams together, following **Diagram 2** in "Joining Seams" on page 102.

Step 2: With the right side facing and using the circular needle and color Z, begin at the left shoulder to pick up and knit 13 stitches evenly spaced along the left side of the front neckline. Knit the 20 stitches from the stitch holder at the center front neck and pick up and knit 13 stitches on the right side of the front neck. Knit the 34 stitches from the stitch holder at the center back neck (80 stitches total).

Step 3: Place a marker to indicate the beginning of the round. Work around in K1, P1 ribbing for 1½ inches. Bind off loosely in ribbing.

Finishing

Step 1: Fold each sleeve in half and mark the center of the top edge with a small piece of yarn.

Step 2: Place markers 9½ (9¾, 10) inches down each side from the shoulder seams. Matching the center sleeve to the shoulder seam, set in the sleeves between the markers.

Step 3: Join the underarm and side seams, following **Diagram 3** in "Joining Seams" on page 102.

Step 4: Weave in all loose ends on the wrong side of the fabric.

Boxing Day Front/Back Chart

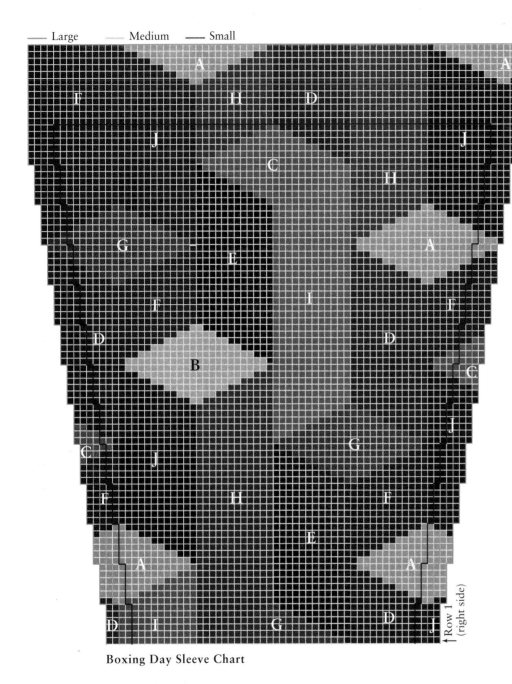

Boxing Day Sleeve Chart

Wreaths

When we moved into our old house, it was practically buried in boxwood hedges that had gone unclipped for many years. The boxwoods had grown together across the path leading to the front door, and the ones planted under the windows had grown so tall one could no longer see in or out of many windows. Never having done much gardening, for the first few years I was afraid to touch the boxwoods for fear they would die. Then we had a visit from a Scottish friend who has beautiful gardens with yew and boxwood hedges surrounding his garden beds. He was clearly aghast at the state of our boxwoods. He persuaded me to let him tackle one particular bush that was obscuring the view from the kitchen window. He hacked and sawed the bush and stripped it of most of its leaves. I stared at the hedge when he finished and couldn't believe my eyes. Yes, I could now see out the kitchen window, but what remained of the boxwood was bare stubs of branches. I smiled politely and thanked him, but inside I was sick. For months I stared at those stubby sticks wondering how he could have done such a thing to my precious bush. But miraculously, the bush did not die, it flourished—and two years later not only was it the fullest and prettiest one in our yard, but it was also a manageable size.

After that I became braver about clipping boxwoods. I realized I wasn't going to kill them, and that the more I clipped, the prettier they became—and that a very good time to cut some branches was at Christmas. Little by little, I began to learn more about gardening and pruning, and I also began making boxwood wreaths.

Now I make 30 to 40 boxwood wreaths every Christmas. I have it down to a system where I can complete a basic wreath in about 15 minutes. Most of the wreaths decorate the front gate, doors, and windows of our home, but I also make wreaths to give to family and friends as early Christmas gifts. My sister and niece live in the high desert of Oregon where fresh greens at Christmastime are scarce. Each year I send them a basic boxwood wreath that they can decorate as they choose. I use boxwood clippings, holly branches, and magnolia leaves as packing material and put it all in a box lined with a large plastic bag. I sprinkle the contents of the bag with water, seal it tight, and mail the package the same day I cut the greens and make the wreath. The wreaths and extra greens arrive at their destination quite fresh and very welcome.

If you don't have boxwood, look around your yard to see what evergreens you do have. The same principle for making a boxwood wreath can be used for any greens—pine, fir, hemlock, juniper, and holly. Make the clumps of greens about the same size as the clumps of boxwood listed here. If you have no evergreens in your yard, check with a local nursery or your state extension service to find out which varieties will grow in your area. In just a year or two

A Log Cabin Christmas

Our old log cabin was built in approximately 1770. It was most likely the first dwelling on the original tract of land, put together hurriedly to house a family as they then began clearing land, planting crops, and building the main house that would become the center of their plantation.

The first Christmas after we removed all the paint, mortar, and cement from the cabin and restored it back to its original log walls, I decided it would be fun to make a wreath for the door with materials found near the cabin that would have been growing wild when the first settlers arrived—they would not have had apples or other fruits to decorate the wreath their first winter. I went for a walk to see what I could find.

you will be able to cut greens from these plants for your holiday decorating. Many kinds of holly will produce an abundance of bright red berries just a year or two after planting. Pruning them at Christmastime encourages new and bushier growth. You'll get a tremendous amount of pleasure in being able to go into your own yard and cut fresh greens to decorate with during the holidays.

One of the most exciting finds was bright purple beautyberries (*Callicarpa* spp.). It is hard to imagine that these brightly colored purple berries are natural. They make a very interesting splash of color in the otherwise muted shades of winter.

Beneath dense undergrowth I found some sturdy vines with deep purple berries clustered at intervals along the vines. Careful not to get too scratched by the multitude of briars on the vines, I cut several to take back to the house. I pored over various books trying to find the name of these berries that were the size and color of blueberries. Finally I asked my friend Wendy Maddox, who grew up in Virginia and has a wealth of knowledge about everything that grows here. She said it was a weed called sweet brier. I then looked it up in some of my books and discovered that it is actually a type of wild rose, *Rosa eglanteria* (sweet brier rose) and is one of the many species of roses from which today's modern roses have been developed. I gained a newfound appreciation of this "weed." Since I love roses and grow many varieties, I now consider this one part of my collection.

I was also pleasantly surprised to see that the juniper trees that were growing by the edge of the pond had an abundant supply of delicate blue berries, and the tall stately hemlocks had produced a marvelous bounty of tiny, perfectly shaped cones. Armed with all of these found materials, I began creating a wreath. Hopefully, you will be able to find these or similar materials; if not, gather what you do find and have fun creating a special wreath of your own.

Basic Boxwood Wreath

There are hundreds of ways to decorate a boxwood wreath but, after making the basic wreath, you may decide to leave it unadorned. Plain ones look great hanging inside or outside on doors and windows; hung around a wall sconce; or set flat on a table with a hurricane globe and candle, flowers, or other decoration inside. Once you've mastered the basic boxwood wreath shown here, you can move on to the decorated ones that follow. My preference is to decorate wreaths with as many fresh and natural ingredients as possible. I would much rather put

bright red apples on a wreath than add a red bow to it. Decorating with fruit takes very little time yet can be most impressive.

All of my boxwood wreath variations use fresh fruit as decoration. These wreaths are best hung outside. In order for the fruit to be attached to the wreath, it must be pierced, and the warmth of your home's interior will cause the fruit to rot much more quickly than if the wreath is hung outside. Outdoors, it should keep up to three weeks (assuming the squirrels and deer stay away).

You Will Need

About 80 sprigs of boxwood, each about 7 inches long (about ½ bushel or one grocery bag)

16-inch wire wreath frame (available from craft and hobby stores)

Spool of 26-gauge floral wire

Wire cutters

Pruning shears

Making the Wreath

Step 1: Wrap the end of the wire from the spool securely around one of the wires near the top of the frame. Do not cut the wire from the spool. I find it easiest to make this wreath when I'm sitting at a table with the bottom part of the wire frame in my lap and the top part resting against a table. I turn the frame as I go so that I am always working at the upper part of the wreath.

Step 2: Gather three or four fairly uniform sprigs of boxwood and, holding the bundle close to the place where the wire was attached to the frame, firmly wrap the wire two or three times around the base of the boxwood sprigs, as shown in **Diagram 1A**.

Step 3: Lay the bundle on the frame and wrap the wire two or three times around the boxwood sprigs and the wire frame, as shown in **Diagram 1B**.

Step 4: Gather another bundle of boxwood sprigs approximately the same size as the first and hold the bundle close to the stems of the previously wired bundle. Once again, wrap the wire around the stems of the sprigs, then lay the bundle on the wire frame, overlapping the first bundle by about 4 inches, as shown in **Diagram 1C**. Secure the bundle to the frame with the spool wire, as described in Step 3.

Diagram 1

Gathering the Boxwood

When gathering boxwood, I don't worry about taking uniform cuttings, but simply concentrate on where the bush needs to be trimmed. Later, when making the wreath, I break the cuttings into sprigs approximately 7 inches long. To maintain freshness, make the wreath on the same day you gather the boxwood. If you are not ready to hang the wreath immediately, keep it in the garage or outside.

Step 5: Continue adding bundles of boxwood to the frame until the entire frame is covered with boxwood. (For a 16-inch wreath you will need approximately 20 bundles.) Tuck the last bundle under the first and carefully secure it to the wreath.

Step 6: Turn the wreath over so that the right side is facing down, bring the wire to the back, and cut it off, leaving a 2-inch tail. Tuck the wire tail into the frame, wrapping it firmly around one of the frame wires. Or make a loop of the wire to use for hanging. I usually just slip one of the frame wires over a nail or use a wreath hanger that will catch on the wire frame.

Adding Fruit to the Basic Wreath

Step 1: For apples, lemons, limes, and oranges, insert an 18-inch piece of 16-gauge wire directly through the middle of the piece of fruit. Depending on the look you want to achieve, you may want the side of the fruit facing out or the stem or bottom ends facing out. If you want the side facing out, insert the wire vertically down through the core of the fruit, as shown in **Diagram 2A**. If you want the stem or bottom facing out, insert the wire horizontally through the middle of the fruit, as shown in **2B**. Once the wire is inserted through the fruit, bend it down on both sides into a U-shape.

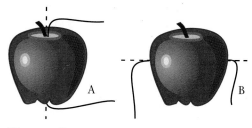

Diagram 2

Step 2: Position the piece of fruit on the wreath and push the ends of the wire through the wreath. Carefully twist the wire together at the back of the wreath, taking care to twist it firmly enough to keep the fruit from flopping down, but not so tight as to cause the wire to slit the fruit.

Step 3: For pineapples, insert an 18-inch piece of 16-gauge wire horizontally through the pineapple, about one-third of the way up from its base, as shown in **Diagram 3**. Bend the ends down into a U-shape.

Step 4: Tightly wrap a 24-inch piece of 26-gauge wire two or three times around the neck of the pineapple directly below the leaves, twisting the two ends securely together at the back side of the pineapple and leaving tails at least 5 inches long.

Step 5: Lay the pineapple on the wreath with its side facing out. Push the wires on both the base and neck of the pineapple through the wreath to the back, as shown in **Diagram 4**. Carefully twist the wires tightly around the wreath frame to secure.

Diagram 3

Diagram 4

Quick and Easy Decorating with a Plain Boxwood Wreath

▲ Hang three or more wreaths in a bay window, or hang a single wreath in a smaller window. Use a ribbon made from wide red satin, velvet, or fabric to hang the wreath. Or choose a border print fabric with Christmas colors, and line the border strip with another piece of the border print or with a contrasting fabric. The photograph on page 213 shows plain wreaths hanging inside a window.

▲ Place a 12-inch wreath flat on a table to use as a centerpiece with a hurricane lamp with a candle inside, a vase of flowers, or, for a special touch, a pot of early-blooming narcissus.

▲ Hang individual plain wreaths on the outside of windows to decorate the house exterior. The size of the wreath should be in proportion to the window. It is best for the wreaths to cover the window almost to the frame, but not to extend onto the frame.

*A*pple and Holly Boxwood Wreath

The old door where I hang an apple-and-holly wreath is 39 inches wide, which is wider than most, so I use a 24-inch wire frame with 16 apples. For a smaller door, you might want to use a 21-inch frame with 14 apples. These directions are for the wreath with the 24-inch frame.

You Will Need

24-inch basic boxwood wreath

16 medium-size Red Delicious apples

16 sprigs of holly

16 pieces of 16-gauge wire, each 18 inches long

Pruning shears

Making the Wreath

S t e p 1 : Make a 24-inch boxwood
wreath, following the instructions for
the "Basic Boxwood Wreath" on page
122. For this larger wreath, however,
you will need a 24-inch wire wreath
frame and about ¾ bushel of boxwood
clippings, cut into sprigs about 7
inches long.

S t e p 2 : Following the instructions for
"Adding Fruit to the Basic Wreath" on
page 124, add four apples (with the
stems facing outward) to your wreath
with one each at the noon, 3 o'clock, 6
o'clock, and 9 o'clock positions, as
shown in the diagram. Take care to ensure that these first four apples are sit-
uated at exact quarter sections of the
wreath.

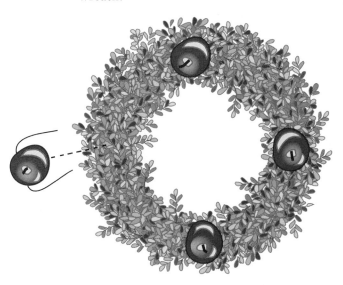

Gathering the Holly

When gathering holly, cut a
branch or twig that has several
berries clustered together. In
order for the red of the berries to
stand out as much as possible,
the holly leaves and extra stems
should be eliminated. Use small
pruning shears to carefully (so as
not to cause any
berries to fall
off the branch)
cut all leaves
and twigs from
the holly above
the clump of
berries. Cut just
the leaves below
the berries,
leaving an
approximately
4-inch woody
stem.

S t e p 3 : Evenly space three more apples
in each quarter section until you have
16 apples evenly spaced around the
wreath.

S t e p 4 : Carefully take the sprigs of
holly and push the 4-inch woody stems
through the outer part of the wreath
between the apples. The stems should
remain secure as long as they are long
enough to penetrate the gaps between
the sprigs of boxwood on the wreath
frame.

Boxwood Wreath with Mixed Fruit

Each year my mixed fruit wreath is a little different. I like to experiment depending on the fruit available. You might try other variations on your own by adding such materials as pinecones, lotus pods, holly leaves and berries, limes, 'Lady' apples, or kumquats.

You Will Need

24-inch basic boxwood wreath

1 large Red Delicious apple

2 small pineapples

10 lemons

4 blood oranges

17 pieces of 16-gauge wire, each 18 inches long

2 pieces of 26-gauge wire, each 24 inches long

Making the Wreath

S t e p   1 : Make a 24-inch boxwood wreath, following the instructions for the "Basic Boxwood Wreath" on page 122, but using a 24-inch wire wreath frame and about ¾ bushel of boxwood clippings, cut into 7-inch-long sprigs.

S t e p   2 : Follow the instructions for "Adding Fruit to the Basic Wreath" on page 124 for wiring all of the fruit onto this wreath. Start by wiring the large apple to the top of the wreath with the stem pointing outward.

S t e p   3 : Wire the two pineapples to the top portion of the wreath, angling the pineapples on each side of the apple, as shown in the photograph on the opposite page.

S t e p   4 : Wire four lemons in a square at the bottom of the wreath exactly opposite the apple. Then wire two blood oranges to either side of the lemons, centering them between the lemon rows, as shown in the diagram.

S t e p   5 : Wire three lemons and one blood orange just below the base of each pineapple, as shown in the photograph.

*B*asic Evergreen Wreath

Wreaths can be made from pine, hemlock, juniper, and other fir trees in much the same way as they are made from boxwood. The directions here are for a basic juniper wreath with two variations, but if you do not have juniper readily available, try the wreath with other evergreen materials.

You Will Need

About 100 sprigs of juniper (or other evergreen sprigs) with berries, each 8 inches long

18-inch wire wreath frame (available from craft and hobby stores)

Spool of 26-gauge wire

Wire cutters

Making the Wreath

Step 1: Sort through the sprigs of juniper, separating the ones that have more berries. Set these aside.

Step 2: Wrap the end of the wire from the spool securely around one of the wires at the top of the wreath frame. Do not cut the wire from the spool.

Step 3: Take four fairly uniform sprigs of juniper approximately 8 inches long and gather them into a bundle. Place two heavily berried sprigs of juniper from the set-aside group on top of the bundle. Holding the bundle close to the place where the wire was attached to the frame, firmly wrap the wire two or three times around the base of the juniper sprigs. (See **Diagram 1** on page 123 for this wiring technique.)

Step 4: Lay the bundle onto the frame and wrap the wire two or three times around both the juniper sprigs and the wire frame.

Step 5: Gather another bundle of juniper sprigs approximately the same size as the first and hold the bundle close to the stems of the previously wired bundle. Once again, wrap the wire around the stems of the sprigs, then lay the bundle on the wire frame, overlapping the first bundle by about 4 inches. Secure the bundle to the frame with the spool wire, as described in Step 4.

Step 6: Continue adding bundles of juniper to the frame until the entire frame is covered with juniper (you will need approximately 16 bundles). Tuck the last bundle under the first and carefully secure it to the wreath.

Juniper Wreath with Woodland Materials

The materials for this wreath were gleaned from my many walks around our yard. We have juniper, hemlock, sweet brier roses (*Rosa eglanteria*), and beautyberry (*Callicarpa* spp.) all within picking distance of our cabin. But you don't need the same materials to make a wreath like this one. Start with juniper sprigs and see what you have on hand to add for decoration.

You Will Need

18-inch juniper wreath

Several branches of hemlock with cones, or other tiny pine cones (approximately 60 cones total)

Several vines of sweet brier rose (*Rosa eglanteria*) with berries to total about a dozen clumps

About 24 stems of beautyberry (*Callicarpa* spp.) with berries attached

Spool of 26-gauge wire

Wire cutters

Pruning shears

Making the Wreath

S t e p   1 : Make an 18-inch juniper wreath, following the instructions for the "Basic Evergreen Wreath" on page 130.

S t e p   2 : Divide the beautyberry into two bundles of 12 stems each. For each bundle, cut a piece of wire about 18 inches long and wrap the middle part of the wire tightly three times around the stems, as shown in **Diagram 1A**. Twist the two ends of wire together tightly to secure.

S t e p   3 : Push the wire ends of each bundle through the wreath at the top right and left, with the stem ends facing each other and the branches of berries draping a little over halfway down the wreath, as shown in **Diagram 1B**.

S t e p   4 : Prepare two bundles of tiny cones with six sprigs of hemlock cones per bundle. First find hemlock sprigs with as many cones clustered together as possible. Trim as much of the hemlock needles from the sprigs as you can without damaging or breaking off the cones. Working with the spool wire, wrap the wire tightly two or three times around two of the hemlock sprigs, leaving at least an 8-inch tail of wire, as shown in **Diagram 2A**.

S t e p   5 : Take two more sprigs of hemlock cones and, working with the same wire, hold the sprigs close to the first group, overlapping them so that the cones of the third and fourth sprigs lie just above the first two. Wrap the wire

Diagram 1

first around the new sprigs two or three times and then around the first sprigs. Finally, take the last two sprigs of hemlock cones and wire these in the same manner. When you are finished, the cones should be sprayed out in a branch approximately 8 inches long.

S t e p 6 : Cut the wire from the spool, leaving an end about 8 inches long. Repeat steps 4 and 5 to make a second bundle of cones approximately the same size as the first.

S t e p 7 : Gently place the two bundles of hemlock cones on top of the beauty-berry at the top of the wreath so that the stem ends cover the stem ends of the beautyberry, as shown in **Diagram 2B**. Push the 8-inch wire ends through the wreath to the back and carefully wire the bundles to the frame.

S t e p 8 : Finally, add the sweet brier rose vines to the wreath. Cut about 10 clumps of sweet brier berries from the vines, leaving stem ends about 4 inches long. The vines of sweet brier are very sturdy, and these ends can be pushed directly through the wreath and held in place by the juniper branches and wreath frame wires. If you prefer, you can wire the ends to attach them to the wreath. These sweet brier berries are attached near the top of the wreath so that they cover the stem ends of the beautyberry and hemlock.

Diagram 2

134 Christmas with Jinny Beyer

*G*rapevine Wreath with Lotus Pods, Rose Hips, and Pomegranate

This is a good wreath for inside the house. Even though the pomegranate is fresh, it does not rot when pierced as other fruit does. In fact, both the rose hips and the pomegranate dry nicely, and the wreath will last indefinitely. Because of the rustic nature of this wreath, I like to hang it on an old wooden door. The wreath can be hung square or slightly askew, which is my preference.

You Will Need

About 50 feet of grapevines, approximately ½ inch in diameter

1 large pomegranate

3 large lotus pods (available at craft or florist supply stores)

24 sprigs of wild rose hips or holly, each about 10 inches long

Spool of 26-gauge wire

1 piece of 16-gauge wire, 18 inches long

Wire cutters

Making the Wreath

Step 1: Hold the thickest part of one vine in one hand and loop the vine around into a circle approximately 15 inches in diameter. Take hold of the looped piece and wrap the remaining vine around the circle. When all of the length of vine has been used up, carefully tuck the end between two of the vines in the wreath. Repeat for additional vines. Wire in place if necessary.

Step 2: Tightly wrap a piece of the 26-gauge wire two or three times around six sprigs of rose hips, leaving about 6 inches of wire on either end. Try to have the rose hips fan out a little so they have an airy, delicate look. Make three more bundles in the same way. If you are using sprigs of holly instead of rose hips, be sure to remove all the holly leaves first.

Step 3: Wire two of the bundles of rose hips to the top of the wreath, with the stem ends facing each other and the hips trailing delicately down the side of the wreath.

Step 4: Carefully thread a piece of the 26-gauge wire through the base of each lotus pod, about 1 inch up from the bottom. Bend the wires down into a U-shape. (See "Adding Fruit to the Basic Wreath" on page 124.)

Step 5: Wire one lotus pod to the top of the wreath by pushing the two ends of wire through the grapevine and twisting them together at the back. Place the lotus pod so it covers the stem ends of the rose hips.

Step 6: Insert the 16-gauge wire through the middle of the pomegranate from side to side and bend it into a U-shape. Place the pomegranate at the bottom of the wreath directly opposite the lotus pod, with the stem end facing out. Push the wire ends through the grapevine wreath and gently twist them together at the back of the wreath.

Step 7: Wire the two remaining lotus pods to the wreath on either side of the pomegranate, as shown in the diagram.

Step 8: Gently tuck the last two groups of wild rose hips into the bottom of the wreath, between the grapevines and behind each of the two lotus pods, so that the hips fan upward into the hole in the center of the wreath.

Grapevine Wreath with Ivy and Holly

You Will Need

About 50 feet of grapevines, approximately ½ inch in diameter

2 lengths of fresh English ivy vine, each 8 feet long

8 sprigs of holly

Pruning shears

Making the Wreath

Step 1: Follow the instructions in Step 1 on page 135 to make a 20-inch grapevine wreath.

Step 2: Tuck the end of the first length of ivy vine between some of the grapevines. Gently weave it over and under the grapevines, twisting the ivy as you wind it around the wreath so that the leaves face outward, as shown in the diagram. Continue weaving in and out until you have used the entire length of ivy. Tuck the end into the wreath. Repeat with the second piece of ivy vine. No wiring should be necessary.

Step 3: Prepare the holly springs according to the instructions in "Gathering the Holly" on page 127. Evenly space the holly sprigs around the wreath and secure them by pushing their stem ends through the grapevine.

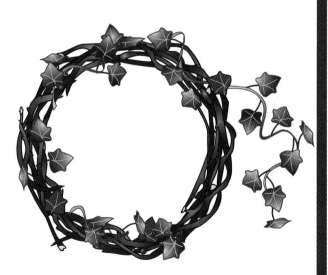

When our children were small, we always took a drive around the neighborhood one night just before Christmas to see how people decorated their houses. It always struck me that something as simple as a tastefully placed wreath could make a home very cozy and inviting.

You do not need to go to a lot of elaborate expense to decorate your house and yard for the holidays. Put a wreath on the door and pile an old wheelbarrow or iron kettle with greens and holly. Put pine boughs and fresh fruit on a windowsill, make a swag over a doorway with pine roping, or try one of the plaques shown in this chapter. Once the wooden bases for these plaques are cut, they are very easy and quick to make (even though they look quite complicated), and they will stay looking fresh outside for more than two weeks. If you do not have magnolia leaves or boxwood available where you live, substitute other evergreen leaves or pieces of fir or pine.

I find many of the materials for outside decorations just by taking a walk around my yard and through the neighborhood. Take a walk near your home and see what you can find. Keep an eye out for pods, cones, and other materials to add a different look to these projects.

$\mathcal{P}$ine Roping

Pine roping is readily available wherever Christmas trees are sold. When I am in a rush, I will often purchase roping for my decorations, but I prefer to make my own because it is much fresher, will last longer, and is not as skimpy as the store-bought roping. These directions are for pine, but roping can be made from any evergreen material—or from combinations of different materials.

You Will Need

For 10 feet of roping

About 80 sprigs of white pine, each 10 inches long

12 feet of green twine

Spool of 26-gauge wire

Wire cutters

Making the Roping

Step 1: Make a slipknot in one end of the twine and run an end of the spool wire through the loop. Twist the wire back on itself and secure it so that the twine and the wire are tightly connected, as shown in **Diagram 1.** Do not cut the wire from the spool.

Step 2: Take three or four 10-inch sprigs of pine and, holding them close to where the wire and twine join, wrap the wire tightly around the ends of the sprigs two or three times, as shown in **Diagram 2.**

Step 3: Place the sprigs on the twine and wrap the wire two times around the sprig ends and the twine, as shown in **Diagram 3.** Be careful not to wrap around any of the needles, only the stems. This will ensure roping that is fuller as well as more secure.

Step 4: Make another bundle of pine sprigs approximately the same size as the first. Once again, wrap the wire tightly around the sprig ends first, and then around the twine, facing the same direction as the first bundle and overlapping the previous bundle by about 4 inches (enough to cover the stem ends of the first bundle).

Diagram 1

Quick and Easy Pine and Juniper Roping

To trim the door of our cabin, I made a length of pine roping approximately 20 feet long. I attached one layer of roping down each side of the door and two layers across the top of the door. I then took 10-inch branches of berried juniper and pushed the ends of the branches between the twine and wire of the pine roping at approximately 12-inch intervals. I tried to balance the branches on either side of the door so that they were equal.

Adding the juniper after making the roping gives you more flexibility for placing the juniper and its berries. Another option is to purchase the basic roping from a nursery or Christmas tree stand and add juniper, boxwood, or other greens to it.

Step 5: Continue adding pine bundles to the roping until you have the desired length. Turn the last bundle in the opposite direction. Tie off the twine and wire, securing them tightly together as you did at the opposite end of the twine.

Diagram 2

Diagram 3

Over-Doorway Apple Plaque with Pine Roping Trim

This is the decoration that I place over one of the main doors into our house. The base of the plaque is a piece of plywood. After you have the plywood cut to size, the remainder of this project can be made in less than half an hour. You can save the plywood from year to year. This project is very impressive—the beauty is that the design looks much more complicated than it really is.

You Will Need

12 feet of pine roping

About 100 sprigs of boxwood, each 4 inches long (about ¼ bushel or half a grocery bag)

24 large Red Delicious apples

1 large pineapple

30 magnolia leaves

16 large pinecones

18 × 72-inch piece of ½-inch plywood

2 pieces of 26-gauge wire, each 12 inches long

27 2-inch finishing nails

Hot-glue gun and glue sticks

Jigsaw

Hammer

Staple gun and staples

Wire cutters

Pruning shears

Nails or screws as needed for hanging

Making the Plaque

S t e p   1 : Make the plywood plaque by cutting an arc from the plywood that is 60 inches wide × 15 inches high. If you do not have a jigsaw, you may be able to have the plywood cut at the lumberyard where you purchase it. Hammer the nails into the plywood as shown in **Diagram 1;** they should protrude about 1½ inches from the board.

S t e p   2 : Cut about 1 inch off the stem ends of the magnolia leaves to prevent them from curling. Staple them to the upper edge of the plaque with the leaves extending beyond the edge by about 2 inches, as shown in **Diagram 2.**

S t e p   3 : Staple the boxwood sprigs over the entire plywood arc so that you cannot see any wood. Be sure to place boxwood right up against the nails.

S t e p   4 : Wrap one end of one piece of

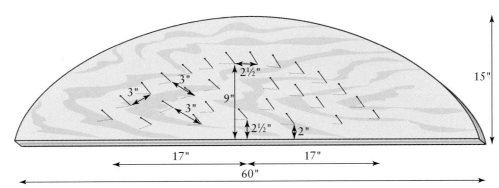

Diagram 1

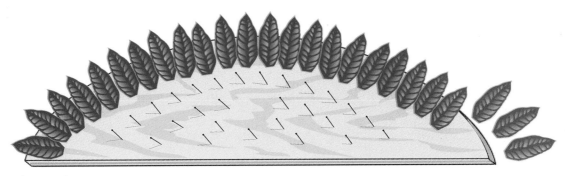

Diagram 2

26-gauge wire around the left-hand nail at the top center of the plywood arc. Then wrap one end of the second piece of wire around the right-hand nail at the top center. Twist each wire around the nail tightly to secure. Attach the pineapple to the center of the plaque, embedding the bottom of the fruit on the bottom center nail and pushing the neck and base of the leaves between the two nails at the top center of the plaque. Bring the two wires around the neck of the pineapple and twist them tightly together, as shown in **Diagram 3.**

Step 5 : Embed one apple, with its side facing out, on each of the remaining 24 nails.

Step 6 : Arrange the 16 pinecones as shown in the photograph on page 142. Place them on their sides, making two rows of four on each side of the pineapple greens. Once they are arranged evenly, glue them to the plaque with the hot-glue gun.

Step 7 : Make 12 feet of pine roping, following the instructions in "Pine Roping" on page 140. Arrange a double row of pine roping across the top of the door frame and, if necessary, staple or tack it in a few places to hold it.

Step 8 : Gently prop the plaque on top of the door frame and lean it slightly backward. The weight of the fruit should hold it in place, but for safety, secure it with a nail, or put two screws on the back of the plaque to which you can attach wire, then hang it on a nail.

Diagram 3

Apple Plaque with Double Swag

This decoration is made with three separate pieces—the plaque in the center, and two swags on either side. Each of them could be used separately.

The apple plaque alone could be hung on a door, and the two swags could be hung underneath windows at either side of the door.

You Will Need

For the apple plaque

About 40 sprigs of boxwood, each 4 inches long

1 pineapple

9 large Red Delicious apples

8 large magnolia leaves

13 medium-size magnolia leaves

10 × 16-inch piece of ½-inch plywood

2 pieces of 26-gauge wire, each 12 inches long

12 2-inch finishing nails

Picture hook and picture hanger

Staple gun

Jigsaw

Hammer

Wire cutters

Pruning shears

Making the Plaque

S t e p 1 : Hammer the nails into the ply-wood as shown in **Diagram 1;** they should protrude about 1½ inches from the board.

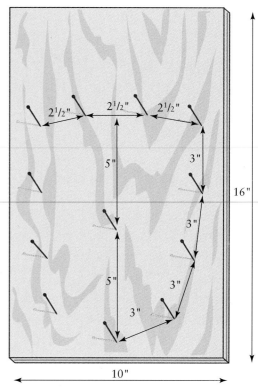

Diagram 1

S t e p 2 : Cut about 1 inch off the stem ends of the magnolia leaves to prevent them from curling, then staple them to the outside of the plaque. The eight large leaves should be evenly spaced around the top of the plaque (beginning just opposite the top two nails), with the leaves extending beyond the wood by about 3 inches. The 13 medium leaves should be stapled around the bottom of the plaque with the edges extending over the wood by about 1½ inches.

S t e p   3 : Staple the boxwood sprigs over the surface of the wood, making sure to cover the cut ends of the magnolia leaves.

S t e p   4 : Wrap one end of one piece of 26-gauge wire around the left-hand nail at the top center of the plywood. Then wrap one end of the second piece of wire around the right-hand nail at the top center. Twist each wire around the nail tightly to secure. Attach the pineapple to the center of the plaque, embedding the bottom of the fruit on the center nail and pushing the neck and base of the leaves between the two nails at the top center of the plaque. Bring the two wires around the neck of the pineapple and twist them tightly together (see **Diagram 3** on page 144).

S t e p   5 : Embed one apple, with its stem facing out, on each of the nine remaining nails.

S t e p   6 : Use the picture hook and picture hanger to hang the plaque centered underneath a window.

You Will Need

For one under-window swag

About 80 sprigs of boxwood, each 6 inches long (about ½ bushel or one grocery bag)

20 large magnolia leaves

9 medium-size Red Delicious apples

2 large pinecones

8 × 50-inch piece of ½-inch plywood

9 2-inch finishing nails

4 1-inch finishing nails

4 pieces of 26-gauge wire, each 18 inches long

2 hooks and 2 screw eyes

Hammer

Wire cutters

Pruning shears

Making the Swag

S t e p   1 : Cut the plywood to the dimensions and shape shown in **Diagram 2** on page 148. Hammer the 2-inch nails into the plywood as shown; they should protrude about 1½ inches from the board.

S t e p   2 : Hammer the 1-inch nails into the plywood with two nails at each top corner, as shown in **Diagram 3** on page 148. Then wrap a pieceof 26-gauge wire around each nail, leaving a fairly long tail.

Step 3: Cut about 1 inch off the stem ends of the magnolia leaves to prevent them from curling, then staple them to the lower edge of the crescent, tips pointing out, as shown in the photograph on page 145.

Step 4: Staple the boxwood sprigs across the top of the crescent, making sure to cover the cut ends of the magnolia leaves.

Step 5: Embed one apple, stem side facing out, on each nail. Place one pinecone over each set of 1-inch nails at the top corners of the crescent. Wrap the wires around the pinecones, under their petals, to secure them to the plywood base.

Step 6: Screw the hooks underneath your windowsill, then install the screw eyes in the back of the swag. Hang the swag.

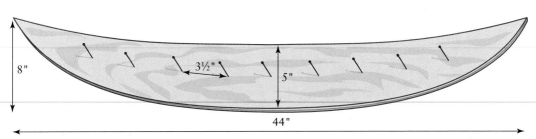

8"   3½"   5"

44"

Diagram 2

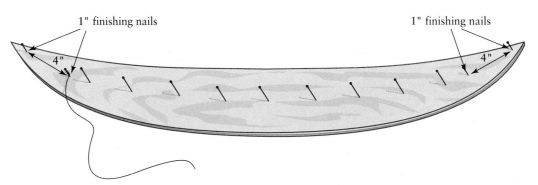

1" finishing nails   1" finishing nails

4"   4"

Diagram 3

Spruce Up Outdoor Windowsills

A few greens and some fruit can transform a windowsill in minutes. I discovered this when I decided to decorate the two small windows on either side of our main door. After hanging the apple wreath on the door and the apple plaque above the door, I balanced out the overall design by adding some fruit to the sill on either side of the door (see page 138 for a photograph of the full doorway). A few small branches of hemlock, a pineapple in the middle, and two bright red apples complete the picture.

For the window next to the cabin door, I wanted to balance out the purple tones from the beautyberry (*Callicarpa* spp.), juniper, and sweet brier rose (*Rosa eglanteria*) berries, so I chose some black plums to place on a bed of pine needles. You can see how nicely this turned out in the photograph on page 141.

Here are two other ways I spruce up my windowsills during the holidays.

▲ I place a garland of juniper and boxwood roping along the edge of the kitchen windowsill, with brightly colored apples spaced amid the roping.

▲ I place candlesticks on each windowsill inside the house to be viewed by passersby from the outside. It really adds an appealing, welcoming glow to the outside of the house. You can see the full effect of this simple treatment in the photograph on page 145.

The Christmas Tree

Traditionally in both my family and my husband's, trimming the tree is a special occasion. That is when the first Christmas cookies are brought out, the lights strung, Christmas carols played, and, as each ornament is hung, fond memories of Christmasses past fill our thoughts. The first Christmas after John and I were married was also the first one away from our families. About two weeks before Christmas, we received a check from my parents with a note saying that the money was to be used to buy ornaments for our first tree. Since we had nothing, we purchased a string of lights and a few shiny balls. I was especially moved by the thought, as we were separated by a continent and John and I were beginning to build our own Christmas traditions.

Our next Christmas was spent in Sarawak on the island of Borneo. We added to our small collection of tree ornaments with distinctive Malaysian- and Chinese-style decorations. That year began the tradition of our Christmas tree. Those first years I supplemented the few new decorations we purchased with ones I made. As the years progressed, with the exception of the lights and shiny balls, our tree became a memory of ornaments purchased in places we had lived or visited and ones made by friends, local craftspeople, and me. In this chapter, I share with you some of the ornaments I have made through the years.

Miniature Cat Ornaments

Most people like cats and, of course, all cat lovers think their cats are more remarkable than anyone else's— and I must admit I am no exception. This ornament was modeled after our favorite cat, whose name is "Cat."

If you are under a time constraint, make the cats with scraps of a variety of cotton prints—one fabric for each cat, or different fabrics on the front and back. Cut out, sew, stuff, and finish them all at the same time—you can make several in an hour. If you have

more time, try the strip-quilted and patchwork variations. Experiment using a variety of different fabrics—several different versions are shown in the photograph. Choose your favorite variation, or make them all. These cats are also great used in place of a bow on a package. Then the person who receives the gift can save the cat and use it for an ornament the following year.

You may want to review "Making and Using Templates" on page 74 before beginning this project.

You Will Need

For each cat ornament

2 5 × 8½-inch pieces of fabric (for the large cat)

2 4 × 7-inch pieces of fabric (for the small cat)

Small scraps of fabric (for the patch-work and strip-quilted cats); use scraps left over from other projects or whatever you have on hand

Handful of polyester stuffing

#8 pearl cotton

10 inches of ⅛-inch ribbon for the bow

Template plastic

Permanent pen

Making the Plain Fabric Cat

Step 1: Using the template plastic, make templates for the cat body and tail using either the **Large Cat Ornament Pattern** or the **Small Cat Ornament Pattern** on pages 156–157.

Step 2: Place two pieces of fabric together with right sides facing. (If you are using one piece of fabric, fold it with right sides facing.) Trace the body template onto the fabric and cut two body pieces (front and back). Trace the tail template onto the remaining fabric and cut two tail pieces.

Step 3: Pin the two body pieces right sides together and begin stitching at the bottom of the cat, sewing a ¼-inch seam allowance. Stitch across the bottom and all around the cat, leaving a 1½-inch opening at the base of the cat where the tail will be attached.

Step 4: Trim the seams and clip the ears, the curve of the back, and the front foot, as shown in **Diagram 1.** Turn the cat right side out and, using the blunt end of a wooden skewer, push carefully into the ears to make sure they are turned completely and are pointed.

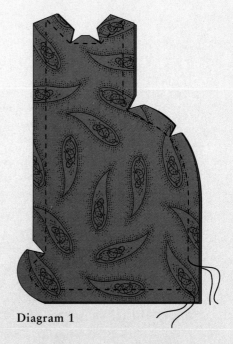

Diagram 1

Step 5: Pin the two tail pieces together and stitch all around, leaving an opening at the end. Turn right side out.

Step 6: Stuff the cat and tail with the polyester filling. Do not stuff the tail too tightly because it will need to be bent. Insert the tail into the opening at the base of the cat and whipstitch the opening closed.

Step 7: Bend the tail toward the front of the cat and tack the tip of it to the body. If you are making several cats, plan to have them turning in different directions. In other words, sometimes bend the tail toward the front of the cat and sometimes toward the back.

Step 8: To finish, use the ribbon to tie a bow around the neck of the cat. Then thread a 10-inch piece of pearl cotton through the top of the head to form a hanging loop. Tie it off.

Making the Patchwork Cat

Step 1: Using the template plastic, make templates for the four patchwork pieces using the **Large Cat Patchwork Templates** or the **Small Cat Patchwork Templates** on pages 156–157.

Step 2: Select four different fabrics to use. Fold each piece with right sides together and use one template for each of the fabrics. Trace the templates onto the fabric and cut two pieces from each fabric (a front and a back).

Step 3: So as not to get confused and to make sure that all the pieces are cut correctly, lay the pieces out in order. Sew them together according to **Diagram 2.**

Step 4: Press. Using the pearl cotton, finish the seams with feather stitching embroidery, as shown in **Diagram 3.**

Step 5: Finish the cat by following Steps 3 through 8 in "Making the Plain Fabric Cat" on page 153.

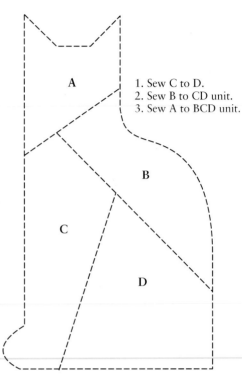

1. Sew C to D.
2. Sew B to CD unit.
3. Sew A to BCD unit.

Diagram 2

Diagram 3

Making the Strip-Quilted Cat

Some strip quilting is done with batting, and the piece is quilted while the stitching is being done. These cats are so small that the addition of batting would add too much bulk, and the ears and feet would be difficult to define. I use a fabric base and do the strip work directly on the fabric.

S t e p   1 : Using the template plastic, make templates for the cat body and tail using either the **Large Cat Ornament Pattern** or the **Small Cat Ornament Pattern** on pages 156–157.

S t e p   2 : Place two pieces of scrap fabric with right sides together. (If you are using one piece, fold it with right sides facing.) Trace the body template onto the fabric and cut two body pieces (a front and a reverse). Trace the tail template onto the fabric you want to use for the tail and cut two tail pieces.

S t e p   3 : Cut narrow strips about 3 inches long and ¾ to 1¼ inches wide out of a variety of scraps. A few pieces of shiny fabric such as lamé add sparkle when the ornament is on the tree. You will need approximately 10 strips for each side of the small cat and 13 for each side of the large one.

S t e p   4 : Working from the center of the cat toward either side, place one of the wider strips at an angle across the scrap fabric front so that the strip crosses where the back hump of the cat curves downward. With right sides together, sew one strip to either side of this first strip, angling them so that

they are slightly wider at the back hump. Open the strips out and press them flat with a hot iron. Following **Diagram 4,** continue adding strips until the fabric base is completely covered. I do both the front and back of the cat at the same time, as I can add two strips on each piece (four total) before going to the iron for pressing. If I am making several cats at one time, I sew strips to fabric bases for several cats before doing the pressing. This saves getting up and down all the time. (For more details on strip quilting, see "Strip Quilting" on page 86.)

Diagram 4

S t e p   5 : With the wrong side facing you, trim off the strips that extend beyond the cat shape. Finish the cat by following steps 3 through 8 in "Making the Plain Fabric Cat" on page 153.

Tail placement

Small Cat Ornament Pattern

Small Cat Patchwork Templates

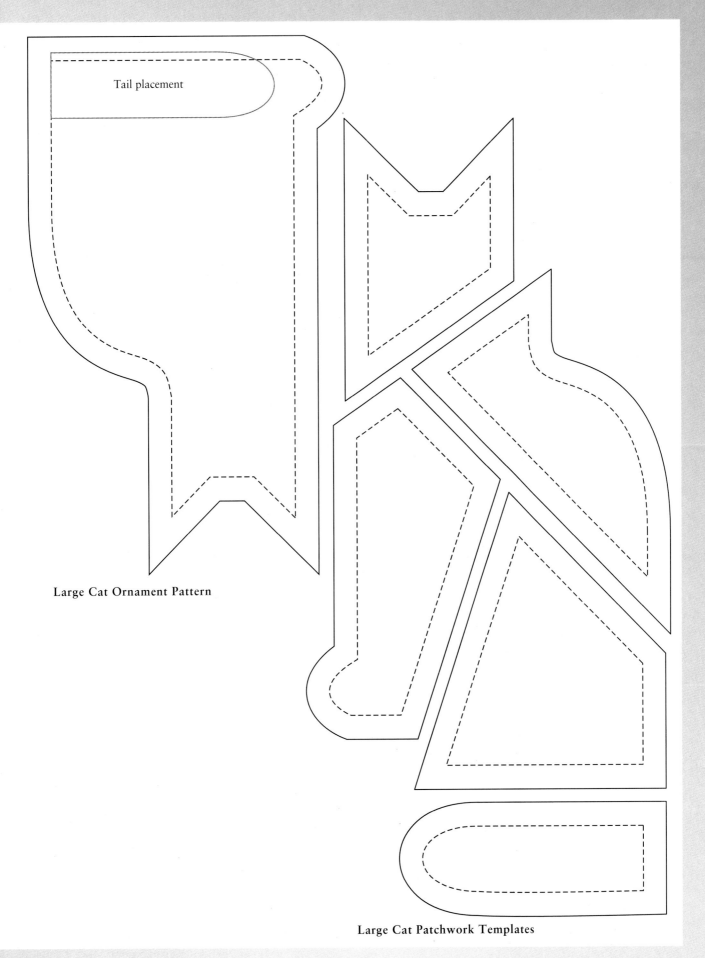

Tail placement

Large Cat Ornament Pattern

Large Cat Patchwork Templates

Miniature Stocking Ornaments

These little stockings can be hung on a tree, placed on packages, or given as gifts with tiny presents placed inside. In contrast to the cat ornaments, I do like to use batting with these stockings, as it adds more body. You can make the stockings as elaborate or as simple as you like. Very quick versions can be made using a whole piece of cloth with a scrap of border print fabric for the cuff. Other versions can use crazy patch or strip techniques with embroidery, trim, or border accents. You may want to review "Making and Using Templates" on page 74 before beginning this project.

You Will Need

For both stockings

5 × 8-inch piece of fabric for the plain stocking

Variety of small leftover fabric scraps for the crazy-quilted or strip-quilted stocking

2 5 × 8-inch pieces of fabric for the linings

2 5 × 8-inch pieces of batting

2 6 × 3½-inch (finished width) strips of miniature border print fabric (or fabric of your choice) for the cuffs

2 10-inch lengths of pearl cotton

Template plastic

Permanent pen

side of the front and back stocking pieces. With right sides together, pin the front and back stocking pieces to each other and stitch around the stocking with a ¼-inch seam allowance, leaving the stocking open at the top. Clip the seam at the indentation at the top of the toe, as shown in **Diagram 1,** and turn the stocking right side out.

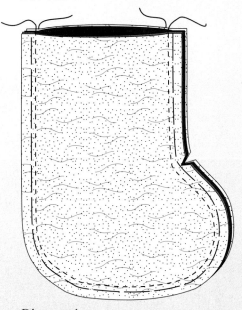

Diagram 1

Making the Plain Stocking

S t e p 1 : Using the template plastic, make a template for the stocking using the **Stocking Ornament Pattern** on page 161. To make a template for the cuff, draw a 3½ × 5-inch rectangle. Add a ¼-inch seam allowance to all sides to complete the template.

S t e p 2 : Fold the fabric for the stocking and the lining in half. Trace the template onto the fabric and cut two stocking pieces (front and back) and two lining pieces (front and back). Cut the cuff from the border print strip.

S t e p 3 : Cut two stocking pieces from the batting.

S t e p 4 : Using a ⅛-inch seam allowance, baste the batting pieces to the wrong

S t e p 5 : With right sides together, pin the front and back lining pieces together and stitch around the edge with a ¼-inch seam allowance. Leave the stocking lining open at the top. Do not turn right side out.

S t e p 6 : Push the stocking lining into the stocking. Pin the top edges together and stitch the lining and stocking together ¼ inch in from the edge.

Step 7: With right sides together, stitch the short edges of the cuff together, as shown in **Diagram 2** on page 160. Press the seams open. Turn the loop right side out, then fold in half lengthwise with wrong sides together. Press.

Diagram 2

Step 8: With the raw edges facing up, insert the cuff into the stocking and pin the raw edges of the stocking and lining to the raw edges of the cuff. Stitch together ¼ inch from the edge. Bring the cuff out of the stocking and fold over the outside.

Step 9: Thread the pearl cotton through the top of the cuff at the back of the stocking to form a hanging loop. Tie it off.

Making the Crazy-Quilted or Strip-Quilted Stocking

Step 1: For the strip-quilted stocking, cut narrow strips about 3 inches long and ¾ to 1¼ inches wide out of a variety of scraps. You will need approximately 13 strips for each side of the stocking. For the crazy-quilted stocking, cut the fabric into random-size patches. You will need approximately seven patches for each side of the stocking.

Step 2: Using the template plastic, make a template for the stocking using the **Stocking Ornament Pattern** on the opposite page. Trace the template onto the lining and the batting and cut two stocking pieces (front and back) from each. To make a template for the cuff, draw a 3½ × 5-inch rectangle. Add a ¼-inch seam allowance to all sides to complete the template. Cut the cuff from the border print strip.

Step 3: Strip-quilt or crazy-quilt directly onto the front and back pieces of batting. (See "Strip Quilting" on page 86 and "Crazy Patch Quilting" on page 86 for detailed instructions.) When all the fabric has been sewn to the batting, turn to the wrong side and trim the stocking to the size of the batting.

S t e p 4 : To embellish the crazy-quilted stockings, I often add feather stitching in a fine pearl cotton (see **Diagram 3** on page 158). This looks particularly nice on the velveteen stockings. On other stockings I've used mini strips of border print fabrics for embellishment.

S t e p 5 : With right sides together, pin the front and back stocking pieces to each other and stitch around the stocking with a ¼-inch seam allowance, leaving the stocking open at the top. Clip the seam at the indentation at the top of the toe, as shown in **Diagram 1** on page 159, and turn the stocking right side out.

S t e p 6 : Follow Steps 5 through 9 on pages 159–160 to finish the stocking.

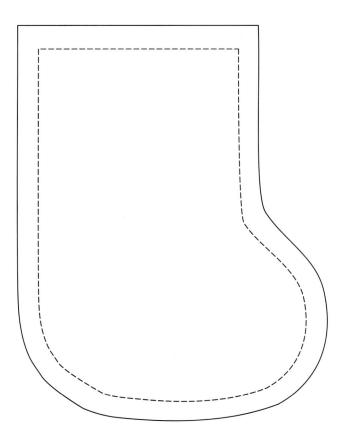

Stocking Ornament Pattern

Miniature Boxwood Tree

It is often nice at Christmastime to have a small tree as a tabletop decoration. This miniature boxwood tree is easy to make, lasts a long time, and will add a nice touch of Christmas green to any room of your house. If you keep water in the dish, this tree will stay fresh looking for more than three weeks.

I have decorated my tree with dried pink pepperberries and a wooden star for the top, but many different items could be used to decorate your miniature tree. Some possibilities include miniature lights, strings of cranberries, or dried miniature roses. You can also decorate your tree with miniature dried kumquat slices. For an added touch of interest, set your tree on a miniature tree skirt like the one shown here. (See "Miniature Tree Skirt" on page 164 for directions to make this project.)

You Will Need

About ¾ bushel (1½ grocery bags) of boxwood sprigs, ranging in size from 5 to 10 inches in length

12-inch sprig of boxwood for the top of the tree

75 4-inch clumps of dried pink pepperberries for decoration (optional)

Wooden star on a stiff wire stem (optional)

8 × 4 × 3½-inch block of Oasis floral foam

Plastic dish that will hold the foam upright

Bread knife

Making the Tree

Step 1: Shape the floral foam into a soft cone shape. This makes it easier to get the correct proportions of the tree. Beginning at about the center of the foam and working toward what will be the top of the tree, slice each of the four sides on an angle so that about ¾ inch is taken off the corners, as shown in **Diagram 1**.

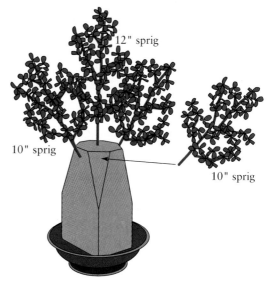

Diagram 2

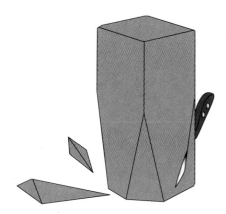

Diagram 1

Step 2: Gently smooth the corners of the foam with the knife, cutting just a little off to round the hard edges.

Step 3: Fill a sink or large pan with water and let the foam soak for about five minutes or until it fills with water.

Step 4: Set the foam upright into the plastic dish and begin building the tree, working from the top of the tree downward. Take the 12-inch sprig of boxwood and place it straight up in the top of the tree, as shown in **Diagram 2**. About 1 inch down from the top, evenly space three 10-inch sprigs of boxwood, facing upward.

Step 5: Insert several 5-inch sprigs of boxwood around the foam, facing slightly downward and just below the larger sprigs. Make sure you use enough pieces to cover the foam.

Step 6: Continue building the tree in this manner, working with longer sprigs of boxwood as you get to the bottom of the tree, until you have a row of 10-inch sprigs around the very bottom.

Step 7: If desired, decorate the tree with pepperberries by gently inserting the stem ends of the pepperberry clumps into the boxwood to hold them in place.

Step 8: If you want to add a star, poke the wire at the end of the star into the foam at the top of the tree.

*M*iniature Tree Skirt

This easy-to-make tree skirt fits nicely under a miniature
tabletop tree. Review "Working with Border Prints" on page 77
and "Making and Using Templates" on page 74 before beginning
this project.

Skill Level: Beginner
Size: Finished tree
skirt is 22½ inches
from side to side

You Will Need

½ yard of a Christmas print for the equilateral triangles

1 yard of border print fabric with at least two repeats of a 1¼-inch (finished width) stripe and at least 3 repeats of a 1½-inch (finished width) stripe

¾ yard of fabric for the backing

25 × 30-inch piece of batting

Template plastic

Permanent marker

Making Templates

Step 1: Follow steps 1 through 4 of "Drafting an Equilateral Triangle" on page 167 to make Template A. Your triangle will have a 9¼-inch side and a height of 8 inches. Add a ¼-inch seam allowance to each side of the drafted triangle. For Template B, cut a 1¼ × 9¾-inch rectangle. Add ¼-inch seam allowances to all sides.

Step 2: Use the full-size pattern pieces on page 166 to make templates for the long outer border (C) and the corner border piece (D). Note that the pattern for C is one-half the template; flip your template plastic to complete Template C. Seam allowances are included in the printed patterns.

Cutting

Position the arrows on the templates along the straight grain of the fabric.

From the Christmas print, cut:
6 A triangles

From the 1¼-inch border print, cut:
6 border bands (B)

From the 1½-inch border print, cut:
6 outer border pieces (C)
6 corner border pieces (D)

Assembling the Skirt Top

Step 1: Refer to the **Tree Skirt Layout** on page 166 as you assemble the top. Sew the triangles (A) and the border bands (B) together until all the pieces are joined. Leave the final seam open.

Step 2: Sew an outer border strip (C) to the base of each triangle, beginning and ending each seam where seam allowances intersect.

Step 3: Sew a corner border piece (D) to the base of each border band, beginning and ending each seam where seam allowances intersect.

Step 4: Sew up the miters between the C and D pieces. Press.

Quilting and Finishing

Step 1: Place the wrong side of the skirt on the batting. Cut the batting to fit the skirt exactly. Baste together.

S t e p 2 : With the skirt right side up, stitch together ¼ inch from the outer edge, along a line in the border print.

S t e p 3 : With right sides facing, place the skirt top on the backing fabric and cut the backing to exactly fit the top. Pin together.

S t e p 4 : With the batting side up, use a ¼-inch seam allowance to stitch around the center of the tree skirt, down the side, around the outer edge, and up the other side. Leave a 4-inch opening to turn the skirt right side out. As you stitch around the outer edge, be sure to sew on top of the line of stitching you made in Step 2.

S t e p 5 : Clip the corners, turn the skirt right side out, and press. Use a whip stitch to close the opening.

S t e p 6 : Baste the three layers together, then quilt around the triangles or outline quilt a design in the Christmas print. Quilt along some of the lines in the border print and ¼ inch from the outside edge.

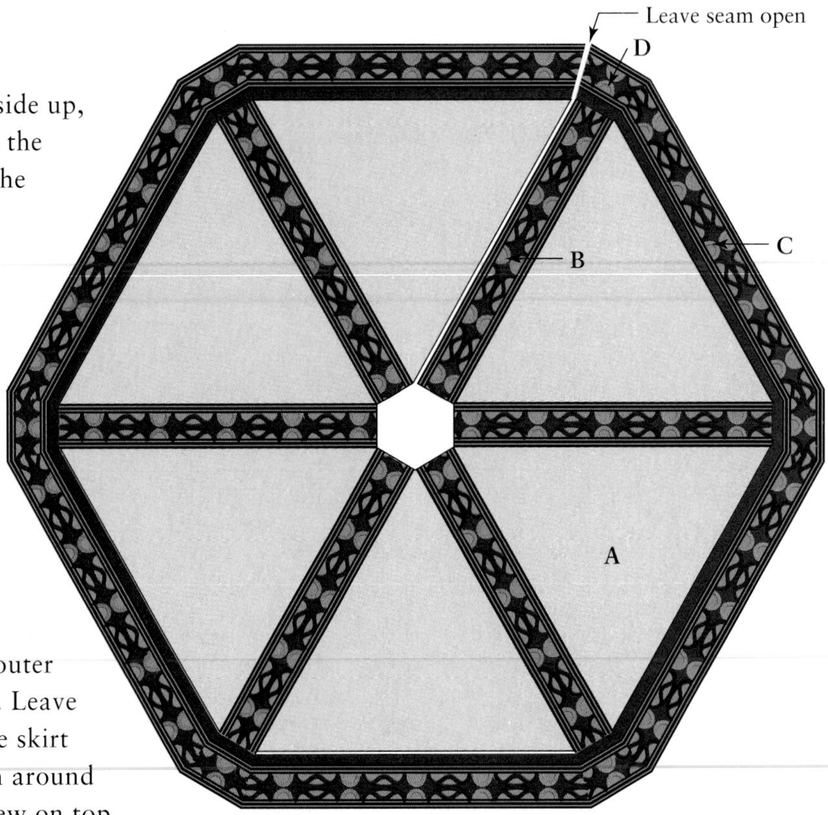

Leave seam open

D

C

B

A

Tree Skirt Layout

D

½ C

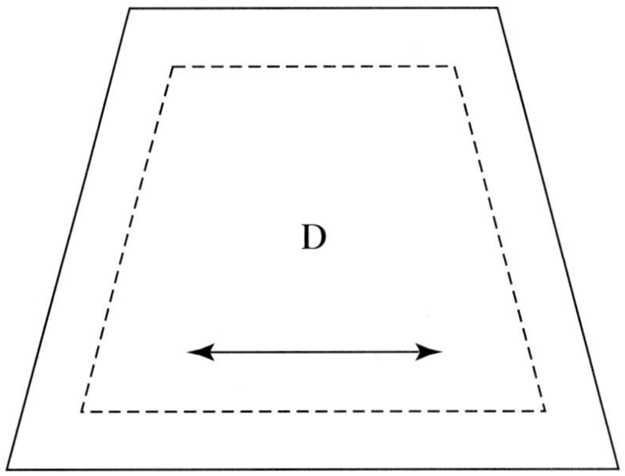

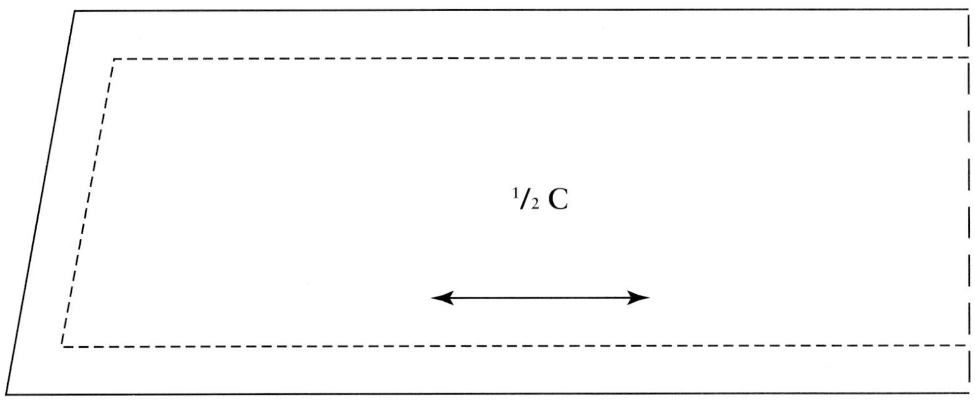

Drafting an Equilateral Triangle

You can use this method to easily draft a triangle of any size. These instructions are for a 30-inch triangle; each project in this book specifies the size triangle needed. Drafting the equilateral triangle is the first step for all the tree skirts.

You Will Need

Piece of newsprint or brown paper that is wider and longer than the triangle you need

Yardstick

Pencil

Drafting the Triangle

1. Measure and mark the length of one side of the triangle along the edge of the paper. In this example, the length is 30 inches. Mark an A at the left end of the line and a B at the right end of the line, as shown in **Diagram 1.**

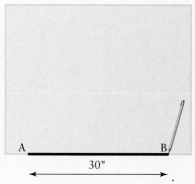

Diagram 1

2. Find the midpoint of the line (here, 15 inches) by folding B over to meet A. Crease the paper all the way up to its top edge, as indicated by the dashed line in **Diagram 2.** Unfold.

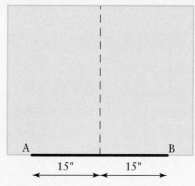

Diagram 2

3. Place the zero end of the yardstick at A and angle it toward the fold line until the 30-inch mark on the yardstick touches the fold, as shown in **Diagram 3.** Mark point C as shown and draw line AC. To cross-check point C, measure to make sure it is 26 inches from the midpoint of the triangle base.

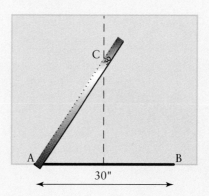

Diagram 3

4. Draw a line from C to B to complete the equilateral triangle, as shown in **Diagram 4.** If you are making a tree skirt with triangles cut from one piece of fabric, this will be your template. Remember to add a ¼-inch seam allowance to each side. *If you plan to piece the triangle, proceed to Step 5.*

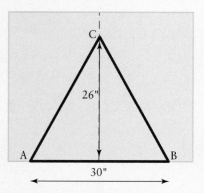

Diagram 4

5. To divide the large triangle into three smaller identical triangles, you must find its center. Determine the midpoint of line AC (by either folding or measuring the line) and connect the halfway mark to point B, as shown in **Diagram 5.** The line will cross the first fold line at the center of the triangle (point D). Make your template from the triangle formed by points CBD.

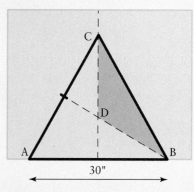

Diagram 5

Flying Geese Border Print Tree Skirt

Skill Level: Beginner to Intermediate

Size: Finished tree skirt is approximately 64 inches from side to side; finished equilateral triangle is 30 inches per side and 26 inches high; finished width of each Flying Geese band is 3½ inches

We like to decorate a large tree at Christmas. The original pattern for this tree skirt came about because I wanted a large skirt that wouldn't be hidden under the tree branches. This easy-to-make skirt is sewn from six equilateral triangles separated by a narrow band of patchwork.

What makes this pattern so versatile is that you can tailor-make your tree skirt to fit your tree. Just vary the size of the triangles, and cut the strips between the triangles to fit.

In this skirt and the Christmas Tree Border Print Tree Skirt on page 174, equilateral triangles are divided into three smaller triangles, then sewn together using identical cuts from a border print fabric.

Before beginning this project, be sure to read "Working with Border Prints" on page 77 and "Making and Using Templates" on page 74.

You Will Need

1 yard of dark green fabric

Scraps of 16 different red prints, each at least 5 × 12 inches

6 yards of border print fabric with a 14-inch stripe and at least two repeats of a 1½ to 2-inch (finished width) stripe

1 yard of coordinating fabric for binding

5½ yards of fabric for backing

Full-size (78 × 99-inch) batting

Template plastic

Permanent marker

Making Templates

Using the template material, follow Steps 1 through 5 in "Drafting an Equilateral Triangle" on page 167 to make Template A (one-third of the equilateral triangle). Use the 30-inch measurement as in the directions. Be sure to add a ¼-inch seam allowance around the outside of the drafted triangle. Make Templates B and C using the full-size patterns on page 172.

Cutting

When you cut the border print triangles, position the template on the fabric with the longest side of the triangle along the straight grain of the fabric. Align it so that a line from the design on the border print falls just within the finished edge. When the three triangles are sewn together to form the large equilateral triangle, its outer edges will be defined by the line.

When working with large pieces, I find it is more accurate to use the first piece I cut as a pattern for cutting the rest. It is usually easier to obtain a perfect match by aligning a fabric triangle with the uncut border print than it is to use a template, especially if the template is not transparent.

From the green fabric, cut:

6 2¼-inch inner border strips from the length of the fabric

192 C triangles, making sure you position the arrows on the template along the straight and cross grains of the fabric

6 2½ × 4-inch inner border rectangles

From the red prints, cut:

96 B triangles—6 from each of the 16 prints, making sure you position the arrow on the template along the straight grain of the fabric

From the border print, cut:

6 36-inch outer border strips (width can vary from 2 to 2½ inches, including seam allowances, according to border print width). **Note:** To match the border print pattern at the miters, refer to "Border Prints Framing a Rectangular Quilt" on page 79 and follow the instructions for both the outer border strips and the 6-inch border print pieces below.

18 A triangles. **Note:** To conserve fabric, you can vary the tree skirt design by using different areas of the same border print fabric. Just make sure you cut three *identical* A triangles for each equilateral triangle.

6 6-inch border print pieces (width must match outer border strip width)

6 2½ × 4-inch rectangles, each with the same border print pattern

Assembling the Flying Geese Bands

Step 1: Arrange the red B triangles into six piles with 16 different prints in each pile. Mix up each pile so that the prints are not in the same order.

Step 2: Using one pile of red B triangles, with right sides together, sew the long side of a green C triangle to one short side of the red B triangle, as shown in **Diagram 1.** Press.

Step 3: Sew another green C triangle to the opposite side of the red B triangle. Press. The rectangular unit should look like **Diagram 2.**

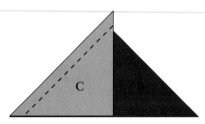

Diagram 1

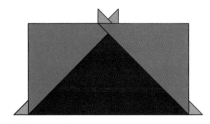

Diagram 2

Step 4: Repeat steps 2 and 3 for all 16 red triangles in the pile.

Step 5: Find the midpoint along the base of the red triangle in a rectangle unit. With right sides together, pin this midpoint to the tip of a red triangle in one of the other rectangle units. Sew together with a ¼-inch seam allowance, taking care not to cut off the triangle point, as shown in **Diagram 3.**

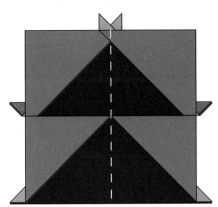

Midpoints must match

Diagram 3

S t e p   6 : Repeat Step 5 to sew all 16 rectangle units together to form a long band.

S t e p   7 : Repeat steps 2 through 6 with the remaining piles of red triangles, making a total of six separate Flying Geese bands.

S t e p   8 : Sew a 2½ × 4-inch border print rectangle to the bottom of each of the six Flying Geese bands.

S t e p   9 : Measure the length of the Flying Geese bands. If they are not 30½ inches long (this includes a ¼-inch seam allowance at each end), sew a 4-inch wide piece of border print or green fabric to the top of each band. To determine the height of the additional piece, subtract the length of the band from 30½ inches, then add back ½ inch (to allow for seam allowances).

Assembling the Equilateral Triangles

S t e p   1 : Align two border print A triangles with right sides together, making sure the designs are matched. Pin the triangles together along a short side. Using a ¼-inch seam allowance, sew along the pinned side, beginning at the long base of the triangles and stopping where seam allowances intersect on the opposite end, as shown in **Diagram 4.**

S t e p   2 : Pin the third triangle to the first two triangles, making sure the designs match. Sew along the short side from the base of the triangle to the point at the center where seam allowances intersect. Pivot and continue sewing down the remaining side, as shown in **Diagram 5.** Remove the pins and press.

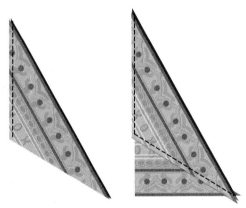

Diagram 4   **Diagram 5**

S t e p   3 : Repeat Steps 1 and 2 to assemble the five remaining equilateral triangles.

Assembling the Skirt Top

S t e p 1 : Sew the equilateral triangle units and Flying Geese bands together, as shown in the **Tree Skirt Layout.** Leave the final seam open.

S t e p 2 : Fold a 2¼-inch green inner border strip in half lengthwise to find the midpoint. Match this midpoint with the midpoint of an A triangle. With right sides together, pin and sew onto the tree skirt, leaving ¼ inch unsewn at each end of the triangle. (The border will be a little long.) Repeat for the remaining five units.

S t e p 3 : Sew the miters between the green borders. Trim the excess fabric.

S t e p 4 : With right sides together, sew a 6-inch border print piece along the long edge to the bottom of each Flying Geese strip, leaving ¼ inch unsewn at each end of the green rectangle. (The border print piece will be a little long.)

S t e p 5 : Fold an outer border strip in half lengthwise to find the midpoint. Match this midpoint with the midpoint of the green border. Pin and sew as you did for the green border strip. Use the **Miter Angle Template** on the opposite page to mark the miter angle onto the border pieces. Make sure that you mark the cutting line, not the sewing line, then trim the excess and sew up the miters. Note that you will have to flip your template once for each miter.

Quilting and Finishing

S t e p 1 : Prepare the skirt back by cutting the backing fabric in half and sewing the two pieces together along the long sides. Baste the backing, batting, and top together according to the directions in "Layering and Basting" on page 88, disregarding the skirt opening.

S t e p 2 : Quilt the tree skirt as you like. The one shown on page 168 was quilted in the ditch around each of the triangles and each of the seams. Some of the designs in the border print fabric were outline quilted. After the quilting is complete, cut the backing and batting along the opening in the skirt.

S t e p 3 : Cut the bias binding and sew it to the tree skirt according to the directions in "Bias Binding" on page 91.

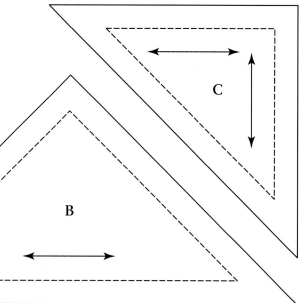

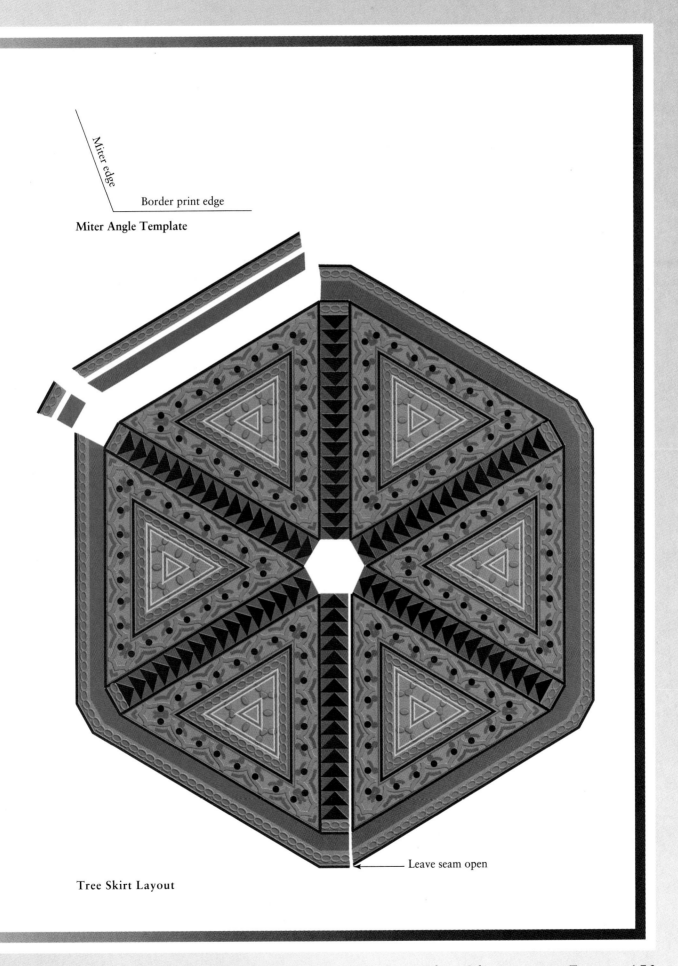

Miter edge

Border print edge

Miter Angle Template

Leave seam open

Tree Skirt Layout

Christmas Tree Border Print Tree Skirt

Robin Morrison used bands of Christmas trees to separate the equilateral triangles in her variation of my Flying Geese tree skirt. The bands contain less patchwork and the outer border has been eliminated, making this skirt faster to construct than my version.

Fabrics

6 yards of border print fabric with a 14-inch stripe

⅛ yard each of five different green prints

¼ yard of red print

1 yard of coordinating fabric for binding

5¼ yards of fabric for backing

Full-size (78 × 99-inch) batting

Skill Level: Beginner to Intermediate

Size: Finished tree skirt is 58 inches from side to side; finished equilateral triangle is 30 inches per side and 26 inches high; finished width of each Christmas Tree band is 3½ inches

Making Templates

Step 1: Follow Steps 1 through 5 in "Drafting an Equilateral Triangle" on page 167 to make Template A (one-third of the equilateral triangle). The finished equilateral triangle for this version is exactly the same as the one used in the Flying Geese Border Print Tree Skirt—30 inches per side and 26 inches high.

Step 2: Use the full-size patterns on page 176 to make Templates J and K. Note that Template K is reversed (KR) for some cuts. Seam allowances are included in both templates.

Cutting

Position the arrows on the templates along the straight grain of the fabric. Handle the cut triangles carefully to avoid stretching the bias edges.

From the red fabric, cut:
30 K triangles
30 KR triangles

From the green prints, cut:
30 J triangles—6 from each of the 5 prints

From the border print, cut:
18 A triangles. **Note:** To conserve fabric, vary the tree skirt design by using different areas of the same border print fabric. Just make sure you cut three *identical* Template A triangles for each equilateral triangle.
6 4-inch-square pieces, each with the same border print pattern

Assembling the Christmas Tree Bands

Step 1: Arrange the green J triangles into six piles with five different print

triangles in each pile. Mix up each pile so the prints are not in the same order.

Step 2: Using one pile of green J triangles, with right sides together, sew the long side of a red K triangle to the right side of a J triangle, as shown in **Diagram 1.** Press. Sew the long side of a red KR triangle to the left side of the green triangle, as shown. Press.

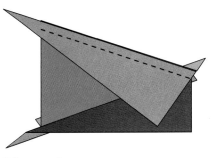

Diagram 1

Step 3: Repeat step 2 for the remaining four green triangles in the first pile.

Step 4: Find the midpoint along the base of the green triangle in a rectangle unit. With right sides together, pin this midpoint to the tip of a green triangle in another rectangle unit. Sew together with a ¼-inch seam allowance, taking care not to cut off the triangle point, as shown in **Diagram 2.**

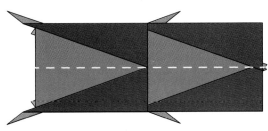

Midpoints must match
Diagram 2

Step 5: Repeat Step 4 to sew all five tree units together to form a long band.

Step 6: Repeat Steps 2 through 5 with the remaining green triangles, making a total of six Christmas tree bands.

Step 7: Sew a 4-inch border print square to the bottom of each of the tree bands. Each band should now measure 30½ inches long.

Assembling the Equilateral Triangles

Follow Steps 1 through 3 in "Assembling the Equilateral Triangles" on page 171.

Assembling the Skirt Top

Sew the equilateral triangles and Christmas Tree bands together, alternating them until all six large triangles and patchwork bands are joined together, as shown in the **Tree Skirt Layout.** Leave the final seam open.

Quilting and Finishing

Step 1: Prepare the tree skirt back by cutting the backing fabric in half and sewing the two pieces together along the long sides. Baste together the backing, batting, and top according to the directions in "Layering and Basting" on page 88. Baste the layers together as if there were no opening.

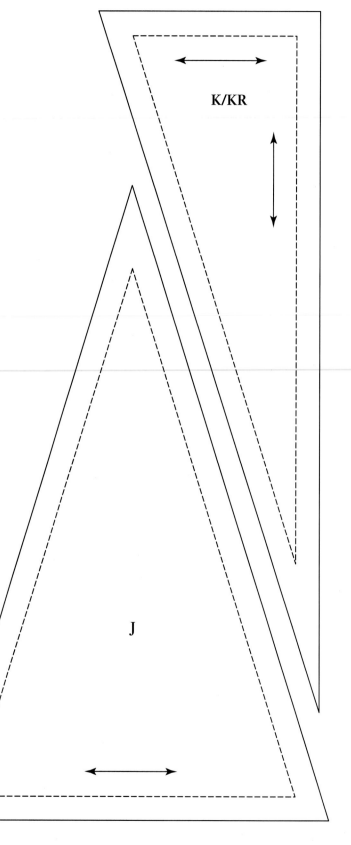

S t e p   2 : Quilt the tree skirt as you like. The skirt shown on page 174 was quilted ¼ inch in from the edges of the patchwork trees and background pieces, and along some of the lines and designs in the border print fabric.

After the quilting is complete, cut the backing and batting along the opening in the skirt.

S t e p   3 : Cut the bias binding and sew it to the tree skirt according to the directions in "Bias Binding" on page 91.

Leave seam open

Tree Skirt Layout

Inside Decorations

In the 1930s a man named Rixey Smith bought the old farmhouse where we now live. At that time the house was in very poor shape, but Rixey's hobby was restoring old buildings, and he was excited about the prospect of renewing it. About this same time, Rixey got married, and his ushers gave him an old log structure for a wedding present. It was a 150-plus-year-old "mail tavern" from Ruby, Virginia. A mail tavern is a way station—a place for weary travelers to stop, send their mail, and have a bite to eat. They could even throw their gear on the floor upstairs and rest for the night. Rixey Smith had the tavern moved and attached to the back end of the house. That log structure became the dining room that you see here, and it is a wonderful place to have a holiday meal.

As Christmas approaches I always want to give the house a festive look, but, as usual, time is very short. It is amazing, however, how quickly you can add a holiday touch to a mantel, shelf, windowsill, table, or any other area. A few greens, some fresh fruit, and dried pods or flowers—along with supplies that can be saved from year to year—can quickly make the transformation. Once you have the basic supplies, each of the decorations in this chapter can be done in less than 20 minutes. In fact, in half a day you can do all of these projects and add a festive look to every room in your house.

Apple and Grape Table Tree

This arrangement is very easy to make—and the best news is that it takes very little time. It makes a spectacular centerpiece and should keep for up to one week. This is the decoration that I use on the large pine table in our dining room. It's best to make this centerpiece right at the table where it will reside because it is heavy and difficult to move once it is made.

You Will Need

About 40 sprigs of boxwood, each 4 inches long

20 medium-size Red Delicious apples

About 40 magnolia leaves

1 pineapple

2½ pounds of black grapes

½ pound of red grapes

9 floral pins

6½ × 20-inch piece of plywood

1 cone-shaped wooden form*

Pruning shears

*Available through Colonial Williamsburg, 210 Fifth Avenue, P.O. Box 3532, Williamsburg, VA 23187-3532; (800) 446-9240. Ask for the 8½-inch-tall wooden cone studded with six rows of nails.

Step 1: Place the piece of plywood on the table and center the wooden form in the middle of it.

Step 2: Put eight of the apples around the bottom of the form, pushing them onto the nails, as shown in **Diagram 1.**

Diagram 1

S t e p 3 : Make a second row of apples above the first, this time using seven apples. Then make a third row of five apples.

S t e p 4 : Cut the stem and about ¾ inch off the end of each magnolia leaf. This helps to prevent the leaves from curling.

S t e p 5 : Begin arranging the magnolia leaves on the board. Start with the two longest leaves and tuck them under the tree base, as shown in **Diagram 2.**

S t e p 6 : Arrange three leaves on each side of the board, tucking the middle one in a bit, as shown in **Diagram 3.**

S t e p 7 : Tuck two leaves between the leaves on either end of the board, pushing the leaves under the existing ones. Continue tucking magnolia leaves between existing leaves until the board is completely covered with overlapping leaves, as shown in **Diagram 4.**

S t e p 8 : Carefully wash the pineapple leaves, removing any waxy residue. Cut the leaves and about 1½ inches of pineapple off the top. Place this in a bowl of water for a few minutes, then embed it on the nails at the top of the form. Do not cut any discolored tips off the leaves—this will cause moisture to drain from the leaves and they will turn brown.

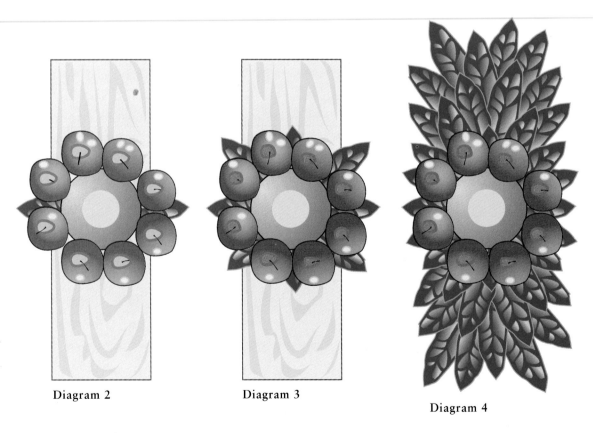

Diagram 2

Diagram 3

Diagram 4

Step 9: Cut the black grapes into 11 clumps, each approximately 3½ inches long. Put a floral pin through the stem at the top of one of the clumps, and carefully push the pin into the base of the pineapple near the leaves, as shown in **Diagram 5**. Continue until all but two clumps of black grapes have been placed around the pineapple.

Variations on a Theme

There are many variations to the Apple and Grape Table Tree. One possibility is to eliminate the grapes altogether and put a whole pineapple on top of the tree. Or eliminate the pineapple and put another apple on the top. Instead of having the decoration elongated, you could make it on a round plate, with the magnolia leaves lining the plate. Try these variations or experiment with your own.

Diagram 5

Step 10: Carefully tuck the boxwood sprigs between the apples so that the tree form is not visible, as shown.

Step 11: Place the remaining two clumps of black grapes on top of the magnolia leaves at either side of the tree base. For the final touch, put a slightly smaller clump of red grapes on top of each clump of black grapes.

Mantel Decoration with Greens and Mixed Fruit

This decoration is quick to make, yet impressive. It will keep about 10 days. If you want it to keep longer, check the fruit periodically and replace any that are beginning to turn brown.

You Will Need

2 pine boughs, each 20 inches long (I prefer using short-needled boughs for this arrangement, such as Frazier fir or Norway spruce)

2 pine boughs, each 15 inches long

About 15 pine boughs, each 10 to 12 inches long

13 bleached okra pods (available through floral supply houses)

9 small Red Delicious apples

5 limes

7 magnolia pods (or large pinecones)

2 pieces of Oasis floral foam, each 9 × 4 × 3 inches

2 plastic rectangular dishes to hold foam

Floral tape

9 #12 bamboo skewers

5 #10 bamboo skewers

Pruning shears

Making the Mantel Decoration

Step 1: Soak the two pieces of Oasis in water for about 5 minutes. Put them into the plastic dishes and center them side by side in the middle of the mantel. Tape them securely to the mantel. This decoration can get top-heavy, so be sure it is taped well.

Step 2: Cut any branchlets off the cut ends of the pine boughs, leaving about 3 inches of stem clear. Starting with the two 20-inch boughs, insert them into either end of the foam, almost horizontally, so the ends of the boughs are resting on the mantel, as shown in **Diagram 1** on page 186. Add the 15-inch boughs slightly in front of the first two. Then, still working close to the mantel, add five 10-inch pieces evenly spaced across the front.

Step 3: Add five pine boughs across the back, arranging them so that the middle one stands a little higher and the others curve down to meet the ones that are already secured, as shown in **Diagram 2** on page 186.

Step 4: Fill in across the front with the remaining boughs. Do not worry that you may still be able to see some of the foam. The fruit will hide a lot of it and, if there is still some showing once all of the other items have been added, then you can fill in with pieces of pine.

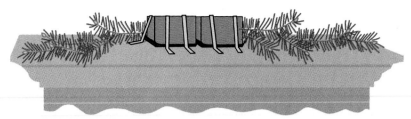

Diagram 1

Diagram 2

S t e p 5 : Add the magnolia pods next, then the okra pods. (See the photograph on page 184 for placement of these materials.) The stems of the magnolia pods and the okra pods can be inserted directly into the foam.

S t e p 6 : Impale the apples with the #12 skewers, pushing one skewer into the bottom of each apple directly opposite the stem. Then insert the skewer into the foam. Do the same for the limes, using the #10 skewers. Rearrange the materials as needed to give balance to the arrangement, using the photograph as a guide.

*K*issing Ball

This boxwood kissing ball looks festive when hung in a doorway or from a chandelier over a table. It takes very little time to make. My sage bush never dies in the winter so I use it fresh-cut for the accent, but dried sage or other dried herbs or mistletoe can also be substituted.

You Will Need

⅓ bushel boxwood sprigs, each 4 inches long

24 holly berry sprigs, each 4 inches long, with all leaves removed (see page 127)

About 20 sprigs of fresh or dried sage, each 4 inches long

4 × 4 × 4-inch piece of Oasis floral foam

16 × 16-inch piece of chicken wire

8-inch piece of 26-gauge wire

3½ yards of ¼-inch-wide satin ribbon

Floral pin

9-inch-wide piece of cardboard (or a thin book)

Pruning shears

Making the Kissing Ball

S t e p   1 : Wrap the chicken wire around the Oasis foam as if you were wrapping a package.

S t e p   2 : Soak the foam in a pot of water for about 5 minutes, then let it drain in the sink for about 30 minutes until all the excess water has run out.

S t e p   3 : Cut about 1 yard of ribbon, string it through a piece of the chicken wire on what will be the top of the kissing ball, and hang it from a hook or lamp. (It is best to have the ball hanging while working on it—you can get a much better shape and balance.)

Step 4: Insert the boxwood sprigs through the chicken wire and into the foam, as shown in **Diagram 1.** Continue until the form is completely covered with boxwood. If necessary, "trim" the ball into a nice uniform shape by cutting back any sprigs that stick out a little too far.

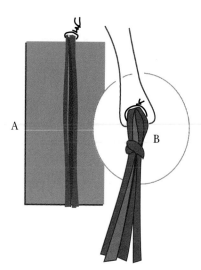

Diagram 2

Diagram 1

Step 5: Insert the holly and sage sprigs, evenly spacing them throughout the ball.

Step 6: To make ribbon streamers, take the remaining length of ribbon and wrap it around the cardboard or book several times, then put the piece of wire through all the ribbon pieces and twist tightly, as shown in **Diagram 2A.**

Step 7: Pull the ribbon off the book and make a single knot in the end with the wire, as shown in **Diagram 2B,** then cut the remaining ends evenly.

Step 8: Insert the floral pin through the loop of the ribbon where the wire is attached and cut off the wire. Find the bottom of the ball (exactly opposite where the ribbon is attached at the top) and insert the floral pick. Check to make sure that the ribbon streamers are hanging directly at the bottom of the kissing ball.

Stairway Roping

Nothing can be more attractive than a swag of greens draping a stairwell. This one is surprisingly easy to make and, if you use newly cut greens, it should look fresh for more than two weeks.

You Will Need

For 3 feet of basic roping

> 9 sprigs of boxwood, each 8 inches long
>
> 9 sprigs of juniper, each 10 inches long
>
> 40 inches of green twine
>
> 40 inches of 26-gauge wire

For the decoration

> 3 clumps of fresh pepperberries (*Callicarpa* spp.) for every 3 feet of roping (usually available from florists at Christmastime, or substitute holly or nandina (*Nandina domestica*) berries
>
> 3 or 4 sprigs of fresh pepperberries, each 12 inches long, for the newel post
>
> 1¾ yards of a border print fabric with at least three repeats of a 4-inch (finished width) stripe
>
> 1¾ yards of contrasting fabric for the bow lining
>
> Fabric stiffener
>
> Spool of 26-gauge floral wire
>
> Wire cutters
>
> Pruning shears

Making the Roping

Step 1: Measure your banister and determine how many feet of roping you will need. Figure that for every 3 feet of banister length you will need 3 feet of roping plus 4 inches for drape. In addition, you will need three separate 22-inch pieces of roping—two for the swag in the middle of the roping and one for the piece at the bottom of the banister.

Step 2: Make bundles of boxwood and bundles of juniper, using about three sprigs for each bundle. Using the twine and floral wire, make the basic roping following the directions for "Pine Roping" on page 140, alternating juniper and boxwood bundles.

Step 3: Attach the roping to the top of the banister with a piece of wire. Bring the roping to the point where you want the center swag and wire it there, as well. Make sure to allow about 4 inches of drape for every 3 feet of roping. To create the appearance of more fullness from below, place the roping so that the ends of the bundles are facing up the stairs. Bring the roping to the bottom of the banister and attach it around the newel post.

Step 4: Take two of the 22-inch lengths of roping and hold them together with the branches pointing down and the edges curling toward each other. Arrange them so they are the same length, then wire them tightly together, as shown in **Diagram 1.** Wire the roping to the portion of the banister where the bow will be.

Diagram 1

S t e p 5 : Attach the third 22-inch piece of roping to the newel post at the end of the banister, once again with the branches facing downward.

S t e p 6 : Cut some of the pepperberries to about 8 inches long. Insert the stem ends through the roping at 12-inch intervals along the entire length.

S t e p 7 : Take the 12-inch-long sprigs of pepperberries and wire them together, then wire them to the newel post, hiding the stems in the roping.

S t e p 8 : Make a bow, following the instructions in "Making the Bow" on this page. Attach the bow to the banister directly on top of the swag.

Making the Bow

S t e p 1 : Cut two 4½-inch-wide × 1¾-yard strips and one 4½-inch-wide × 1¼-yard strip from the border print.

S t e p 2 : Cut three strips of lining fabric the same width and length as the border print pieces. With right sides facing, pin a piece of lining to each border print strip. Fold each end at a right angle and cut them off, as shown in **Diagram 2.** Using a ¼-inch seam, stitch around each strip, leaving approximately 3 inches open for turning.

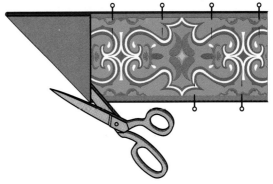

Diagram 2

Diagram 3   Diagram 4   Diagram 5

Step 3: Turn each piece of ribbon right side out and press. Whipstitch the openings closed.

Step 4: Mix the fabric stiffener according to the directions on the bottle. Dip each ribbon in it and allow to dry.

Step 5: With the border print side up, measure about 15 inches from the left end of one of the 1¾-yard-long ribbons. Pinch the fabric together with your right hand. With the print side facing out, make a loop on one side of the pinched section, using about 13 inches of ribbon (this makes a 6½-inch loop). Pinch this loop and hold it with your thumb and forefinger, as shown in **Diagram 3.**

Step 6: On the side opposite the loop, twist the ribbon so the print side is facing out, and use about 13 inches of ribbon to make a second loop opposite the first, as shown in **Diagram 4.**

Step 7: Twist the remaining ribbon around your thumb to make a center loop. Adjust the tails so the print side is facing out. Put a 12-inch length of wire through the center loop and twist it tightly to secure the loops, as shown in **Diagram 5.** Fluff up the loops as desired.

Step 8: Measure about 17 inches from one end of the second 1¾-yard-long ribbons and pinch the ribbon between your thumb and forefinger.

Step 9: Repeat Steps 5 and 6, using 15 inches of ribbon to make each loop. Wire them securely at the center, this time using about 36 inches of wire and leaving excess wire tails. Make sure the loops have the print side facing out and the tails have the lining facing out.

Step 10: Hold the 1¼-inch-yard-long ribbon in the center, letting the ends fall down with the print side facing out. Pinch the center together between your thumb and forefinger and place it behind the bow you just made. Wrap the ends of excess wire from that bow around this new strip, securing the bow and tails together.

Step 11: Place the first bow on top of the second, about ½ inch below the center of the second bow. Bring the longest of the remaining pieces of wire around from behind the second bow, through the knot of the first bow, and to the back again. Do this two or three times to secure the two bows and the tails together. Twist any remaining ends of wire together and cut off the excess. Fluff up the loops until they have a nice, full look.

Add a Splash of Color

Greens, fruit, and holly berries add a splash of color to any shelf, sill, or mantel. Notice the pineapple, apple, and greens mantel decoration in the photograph on page 178, and the pine arrangement on the mantel in the cabin (see page 196). I also like to use an arrangement on my family room mantel of *Euonymus* (spindle tree) greens, large green apples, and sprigs of brightly colored holly berries.

My dining room has six small windows—three on either side of the room. For each of the center windows, I make an arrangement of two 12-inch pine boughs, two apples, and an old lantern. If you don't have a lantern, you can use a candlestick. For the windows on either side of the center ones, I put two 12-inch white pine boughs on each windowsill with the stem ends facing each other. I hide the stems with a large red apple set in the middle.

Decorating with "Found" Items

One of the aspects of holiday decorating that I find the
most fun is to see how many items I already have around the
house or in my yard that can be incorporated into some type of
decoration. I hope the ideas presented here will help you to look
more closely at items you have that can be used in some way.
Look for white plates, pitchers, and bowls; spools of red and
green thread; stacks of red and green fabric; and books with red
or green binding. Put evergreens in an old wheelbarrow with
holly branches on top, or fill a large iron kettle with greens and
holly and place it in the yard.

*M*ost quilters have stacks and
stacks of fabric. A nice touch for a friend
who is also a quilter is to wrap her package in a piece of fabric instead of in
paper. It is useful and also helps the environment.

*F*or one arrangement, I gather all of my quilts
that have red, white, or green in them and stack
them on an old pine shelf. Antique dolls sit on the
top shelf with red ribbons around their waists.
The spool-holder chair has red and green thread,
and I found a white pitcher with a red rose on it
to hold the holly from our yard. A few miniature
green books from the library shelf and old blocks
with the red and green sides facing out add another bit of holiday color. The screen, painted green
and made from wooden shutters hinged together,
has tree motifs cut from the top panels.

To decorate a pine hutch, I found a pincushion shoe with red velvet, stacks of Christmas-colored fabrics, red thread for the old sewing machine, and red and green books from the bookshelves.

Another arrangement I like to make is with my daughter's teddy bears. Bows cut from red and green border print fabrics are tied around their necks. One bear has a knitted scarf made from scraps of yarn left over from one of my sweaters. Red-and-white stocking caps, ginger cookies, and a fire in the brick oven complete the scene.

Border Print Mantel Trim

This mantel decoration fits just as well in a more formal setting as it does in the rustic setting of our cabin. It is one more example of the interesting effects that can be achieved by using border print fabrics.

You Will Need

For a 72-inch mantel

2½ yards of a border print fabric with a 4-inch (finished width) stripe and at least three repeats of a 3½-inch (finished width) stripe

2½ yards of contrasting trim for the lining (If you're willing to piece the lining, 1 yard is enough)

Template plastic

Permanent marker

Double-sided tape

Making Templates

Using the template material, make Template A (one-third of the equilateral triangle), following Steps 1 through 5 in "Drafting an Equilateral Triangle" on page 167. The triangle should be 7¾ inches high with a 9-inch side. Add ¼-inch seam allowances to each side of your finished template.

Cutting and Sewing

Step 1: Each completed equilateral triangle is 9 inches across. These directions are for eight equilateral triangles, to fit a 6-foot mantel. Adjust the number or size of triangles as needed to fit your mantel.

Step 2: Cut three identical triangles from the 3½-inch-wide border print using Template A, following the instructions in "Using Border Prints within Shapes or Blocks" on page 80.

Step 3: Using a ¼-inch seam allowance, sew two triangles together, ending the seam ¼ inch from the center edge of the triangle. Add the third triangle, pivoting your seam to set in the piece at the center, as shown in **Diagram 1.** (See "Piecing Basics" on page 81 for more information about set-in patches.)

Diagram 1

Step 4: Repeat steps 2 and 3 for a total of nine triangles (or the number you need to span your mantel).

Step 5: Use one of the completed border print triangles as a template to cut a lining for each finished triangle. Cut these pieces along the length of the fabric, reserving a long strip of yardage to use for lining the long band.

Step 6: With right sides facing, sew a lining piece to each equilateral triangle, leaving one side unstitched. Use a line from the border print fabric as a sewing guide.

Step 7: Clip the points of all sewn triangles, turn right side out, and press.

Step 8: Cut a 4½ × 84½-inch stripe from the border print fabric, making sure a line from the print falls just inside the ¼-inch seam allowance. Cut the strip so that a motif from the border print will be centered in the middle of the mantel. Mark the center motif with a straight pin. **Note:** Adjust the length of your strip to fit your mantel as needed. The strip should be long enough to span the width of the mantel and wrap around both sides.

Step 9: Working from the center toward the sides, and with right sides together, carefully pin the triangles to the edge of the border print strip, as shown in **Diagram 2.** If you have an odd number of triangles, center a triangle in the middle of the strip. If you have an even number of triangles, two triangles will meet at the strip's center. Be very careful to match up a line from the long border print with a line from the border print on the edge of each triangle. You will have excess border strip at each end.

Step 10: Sew the triangles to the border strip, using a ¼-inch seam. Press.

Step 11: Cut a strip of lining fabric the length and width of the long border strip. Pin the lining so that the triangles are sandwiched between the right sides of the border strip and lining. Sew, starting from the outside edge of the left-hand triangle and using a ¼-inch seam allowance all around the unit, stopping at the outside edge of the right-hand triangle, as shown in **Diagram 3.**

Step 12: Clip the corners, turn right side out, and press. Turn the seam allowance under along the edge of the unstitched border lining. Sew the opening closed and press.

Step 13: Use double-sided tape to attach the trim to the mantel.

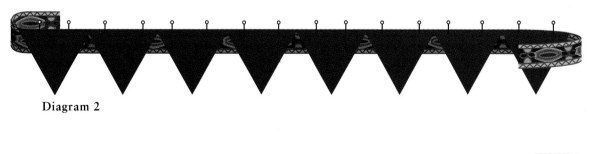

Diagram 2

Diagram 3

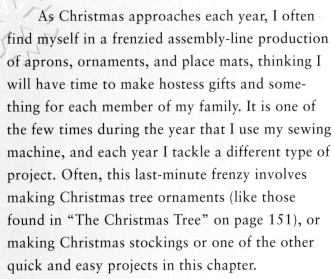

Quick & Easy Patchwork

As Christmas approaches each year, I often find myself in a frenzied assembly-line production of aprons, ornaments, and place mats, thinking I will have time to make hostess gifts and something for each member of my family. It is one of the few times during the year that I use my sewing machine, and each year I tackle a different type of project. Often, this last-minute frenzy involves making Christmas tree ornaments (like those found in "The Christmas Tree" on page 151), or making Christmas stockings or one of the other quick and easy projects in this chapter.

I especially like to do these projects with a friend. I wait for a stormy day, invite a friend over, and make a fire in the wood stove. We cut out the pieces, then take turns sitting at the sewing machine or trimming seams and running to the iron for pressing. If you have the patterns and fabric ready, you will be surprised at what you can accomplish in a single day.

When *you* need a last-minute gift for someone special, try one of the projects in this chapter. You'll be pleased at how quickly you can make a beautiful gift for a friend or loved one.

$\mathcal{B}$order Print Place Mats and Table Runner

The old pine table in our dining room is 10 feet long, which makes it virtually impossible to find tablecloths that fit. Instead, we use place mats, many of which I make from border print fabrics. While the place mats and matching table runner shown here are easy to make, border prints make them look very sophisticated. To make the runner more interesting, create a mirror-image design along the center of the runner and have the "point" on each end barely reach the ends of the table.

Before beginning these projects, review "Working with Border Prints" on page 77 and "Making and Using Templates" on page 74.

Making Templates

Using the template plastic, make templates from pattern piece A on page 206. Half of piece A is provided. To complete the pattern, draw a mirror image of the printed portion on the opposite side of your template material. Be sure to mark the dashed midline of piece A, to serve as a guide for centering the border print. Follow Steps 1 through 4 in "Drafting an Equilateral Triangle" on page 167 to make Template B. The triangle for B should be 6¼ inches high, with a 7¼-inch side. Add ¼-inch seam allowances outside your drawn triangle.

Border Print Place Mat

You Will Need

For four place mats

½ yard of border print fabric with at least three repeats of a 7-inch-wide area

1 piece of batting, 28 × 40 inches

1 yard of fabric for backing

Template plastic

Permanent marker

Cutting and Sewing

Step 1: Use the dashed center line on Template A to center a border print motif at the center of the template. Position the template so that a line from the print falls just within the long edge. Make sure the arrow on the template is parallel to the fabric's straight grain. Draw a portion of the design directly onto the template along the edges marked "side miter" and along the center line. Cut two identical A pieces for each place mat.

Step 2: Place Template B on top of Template A, matching the side miter and border edge sides of both templates. Trace the motif that you drew on Template A onto Template B, as shown in **Diagram 1.** This will help ensure that A and B match at the miters.

Step 3: Place template B on the border print, with the triangle base parallel to the fabric's straight grain. Match the design drawn on the template to the fabric. Cut two identical pieces. Reverse the template and cut two more, again matching motifs. You need two B pieces and two B Reverse pieces for each place mat.

Step 4: Matching the designs at the side miter, sew a B and a B Reverse to the sides of an A piece, as shown in **Diagram 2.** Repeat with a second A piece, mirroring the unit you have just made. Sew the two units together at their long edges and press.

Step 5: Repeat Steps 1 through 4 for each place mat.

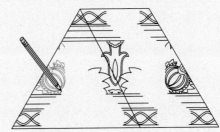

Diagram 1

Diagram 2

Quilting and Finishing

Step 1: Lay a place mat right side up on the batting. Cut the batting to match the top and baste the two together. Since there may be slight variations, repeat this step with each place mat rather than using one place mat as a guide to cutting all the batting pieces.

Step 2: Working from the right side, machine quilt the place mat as desired. I usually quilt along a design in the border print.

Step 3: With the place mat facing up, machine stitch ¼ inch in from the outside edge of the mat, directly on the line you chose for your finished border edge.

Step 4: With right sides together, place a mat onto the backing fabric and cut out the backing to match. Pin together carefully. Repeat with all remaining mats, cutting individual backings to match each one exactly.

Step 5: With the batting side facing up, stitch the pieces together, following the line of stitches that you made in Step 3. Leave a 5-inch opening for turning.

Step 6: Turn the place mat right side out, press, and slip stitch the opening closed. Topstitch all around the outer edge of the place mat, following a line from the border print.

Step 7: Repeat Steps 5 and 6 for each place mat.

Border Print Table Runner

You Will Need

2 5-inch (finished width) strips of border print fabric cut to the length of your table plus 18 inches. (A line from the print should be just within the seam allowance on the side to be placed on the outer edge of the runner.)

1 piece of batting, 10½ inches wide and as long as your table

1 piece of fabric for backing, 11 inches wide and 1 inch longer than the length of your table (this piece can be seamed in the middle)

Template plastic

Permanent marker

Making Templates

Follow Steps 1 through 4 in "Drafting an Equilateral Triangle" on page 167 to make Template C. Use a 5⅞-inch side measurement and a 5-inch height. Add ¼-inch seam allowances to all sides.

Cutting and Sewing

Step 1: Measure the length of your table and determine its midline.

Step 2: Fold one of the long pieces of border print in half crosswise, centering a motif from the print in the exact middle of the fold. Place the fold at the midline of your table, allowing the strip to run the length of one side, as shown in **Diagram 3**. The "border edge" side of the print should face the outer edge of the table, as shown.

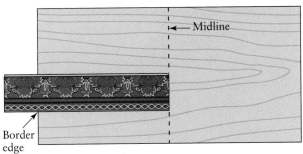

Diagram 3

S t e p 3 : Place template C on the border print, 4 inches from the end of the table, as shown in **Diagram 4.** Mark the angle along the outside edge onto the fabric.

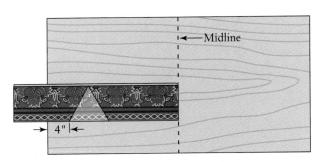

Diagram 4

S t e p 4 : Cut the angle on the top piece of the folded strip. Cut the bottom angle next, after making sure the designs at the top and bottom match exactly. Transfer a design from the border print directly onto template C along the outside edge, to use as a guide for cutting C and C Reverse

pieces later. Unfold the strip. You should have one long strip of border print with a miter at each end, as shown in **Diagram 5**.

Diagram 5

S t e p 5 : Place this mitered strip of border print on top of the second border print strip, matching the design exactly. Cut a second identical strip.

S t e p 6 : Use the remaining pieces of border print to cut two pieces from template C and two from template C Reverse. Be sure to match the motif that you drew at the edge.

S t e p 7 : Sew a C piece to the left end of each strip and a C-Reverse piece to each right end, as shown in **Diagram 6**, matching motifs at the miters.

Diagram 6

S t e p 8 : With right sides facing, pin the two long strips together at the center seam. Carefully match the design and continue pinning along the entire length of the strips. Sew the long seam to make a runner that looks like **Diagram 7**. Press.

Diagram 7

Quilting and Finishing

Follow Steps 1 through 6 on page 204
to quilt and finish the runner.

½ **A**

Full-Skirted Hostess Apron and Matching Potholder

If you have pieces of border print fabric left over from the projects on page 202, use this pattern to make a matching hostess apron and potholder. Review "Working with Border Prints" on page 77 before beginning.

You Will Need

For the apron and potholder

1½ yards of a large-print multicolored fabric for the skirt, pocket, neck band, and bib lining

3 yards of a 4½- to 5-inch-wide strip of border print

6 yards of a 2-inch (finished width) strip of border print for the waistband and ties (make sure you can add a ½-inch seam allowance on each side)

1 15 × 3-inch piece of fusible interfacing

1 20-inch square of 100 percent cotton batting*

Button

Newsprint or brown paper to make the pattern

*Be sure to usc 100 percent cotton batting for this project. Since polyester batting conducts heat, you are more likely to burn your hand if you use it in potholders.

Making Pattern Pieces

Step 1: Enlarge the **Hostess Apron Patterns** on page 211 for the front panel (A), side panels (B), pocket (E), and neck band (F). Transfer the enlarged patterns onto newsprint or brown paper. Add a ½-inch seam allowance to all sides of the patterns shown.

S t e p   2 : To make an accurate border band (D) pattern, fold the side panel pattern in half lengthwise. Measure the finished width of the border print you plan to use around the bottom of the apron, then measure that distance up from the (finished) bottom edge of the side panel, measuring and marking the distance at intervals across its width, as shown in **Diagram 1**. Connect the marks and make a pattern for D, adding a ½-inch seam allowance to all sides.

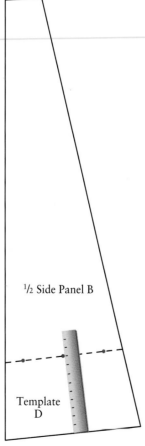

½ Side Panel B

Template
D

Diagram 1

S t e p   3 : Enlarge one triangle of the bib (C) to make a pattern. Add a ½-inch seam allowance to each side.

Cutting

S t e p   1 : From the multicolored fabric, cut one front panel, one side panel, one side panel reverse, one pocket, and two neck bands.

S t e p   2 : Cut two 3-yard lengths from the 2-inch-wide border print, making sure you add a ½-inch seam allowance to each side of the printed strip.

S t e p   3 : Cut four identical C triangles from the wide border print strip, then cut four more identical C triangles for the potholder (set these aside). Position the long side of the pattern so that a line from the border print falls just within the ½-inch seam allowance.

S t e p   4 : Cut eight identical border band (D) pieces from the wide border print, centering a motif from the print at the midpoint of the pattern piece so that the design will match at the seams. Position a line from the border print just within the ½-inch seam allowance on each long side.

Sewing the Apron Skirt

S t e p   1 : To assemble the skirt, use a ½-inch seam allowance to sew the bias edge of a side panel (B) to one side of the center panel (A). Repeat on the opposite side. Press the seams open.

Step 2: Use ½-inch seams to sew the eight border pieces (D) together into one long strip. Press the seams open.

Step 3: Align and pin the right side of the bottom of the border strip to the wrong side of the bottom of the apron panels, matching the seams on the border strip to the seams and angles of the panels. Use a ½-inch seam allowance to stitch the two together, using a line on the strip as a sewing guide. Press the seam open, then fold the border strip to the front of the skirt. Turn under ½ inch, press, and topstitch.

Step 4: To hem the sides of the apron, turn under ¼ inch and stitch. Then turn under ½ inch and press. Stitch down ⅛ inch from the folded edge.

Step 5: Fold the pocket (E) in half crosswise, with right sides together, and sew the aligned edges together with a ½-inch seam allowance, leaving a 2-inch opening at the middle of the seam, as shown in **Diagram 2A.** Press the seam open, then fold the pocket so the seam is in the middle. Sew the two long sides together, as shown in **2B.** This saves quite a bit of time since you do not need to hem the top of the

pocket or deal with getting the edges of the pocket to turn under evenly.

Step 6: Turn the pocket right side out through the opening in the center seam and press. Whipstitch the opening closed, being careful not to catch the back fabric in the stitching.

Step 7: Using pattern piece A on page 211 as a guide, place the pocket, center seam down, onto the skirt. Topstitch ⅛ inch from the edge on all sides except the top.

Step 8: Sew two lines of gathering stitches across the top of the skirt. Draw up the gathers until the width is 15 inches.

Step 9: Find the midpoint of one of the 3-yard pieces of 2-inch (finished width) border print that will be used for the waistband and ties. Find the midpoint of the piece of fusible interfacing and match it with the midpoint of the border print strip. Iron the interfacing to the band according to the manufacturer's instructions.

Step 10: With right sides facing, pin the skirt to the waistband so the gathers do not extend beyond the interfacing. Adjust the gathers and stitch the band to the skirt with a ½-inch seam allowance.

Sewing the Bib

Step 1: Use ½-inch seam allowances to sew together the four border print triangles (C) that form the square bib. Press. Trim excess seam allowances.

A

B

Diagram 2

Step 2: Place the wrong side of the lining fabric on top of the batting. Place the pieced bib right side down onto the lining. Cut the batting and lining to exactly match the bib. Pin the pieces together securely.

Step 3: Fold each of the two neck band strips in half lengthwise, right sides together. Using a ½-inch seam allowance, stitch the long side and across one of the short sides of each band. Turn the bands right side out. Trim the excess seam allowance and press.

Step 4: Insert the unsewn end of a neck band between the lining and border print square on each side of the bib top. Align the raw band ends with the top edge of the bib, and place the sides of the bands just inside the seam allowance on each side, as shown in **Diagram 3.**

Diagram 3

Stitch across the top (catching the neck bands) and down each side, using the stitching line you made in Step 3 as a sewing guide. Leave the bottom open. Trim excess seam allowances, turn the bib right side out, and press. Hand or machine quilt the bib around its outer

edges and following part of the design inside the square.

Step 5: Sew a button near the end of one neckband and two buttonholes near the end of the other neckband, or just plan to tie the bands at the neck.

Step 6: With right sides together, place the midpoint of the bottom of the bib at the midpoint of the waistband. Pin the pieces together and stitch the bib to the waistband with a ½-inch seam allowance.

Step 7: Pin the midpoint of the remaining 3-yard strip of border print to the midpoint of the bottom of the bib, with the right side of the border strip facing the wrong side of the bib. Continue pinning, moving beyond the bib on both sides, matching and pinning the strip to the ends of the waistband. Using a ½-inch seam allowance,

Diagram 4

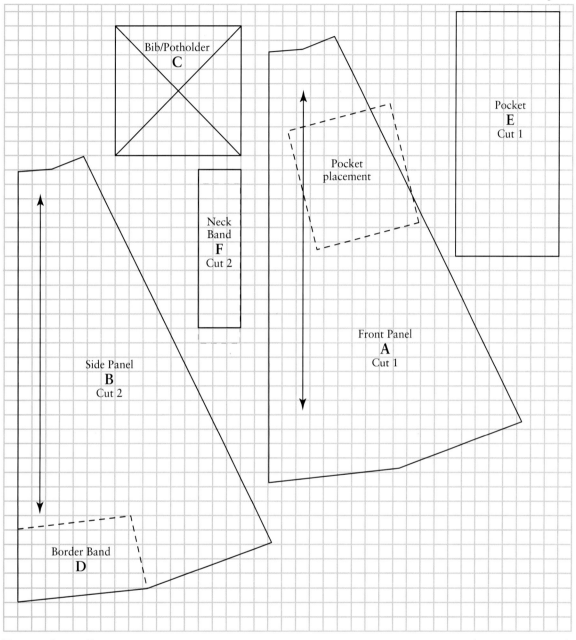

Hostess Apron Patterns

One square=1 inch

and starting where the strip meets the skirt, sew around the edge of the waistband, stopping when you reach the other edge of the skirt. See **Diagram 4.**

S t e p   9 : Trim excess seam allowances, then turn the band ends right side out and press. Turn under ½ inch of the unsewn edge on the waistband and hand stitch in place.

Making the Potholder

S t e p   1 : If you haven't already cut C triangles for the potholder, enlarge one triangle of the potholder (C) on page 208 to make a pattern. Add a ½-inch seam allowance to each side.

S t e p   2 : Cut four identical C triangles from the wide border print strip. Position the long side of the pattern so that a line from the border print falls just within the ½-inch seam allowance.

S t e p   3 : Use ½-inch seam allowances to sew together the four border print triangles (C) that form the potholder. Press. If desired, trim excess seam allowances.

S t e p   4 : Fold the batting in half and lay the potholder square on top of the doubled batting. Cut the shape through both layers of batting.

S t e p   5 : Pin the batting to the wrong side of the potholder square. Use a ½-inch seam allowance to stitch around the entire edge from the front side, using a line in the border print as a guide.

S t e p   6 : To make the hanging tab, cut a 1¼ × 4½-inch rectangular scrap from the border print or multicolored fabric. Fold under the two long edges ¼ inch and press. Fold the entire strip in half lengthwise, wrong sides together, and stitch down the length of the strip. Fold in half crosswise and pin the raw edges to the right side of the potholder in one corner.

S t e p   7 : To make the backing, place the potholder on top of a piece of the multicolored fabric, with right sides together. Cut the backing to the exact size of the potholder.

S t e p   8 : Without separating the pieces, pin in place and sew all around the edge with the batting side up, being sure the hanging tab's edges are securely stitched. Sew along the same line of stitches that you made in Step 5. Leave approximately 3 inches open along one side.

S t e p   9 : Trim the corners. Trim excess bulk in seam allowances. Turn the potholder right side out and press. Close the opening with a whip stitch.

S t e p   1 0 : Quilt as desired. I regard potholders as strictly utilitarian and, becuase they last a very short time, I always machine quilt them. There should be enough quilting to stabilize the cotton batting between the layers so that it will not form lumps when the potholder is washed.

Border Print Throw Pillows

These pillows can be made entirely from border print fabric or from a piece of fabric surrounded by a border print. All these pillows were made from scraps left over from projects in this book, augmented with fabric from my collection. If you have no border print scraps, you should be able to make at least four pillows from 1¼ yards of new fabric.

I recommend you use 100 percent cotton batting or a cotton/polyester-blend batting behind any pillow fronts you plan to machine quilt because they tend to be less slippery than other types of batting.

Review "Working with Border Prints" on page 77 and "Making and Using Templates" on page 74 before beginning these pillows.

Totally Border Print Pillow

You Will Need

Border print fabric scraps (or ¼ yard of fabric)

Cotton or cotton/polyester-blend batting, approximately 10 inches square

Fabric for backing, approximately 10 inches square

Template plastic

Permanent marker

Making Templates

Step 1: For Template A, draw a 6⅜-inch square. Cut the square in half diagonally. Add ¼-inch seam allowances to each side of one triangle to complete the template.

Step 2: For Template B, follow Steps 1 through 4 in "Drafting an Equilateral Triangle" on page 167. The side is 5 inches and the height is 4⅜ inches. Add ¼-inch seam allowances to each side of your triangle to complete the template.

Making the Pillow

Step 1: Using template A or B, follow the instructions given in "Working with Border Prints" on page 77 for making a square or hexagon from a border print fabric. Press the piece.

Step 2: Place the pillow front on a piece of batting and cut the batting to exactly fit the pillow. Baste the wrong side of the pillow front to the batting, using enough stitches to hold the pieces firmly in place.

Step 3: Machine or hand quilt from the top, following a portion of the design in the border print.

Step 4: Complete the pillow, following Steps 1 through 8 in "Make Your Own Pillow Form" on page 217.

Square Pillow with a Border Print Border

You Will Need

Piece of print fabric for the pillow front (size determined by your drawing)

Border print fabric scraps to coordinate with the print

Fabric for the pillow back (1 inch wider and longer than your finished pillow size)

Cotton or cotton/polyester batting (1 inch wider and longer than your finished pillow size)

Template plastic

Permanent marker

Making the Pillow

Step 1: Select a finished pillow size, then draw a square to represent it. Draw diagonal lines from corner to corner.

Step 2: Measure the finished width of the border print that will be visible in the finished pillow, then measure that same distance in from all sides of the square. Draw straight lines to represent the border, stopping at the diagonal lines, as shown in **Diagram 1**, which illustrates a 10-inch-square pillow with a 2-inch finished border.

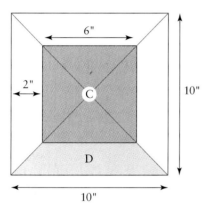

Diagram 1

Step 3: Using the template plastic and the drawing you made in Step 2, make one template (C) for the center square and one template (D) for the side border. Be sure to add ¼-inch seam allowances to all sides of each template.

Step 4: Cut one print A square. Refer to "Border Prints Framing a Square Block or Quilt" on page 78 and cut four identical D borders from the border print fabric, centering a design in the border print on the template.

Step 5: Sew one side border strip to each side of the square, beginning and ending where seam allowances intersect at the miters. Sew up the miters last. Press.

Step 6: Follow Steps 2 through 4 on the opposite page to finish the pillow.

Rectangular Pillow with a Border Print Border

You Will Need

Piece of print fabric for the pillow front (size determined by your drawing)

Border print fabric scraps to coordinate with the print

Fabric for the pillow back (1 inch wider and longer than your finished pillow size)

Cotton or cotton/polyester batting (1 inch wider and longer than your finished pillow)

Template plastic

Permanent marker

Making the Pillow

Step 1: The rectangular pillow is made in a similar manner as the square pillow on the opposite page. Select a finished pillow size, then draw a rectangle to represent it. Position a right angle triangle on your drawing, aligning its angled edge with a corner of the rectangle, as shown in **Diagram 2** on page 216. Draw the miter. Repeat at remaining corners. (An alternate way to find the miters is to fold the rectangle at a corner, aligning adjoining sides, as shown in **Diagram 3.** Unfold and repeat for all sides.)

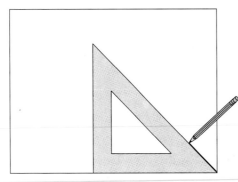

Diagram 2

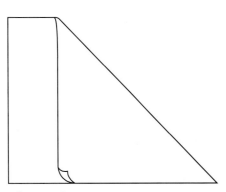

Diagram 3

S t e p   2 : Measure the finished width of the border print that will be visible in the finished pillow, then measure that same distance in from all sides of the rectangle. Draw straight lines to represent the border, stopping at the diagonal lines in the same way as for a square pillow, shown in **Diagram 1** on page 215.

S t e p   3 : Using your template material and the drawing you made in Step 2, make one template (E) for the center rectangle, one template (F) for the side border, and one template (G) for the top/bottom border. Be sure to add ¼-inch seam allowances to all sides of each template.

S t e p   4 : Cut one print E rectangle. Refer to "Border Prints Framing a Rectangular Quilt" on page 79 and cut two F borders and two G borders from the border print fabric.

S t e p   5 : Sew the border print pieces to each of the four sides of the rectangle, beginning and ending where seam allowances intersect at the miters. Sew up the miters last. Press.

S t e p   6 : Follow Steps 2 through 4 on page 214 to finish the pillow.

Make Your Own Pillow Form

After you've spent the time making attractive pillow fronts, don't finish your pillows by using ready-made pillow forms. It is much less expensive to make your own, and the result will be a form that fits your pillow casing perfectly. You might ask why you need a form at all—why not just stuff the pillow casing? I have found that the extra fabric around the inner form helps provide a smoother, lump-free finished pillow. The removable form also makes the pillow casing simple to wash.

You Will Need

For one pillow form

Polyester fiberfill (one 24-ounce bag should fill two 9-inch pillows)

2 pieces of muslin or scrap fabric, each at least as large as your pillow front

Making the Form

Step 1: Complete the pillow front, as described in the project instructions on pages 214 through 216. Make sure all quilting is completed.

Step 2: Place the pillow front on top of the muslin. Using the front as a guide, cut two pillow form pieces the same size as the pillow.

Step 3: Pin the two pillow form pieces with wrong sides together and stitch all around a scant ¼ inch from the edge, leaving an opening of about 4 inches along one side.

Step 4: Turn the pillow form right side out and stuff very tightly with the fiberfill. Make sure to get the fiberfill into the corners. Hand stitch the opening closed.

Step 5: Sew a line of machine stitching all around the edge of the pillow front, exactly where you want to stitch when the back is sewn to the front.

Step 6: Place the pillow front onto the pillow back with right sides together. Cut out the back, using the pillow front as a guide.

Step 7: With right sides together, pin the front to the back. With the pillow front facing you, stitch the front to the back, sewing exactly on the stitching line that you made in Step 5. Leave an opening of about 6 inches along one side.

Step 8: Clip the corners, turn right side out, and push the pillow form inside, making sure the corners of the form fill the corners of the pillow casing. Whip stitch the opening closed.

$\mathcal{B}$aker's Apron

Anyone who likes to cook enjoys receiving a new apron for Christmas. One of my favorite styles is this easy-to-make Baker's Apron. If you are in a hurry, use a pretty floral fabric to make a plain apron, omitting the decorative trim. To save even more time, use grosgrain ribbon for the ties. If you have a little more time, trim the apron with a border print fabric, as shown here.

You Will Need

1 yard of fabric for the apron body and ties

2½-yard strip of a border print fabric (2- to 4-inch finished width) containing mirror image motifs

Piece of newspaper or brown paper

Tracing paper

Making the Pattern Pieces

S t e p   1 : Using the measurements in **Diagram 1,** draw the apron pattern on a piece of newspaper or brown paper. Add a ½-inch seam allowance to all sides of the pattern. Cut out the pattern.

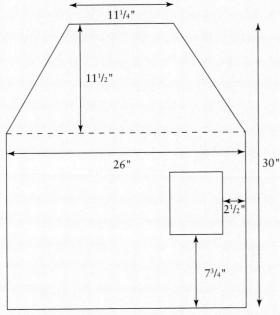

Diagram 1

S t e p   2 : Referring to **Diagram 2,** determine miter lines for the border print trim by folding pattern edge AB to meet edge AC. Then fold edge AC to meet edge BD. Draw lines along the folds.

S t e p   3 : Measure the finished width of your border print fabric. Staying within the finished pattern, draw bands of the same width across the top edges of the apron pattern, as shown in **Diagram 3,** which represents an apron with a 4-inch finished border.

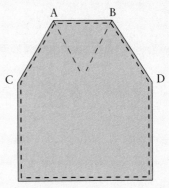

Diagram 2

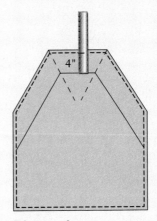

Diagram 3

S t e p   4 : Use tracing paper to make a pattern for the right-side band (the left side is cut by reversing the template). Make a pattern for the top center band. Be sure to add ½-inch seam allowances to all sides of each piece.

Cutting the Pieces

S t e p   1 : Use the pattern to cut out the body of the apron. From the remaining apron fabric, cut two 2½ × 36-inch strips for the ties, one 2½ × 21-inch strip for the neck band, and one 14 × 8-inch rectangle for the pocket.

Step 2: Fold the pattern piece for the center band that you made in Step 4 in half crosswise to find its midpoint. Center the midpoint on a symmetrical motif in the border print. Mark and cut out the center band from the border print fabric.

Step 3: Place the center band fabric on the remaining border print, matching its design with the design on the fabric. Place the side band pattern piece that you made in Step 4 on page 219 on top of the fabric, lining up its left angle with the left side of the center band. Carefully mark and cut out the right-side band.

Step 4: Place the side band cut in Step 3 with right sides facing on the remaining piece of border print, matching the design on both pieces of fabric. Cut out the left-side band. It should be a mirror image of the first.

Step 5: To make the bottom trim, fold the remaining strip of border print in half crosswise, making sure the fold is at the midpoint of a symmetrical motif on the fabric. Finger press and unfold. Cut a strip 26 inches long, with the fold line at its midpoint. Make sure you add a ½-inch seam allowance to each long side of the strip.

Making the Neck Band and Ties

Step 1: Fold the 21-inch strip of neck band fabric in half lengthwise, right sides together. Stitch the long edge and one of the short edges together with a ¼-inch seam allowance. Turn right side out and press.

Step 2: Fold each 36-inch tie strip in half lengthwise, right sides together. Use a ¼-inch seam allowance to stitch the length and across one edge of each. Turn the ties right side out; press.

Assembling the Apron Body

Step 1: Align the right side of the 26-inch band of border print along the wrong side of the bottom of the apron. Pin in place and sew the two pieces together with a ½-inch seam allowance.

Step 2: Fold the band to the right side of the apron and press. Turn under ½ inch of the raw edge on the band and press. Pin the band to the right side of the apron and topstitch in place.

Step 3: Sew the two border print side bands to the center band, ending the stitching where seam allowances intersect on the lower portions of the band, as shown in **Diagram 4.**

Diagram 4

Step 4: Center and pin the neck band to the wrong side of the top of the apron, as shown in **Diagram 5,** being careful not to twist the band. Baste the band in place. Try on the apron to make sure the band length is correct.

Step 5: Still working on the wrong side of the apron, pin the unsewn end of a tie on each side, as shown in **Diagram 5.**

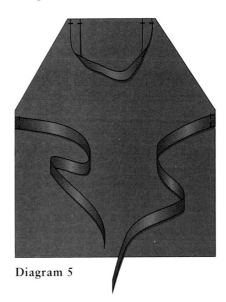

Diagram 5

Step 6: Position the right side of the border print band against the wrong side of the top and sides of the apron. Pin in place, making sure to keep the neck band and tie ends free. Sew up one side, across the top and down the other side, stitching the neck band and ties in place at the same time.

Step 7: Turn the border print band to the right side of the apron and press.

Step 8: Turn under ½ inch of the raw edge of the border band. Press and pin the edge to the right side of the apron. Topstitch in place.

Finishing the Apron

Step 1: To hem the sides of the apron, turn under ¼ inch and stitch. Turn under ½ inch and press. Stitch down very close to the folded edge.

Step 2: Fold the pocket rectangle in half, right sides together, aligning the 8-inch-long edges. Use a ½-inch seam allowance to sew the edge together, leaving a 2-inch opening at the middle of the seam, as shown in **Diagram 2A** on page 209. Press the seam open, then fold the pocket with the seam in the middle and sew the two long edges together as shown in **Diagram 2B** on page 209.

Step 3: Turn the pocket inside out through the opening that was left in the first seam and press. Whip stitch the opening closed, being careful not to catch the fabric on the back in the stitching.

Step 4: Using **Diagram 1** on page 219 as a guide, place the pocket onto the apron. Stitch a continuous seam ⅛ inch from the edge on all sides except the top.

Flying Geese Place Mats, Table Runner, and Potholder

With this place mat style, the patchwork remains visible when the plate is on it, unlike many other mats where the patchwork is often hidden when the mat is in use.

The following instructions result in a table runner approximately 60½ inches long. Lengthen or shorten the runner to fit your own table by adjusting the number of Flying Geese rectangles used in the long strip.

Before beginning this project, be sure to read "Working with Border Prints" on page 77 and "Making and Using Templates" on page 74.

You Will Need

For four place mats, one table runner, and one potholder

2½ yards of a border print fabric containing at least two repeats of a 4¾-inch stripe, four repeats of a 2¼-inch stripe, and one repeat of a 1¾-inch stripe

Scraps of 7 different red prints, each at least 7 inches square

1 yard of dark green print fabric

2 yards of batting*

2 yards of coordinating fabric for backing

*Be sure to use 100 percent cotton batting for the potholder. Since polyester batting conducts heat, you are more likely to burn your hand if you use it in the potholder.

angle to the opposite side of the A triangle, as shown.8

Step 4: Repeat Step 3, assembling a total of 66 rectangular units. Set aside the leftover triangles.

Making Templates

Make templates for the large triangle (A), small triangle (B), and side point (D) using the full-size patterns on page 227. Make a paper pattern for a 2-inch square (C). Note that square C is only used once, at the center of the table runner. For the large rectangle (E) used in the place mat, make a paper pattern 10¾ × 9¼ inches.

Making the Flying Geese Units

Step 1: Cut 9 A triangles from each scrap of red fabric, plus one extra A triangle from five of the red fabrics (for a total of 68 triangles).

Step 2: Cut 134 B triangles from the lengthwise edge of the green fabric.

Step 3: Sew a green B triangle to one side of a red A triangle, as shown in **Diagram 1.** Then sew another B tri-

Assembling the Place Mats

Step 1: Sew seven Flying Geese units together, with red triangles all pointing in the same direction, to make one long band. Repeat, making a total of four long Flying Geese bands.

Step 2: Cut four E rectangles from the lengthwise edge of the green fabric. Pin and sew an E rectangle, right sides together, to each long Flying Geese band, as shown in **Diagram 2.** Sew the two pieces together from the patchwork side to help ensure you do not cut off the side points of the red triangles.

Step 3: See "Border Prints Framing a Rectangular Quilt" on page 79 for instructions on cutting out and adding a 2¼-inch border print border to each place mat.

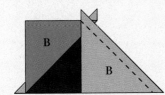

Diagram 1

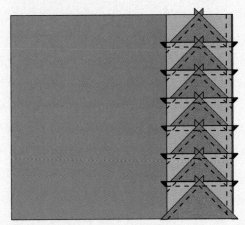

Diagram 2

Quilting and Finishing the Place Mats

S t e p 1 : Lay a place mat right side up on the batting. Cut the batting to match the place mat and baste the two together. Since there may be slight variations, use each place mat as a guide to cut its own batting to size.

S t e p 2 : Working from the right side, machine quilt the place mat as desired.

S t e p 3 : With the place mat facing up, machine stitch ¼ inch from the outside of the mat, directly on the line you chose for your finished border edge.

S t e p 4 : With right sides together, place a mat onto the backing fabric and cut out the backing to match. Pin together carefully. Repeat with all remaining mats, cutting individual backings to match each placemat exactly. Cut the backing pieces along one lengthwise edge of the lining fabric.

S t e p 5 : With the batting side facing up, stitch the backing and place mat together, following the line of stitches that you made in Step 3. Leave an approximate 5-inch opening along one side for turning.

S t e p 6 : Turn the placemat right side out, press, and slip stitch the opening closed. Topstitch all around the outer edge of the placemat, following a line from the border print.

S t e p 7 : Repeat for the remaining three place mats.

Assembling the Table Runner

S t e p 1 : Use the remaining 34 Flying Geese units to sew two more Flying Geese bands of 17 Flying Geese units each.

S t e p 2 : Cut one red C square. Using the green B triangles set aside previously, align the midpoint of the long side of a green B triangle with the midpoint of one side of the red C square. Use a ¼-inch seam allowance to sew the pieces together. Repeat, sewing a green triangle to each side of the square, as shown in **Diagram 3**. Press.

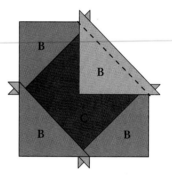

Diagram 3

S t e p 3 : Sew a long band of Flying Geese triangles to opposite sides of the B/C square. The red triangles should point away from the center square, as shown in **Diagram 4**. Sew a single red A triangle to each end of the band. Press the band.

S t e p 4 : Mark the side miter and the center miter directly on Template D along the appropriate edges.

S t e p 5 : Place a strip of the 4¾-inch-wide border print along the Flying Geese strip, centering a motif from the border print at the midpoint of the red square in the middle of the strip. Place pins at each end of the border print, aligning them with the seams of the last red triangle in each strip.

Step 6: Place Template D on the border print with the side miter edge toward the edge of the border print, as shown in **Diagram 5**. Line up the dashed seam line on the template with the pin in the border print (the seam allowance will extend beyond the pin). To align remaining edges, mark some design from the border print directly onto the template along the side miter edge. **Note:** This template is used here for cutting the miter only.

Step 7: Cut the angle along the edge of the border print. Carefully fold the mitered edge over to the opposite end of the strip and, matching pins and the design on the fabric, cut the miter on that end. You should now have one

long strip of border print with a miter at each end.

Step 8: Place this mitered strip of border print on top of the remaining piece of 4¾-inch border print, matching the design exactly, and cut the second strip exactly as the first.

Step 9: Cut two identical D pieces and two identical D Reverse pieces from the remaining border print. Be sure to match the design you traced onto the side miter edge of the template.

Step 10: Sew a D and a D Reverse to the ends of each long strip of border print, as shown in **Diagram 6**. Make sure to match the design in the fabric at the side miter.

Step 11: Carefully pin one long border print strip to one side of the Flying Geese strip, matching midpoints of both strips, and stitch in place with a ¼-inch seam allowance. Begin and end

Diagram 4

Diagram 5

Diagram 6

each seam ¼ inch from the end of the strip. Repeat, sewing the second border strip to the unit. Sew up the miters at each end of the table runner. Press.

Quilting and Finishing the Table Runner

Step 1: Quilt and finish the runner following Steps 1 through 6 on page 224.

Assembling the Potholder

Step 1: Sew the remaining four Flying Geese units together into one strip. Press the strip.

Step 2: Cut a piece of solid green fabric to match the size of the pieced strip. Cut two pieces of 1¾-inch border print to match the length of the pieced strip. (Be sure to add ¼-inch seam allowances to each long side.) Use ¼-inch seams to sew all four pieces together, as shown in **Diagram 7.**

Diagram 7

Step 3: Cut two pieces of 1¾-inch border print to match the width of the partially assembled potholder. (Be sure to add ¼-inch seam allowances on each long edge.) Sew to the top and bottom of the unit, as shown in **Diagram 8.** Press.

Diagram 8

Quilting and Finishing the Potholder

Step 1: Fold the piece of batting in half. Lay the potholder on top of it and carefully cut the batting to match.

Step 2: Pin the batting and potholder together, with the right side of the potholder facing up. Stitch around the entire edge from the printed side, using a line from the border print as a guide.

Step 3: To make the hanging tab, cut a 1¼ × 4½-inch rectangle from the green fabric. Fold under the two long edges ¼ inch and press. Fold the entire strip in half lengthwise, wrong sides together, and stitch down the length of the strip. Fold in half crosswise and pin to the right side of the potholder in one corner, matching raw edges.

Step 4: To make the backing, place the potholder on top of a scrap of the dark green fabric, with batting side up and the patchwork facing the right side of the backing print. Cut the backing to match the size of the potholder.

Step 5: Without separating the pieces, pin in place and sew all around the edge with the batting side up, being careful to catch the hanging tab in the stitches. Sew along the same line of stitches that you made in Step 2. Leave approximately 3 inches open.

Step 6: Trim the corners. Trim excess bulk in seam allowances. Turn the potholder right side out and press. Close the opening with a whip stitch.

Step 7: Quilt as desired. There should be enough quilting to stabilize the cotton batting between the layers so that it will not form lumps when the potholder is washed.

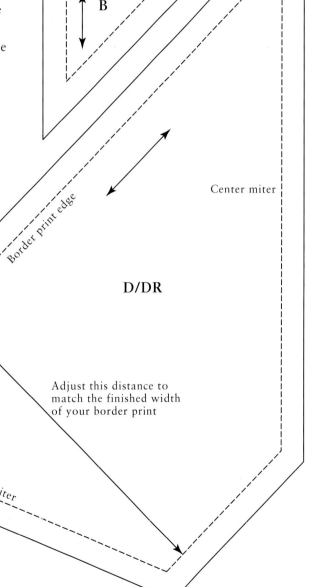

B

Center miter

Border print edge

D/DR

Adjust this distance to match the finished width of your border print

A

Side miter

Flying Geese Templates

*C*at Doorstop

This crazy-patch cat makes a fun gift. He sits upright and is heavy enough to hold a door open. The pattern is a larger version of the tree ornaments on page 152, but with the addition of border print and patchwork trim. Making this cat is a perfect way to use leftover pieces from some of the larger patchwork projects in this book. For a more detailed explanation of the color palette used in this project, see page 7. You will want to review "Making and Using Templates" on page 74 before beginning this project.

You Will Need

Fat quarter (18 × 22-inch piece of fabric) of a large multicolor print for the tail, back, and base

22 print strips, each 1½ × 12 inches, that subtly shade from green to red to brown (11 green strips, and 11 brown and red strips)

Scraps of 9 different red prints, each at least 2 inches square

Scrap of green print, at least 8 inches square

½ yard of firm batting

40 inches of a 1¼-inch-wide strip of border print

½ bag of polyester fiberfill

1-gallon zipper-closure plastic bag

10 to 12 cups of cat box filler or sand

Template plastic

Permanent marker

Making Templates

Step 1: Enlarge the patterns on page 232. Using the template plastic, make templates of the complete cat body shape, the tail (E), and the cat base (F). A ¼-inch seam allowance has been added around the cat body and around pieces E and F.

S t e p   2 : Trace shapes A, B, C, and D on page 232 (within the cat body) onto template material. Trace the ¼-inch seam allowance on the outer edges of each piece, and be sure to add a ¼-inch seam allowance to all remaining sides.

S t e p   3 : Enlarge and make a template from pattern piece G on page 232, which includes a ¼-inch seam allowance.

Cutting the Pieces

S t e p   1 : From the large multicolor print, cut two tail pieces (E and E Reverse), a base (F), and a cat body pattern reverse. Mark or notch the sides of piece F as indicated on the pattern.

S t e p   2 : From the batting, cut two complete cat bodies, a cat base (F) and two 8 × 11-inch rectangles.

S t e p   3 : Cut nine red G triangles and nine green G triangles.

Shading the Print Strips

S t e p   1 : Carefully arrange the 11 green fabric strips from bright green to dark green. Stack in order. Arrange the red and brown strips from dark burgundy to red, then from brick to brown. Make a second stack for these strips.

S t e p   2 : Working directly on one of the 8 × 11-inch pieces of batting, use the shaded green strips to assemble a strip-quilted rectangle. Assemble another rectangle using the red strips and the second 8 × 11-inch piece of batting. See "Strip Quilting" on page 86 for more detailed instructions.

S t e p   3 : Trim the batting even with the strips. Using **Diagram 1** as a guide, lay out and cut pieces A, B, C, and D from the shaded rectangles. Do not cut the area between the ears of piece D until later.

S t e p   4 : Sew a red G triangle to a green G triangle to make a square. Repeat eight more times, then sew the units into a band, as shown in **Diagram 2.**

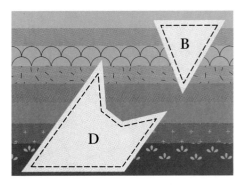

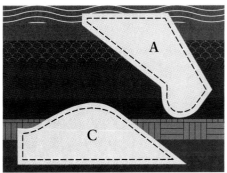

Diagram 1

Diagram 2

Assembling the Cat Front

The cat is assembled using a quilt-as-you-go crazy-patch technique. If the method is new to you, see "Crazy-Patch Quilting" on page 86.

Step 1: Turn one of the cat body batting pieces in the direction you want the cat to face. Using **Diagram 3** as a guide, take piece A that you cut from the shaded strips and place it right side up on the cat body. Pin in place.

Step 2: Cut a 5-inch length of the border print (Border Strip 1) and place it face down on piece A with inside edges aligning, as shown in **Diagram 3**. Stitch ¼ inch in from the edge.

Step 3: Turn the border print strip right side up and press. Place piece B (cut from the shaded strip) face down on the border strip with raw edges aligned, as shown in **Diagram 4**. Stitch ¼ inch in from the edge. Turn piece B right side up and press.

Step 4: Cut an 11-inch length of border print (Border Strip 2) and angle it face down across the cat body, as shown in **Diagram 4**. It will angle across piece A, Border Strip 1, and piece B. Use a ¼-inch seam allowance to sew the strip to the cat body. Flip the strip right side up and press.

Step 5: Place your Flying Geese strip face down on Border Strip 2, with raw edges aligned. Use a ¼-inch seam allowance to sew the patchwork to the cat body. Flip the strip right side up and press.

Step 6: Cut a 9½-inch strip (Border Strip 3) and place it face down on the patchwork strip, aligning it in far enough onto the patchwork to deliberately cut off the points, as shown in **Diagram 5**. Sew to the cat body, turn right side up, and press.

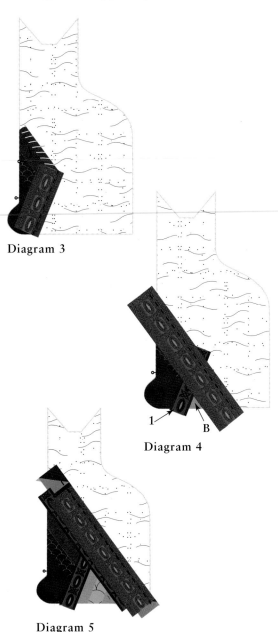

Diagram 3

1   B

Diagram 4

Diagram 5

Step 7: Add piece C in a similar manner, then a 6½-inch strip (Border Strip 4). Add piece D last. Press the entire cat body.

Step 8: Turn to the batting side and trim away fabric that extends past the batting edge, including the excess between the cat's ears.

Finishing the Cat

Step 1: Baste the back of the cat piece to the second piece of cat body batting. Baste the cat base (F) to the cat base batting. Quilt around a portion of the design on the fabric.

Step 2: Pin the cat front and back pieces with right sides together and begin stitching at the bottom of the cat on the foot side. Stitch up the side of the cat, around the head and ears, and down the back, stopping 4½ inches from the bottom, as shown in **Diagram 6.**

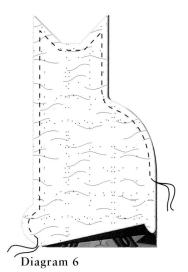

Diagram 6

Step 3: With right sides together, pin the cat base to the bottom edge of the cat, placing the notches at the side seams. Stitch completely around the base.

Step 4: Carefully clip the ears, the curve of the back, and the front foot. Turn the cat right side out. Using a wooden skewer or some other blunt object, push carefully into the ears to make sure they are turned completely and are pointed.

Step 5: Pin the two tail pieces right sides together and stitch, leaving an opening at the end where the tail will meet the body. Turn right side out.

Step 6: Firmly stuff the cat head and body with the fiberfill as far as the 4½-inch opening, and push batting as tightly as you can into the cat's foot.

Step 7: Fill the gallon plastic bag half full with cat box filler or sand. Push all of the air out of the bag and seal. Work the bag into the cavity of the cat. You may have to add or take away some of the fiberfill until you achieve just the right amount of stuffing. Whip stitch the opening, leaving a 1½-inch opening for the tail.

Step 8: Stuff the tail, but not too tightly because it must be bent. Insert the tail into the opening at the base of the cat. Whip stitch closed.

Step 9: Bend the tail toward the front of the cat and tack the tip of the tail to the body.

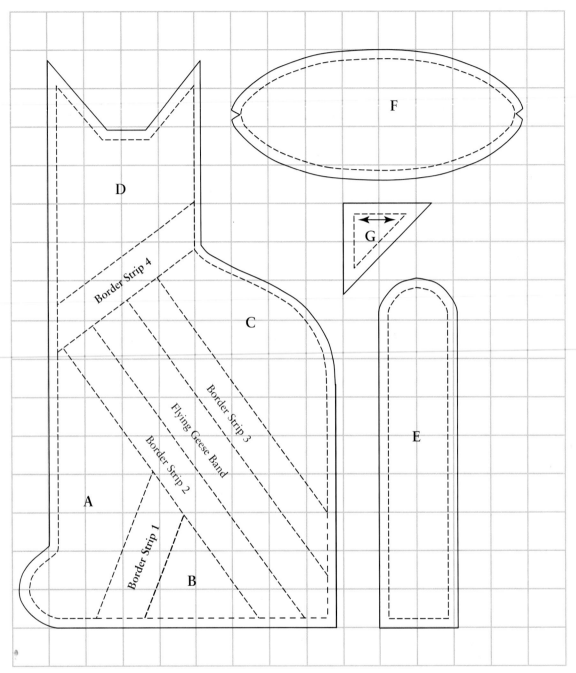

Cat Doorstop Templates

One square = 1 inch

$\mathscr{P}$atchwork Christmas Stockings

Christmas stockings are a lot of fun to make. Once you get started on them, you can devise all kinds of variations. Invite a friend over to share a marathon assembly-line sewing session, making stockings for decorations or gifts. My friend Robin Morrison and I did that one afternoon, and by the time we were finished we had made 12 stockings! Three variations are given here, but use your imagination to create your own designs. For variety, replace the border print strips with lace or ribbon, and add buttons or other special trims.

You Will Need

For each stocking

18 × 20-inch piece of firm batting

18 × 20-inch piece of fabric for the lining

8½ × 17-inch strip of fabric for the band cuff

Materials listed for individual variations

Making a Pattern

Enlarge the stocking pattern on page 239 as indicated. Use the full-size pattern to cut a front and back stocking from the piece of batting, and a front and back from the lining fabric (reverse the pattern to cut one side of the lining). Embellish the stocking using one of the following methods.

Note: Before beginning a crazy-patch or strip-pieced stocking, read more about both methods by referring to pages 85–87. There is only one difference for the instructions here: If you use a firm batting, you do not need to baste the batting to the lining—you can work directly on the batting.

Crazy-Patch Variation

You Will Need

Basic supplies and patterns specified on this page

½ yard of border print fabric with at least four repeats of a 1- to 1½-inch-wide stripe (finished size)

5 9-inch squares of large-scale multi-colored prints (one can be the same fabric used for the cuff)

Making the Stocking

Step 1: Cut the five squares of fabric in half diagonally.

Step 2: Select the fabric you would like to be most prominent, and place one of the triangles right side up on the batting, as shown in **Diagram 1.** Do not worry about being exact. There is a lot of flexibility in the placement.

Step 3: With right sides together, place a strip of border print along the long edge of the triangle, lining up the raw edges, as shown in **Diagram 2,** and pin it in place. Stitch along a line on the border print. Turn the strip right side up and press.

Step 4: Align another border print strip right side down on top of the triangle, as shown in **Diagram 3.** Pin and sew, being careful to keep your stitches on a line in the border print fabric. Turn the strip right side up and press.

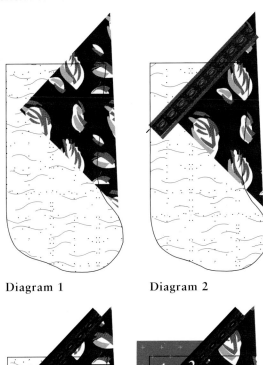

Diagram 1 **Diagram 2**

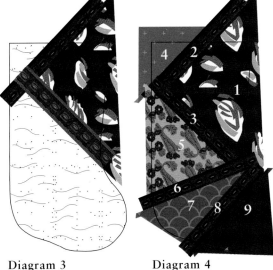

Diagram 3 **Diagram 4**

Step 5: Place another triangle right side down along the edge of the second border fabric and pin, sew, and press. Continue adding pieces of fabric and border print trim to the stocking, using the piecing order shown in **Diagram 4.** When complete, turn to the back of the stocking and trim away excess fabric so that it is even with the batting.

Step 6: Make a stocking back that is a mirror image of the front. Be sure to

orient the batting so that you are making a front and back, not two fronts. I usually work the front and back simultaneously so that there are fewer trips to the ironing board.

Step 7: Finish the stocking by following the instructions in "Completing the Stocking" on page 238.

Shaded Strips Variation

You Will Need

Basic supplies and patterns specified on the opposite page

3 pieces of batting, each 9 × 14 inches

18 cotton prints, each 5 × 9 inches, which subtly shade together from green to red to brown[*]

½ yard of border print fabric with at least four repeats of a 2- to 2½-inch-wide stripe

[*]If you buy ¼ yard of each of the 18 fabrics, you will have enough to make shaded strips for several stockings, as well as leftover pieces for ornaments.

Making the Stocking

Step 1: Carefully arrange the 18 pieces of fabric, arranging them from bright green to dark green, then to black, dark burgundy, red, brick, and brown. Stack them on top of each other and make two cuts, resulting in three strips of each fabric that are approximately 1½ × 9 inches. Do not worry about being exact. The strips are more interesting if they are of random width. Separate the fabric into three stacks of identical strips.

Step 2 : Working directly on each of the three pieces of 9 × 14-inch batting, use the three groups of stacked strips to assemble three shaded strip units. (See "Strip Quilting" on page 86 for more detailed information.)

Step 3 : Trim the strips even with the batting, then cut each unit into triangles, like those shown in **Diagram 5**. You don't have to follow these exact dimensions or shapes.

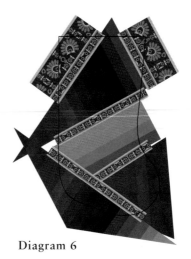

Diagram 6

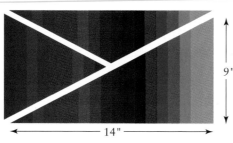

Diagram 5

Step 4 : Sew the triangles directly to the stocking-shaped batting, as described in Steps 2 through 5 on page 234. Refer to **Diagram 6** for approximate placement of triangles and border print strips. Each time a triangle is added, trim it with a strip of border print, as was done in the Crazy-Patch Variation.

Step 5 : Follow Steps 6 and 7 on page 235 to complete the stocking.

Strip and Flying Geese Variation

You Will Need

Basic supplies and patterns specified on page 234

2 pieces of batting, each 9 × 14 inches

18 cotton prints, each 3½ × 9 inches, which subtly shade from green to red to brown

½ yard of border print fabric with at least four repeats of a 2- to 2½-inch-wide stripe

Scraps of 6 different red prints, each at least 3½ inches square

⅛ yard of green fabric

½ yard of the border print strip to use as edging around the cuff

5 × 16-inch strip of fabric for the cuff triangles

Triangle templates A and B on page 227

Making the Stocking

Step 1: Use template A to cut 18 assorted red triangles. Use Template B to cut 36 green triangles.

Step 2: Sew a green B triangle to one side of a red A triangle. Sew another B triangle to the opposite side of the A triangle. Refer to **Diagram 1** on page 223.

Step 3: Repeat Step 2, assembling a total of 18 rectangle units.

Step 4: Sew nine units together, with red triangles all pointing in the same direction, to make one long strip. Repeat for a second strip. One will be used on the stocking front, the other on the back. Press.

Step 5: Carefully arrange the 18 pieces of fabric together from bright green to dark green, then to black, dark burgundy, red, brick, and brown. Stack them on top of each other and cut into two strips approximately 1½ × 9 inches. Do not worry about being exact—the strips are more interesting if they are of random width.

Step 6: Working directly on each of the two pieces of 9 × 14-inch batting, use the two groups of stacked strips to assemble two shaded strip units. (See "Strip Quilting" on page 86 for more detailed information.)

Step 7: Trim the strips even with the batting and then cut each unit once diagonally, as shown in **Diagram 7.**

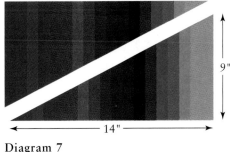

Diagram 7

9"

14"

Step 8: Place the flying geese strip on the stocking-shaped batting, as shown in **Diagram 8.** Sew a border print strip to each side of it, using the same method as for the Crazy-Patch Variation on page 234.

Step 9: Continue to add pieces to the stocking, as shown in **Diagram 8.** Add one shaded strip triangle above the flying geese/border band and one below it. Cut off the excess lower triangle and reserve it for the toe.

Step 10: Add a third border print strip, as shown in **Diagram 8.** Add the leftover shaded unit to the toe.

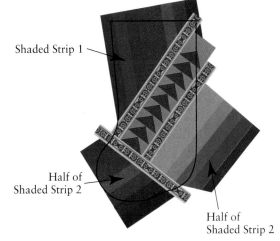

Shaded Strip 1

Half of Shaded Strip 2

Half of Shaded Strip 2

Diagram 8

Step 11: Cut out the band cuff and then cut a strip of border print fabric the length of the cuff. Fold the cuff in half lengthwise and press, then open out again. With right sides facing, position the border print strip as shown in **Diagram 9A,** and carefully pin it in place. Stitch near the top, along a line from the border print. Press the border to the right side, then turn under the raw edge. Press and pin it in place, and top stitch to the cuff, as shown in **9B.**

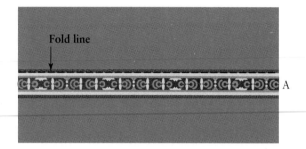

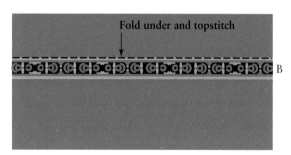

Diagram 9

Step 12: With right sides facing, stitch the short edges of the cuff together. Turn the cuff right side out, fold in half with wrong sides together and press.

Completing the Stocking

Step 1: With right sides facing, pin the completed front and back stocking pieces together. Stitch ¼ inch around the edge, leaving the top open. Clip the seam at the ankle. Turn right side out and press.

Step 2: With right sides together, pin the front and back lining pieces together and stitch ¼ inch from the edge, leaving the top open. Do not turn right side out.

Step 3: Push the lining into the stocking, pin the top edges together, and stitch together ¼ inch from the edge, as shown in **Diagram 10.**

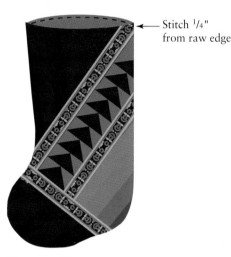

Stitch ¼" from raw edge

Diagram 10

Step 4: If you haven't already cut the band cuff, do so now. With right sides facing, stitch the short edges together. Turn the cuff right side out. Fold in half with wrong sides together and press.

Step 5: With the raw edges facing up, insert the cuff into the stocking, aligning and pinning its edges around the top edge. Stitch together, as shown in **Diagram 11A.** Bring the cuff out of the stocking and fold it over the outside, as shown in **11B.**

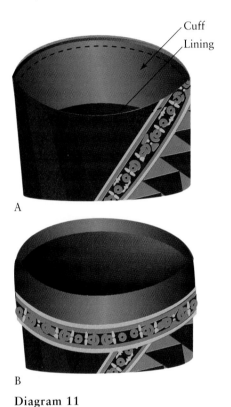

Cuff
Lining

A

B

Diagram 11

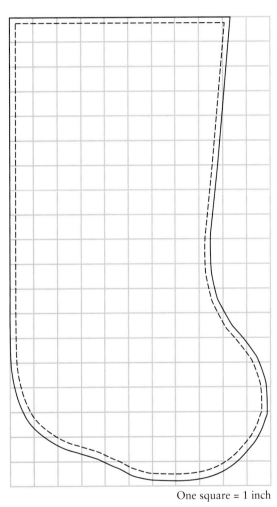

One square = 1 inch

Patchwork Christmas Stocking Pattern

ℋoliday Skirt

The skirt that I'm wearing on the cover of this book is my holiday favorite. I especially like how flattering it is. The six gores are gathered onto a yoke, which means the gathers fall below the yoke instead of at the waist, resulting in a slimmer look. I made my skirt using three fabrics in each gore—a red print fabric for the center panel, a border print framing the red panel, and a dark green fabric surrounding the border print. You can use three fabrics or, for an easier version, cut the gores from a single fabric.

I drafted my own pattern for this skirt, but you can adapt a commercial pattern for a similar look. Look for a pattern that has gores gathered on a yoke. Follow the steps below for making a gore with three fabrics, then incorporate six gores into your skirt pattern. The gores for this skirt are very full and can be gathered to fit any size yoke—you don't need to alter the size of the gores to fit your pattern.

You Will Need

For six three-piece gores

3½ yards of a single border print fabric containing at least four repeats of a 4½-inch (finished width) stripe

1¼ yards of red print fabric

4 yards of dark green fabric

Cutting the Pieces

Step 1: Use 1-inch gridded drafting paper to duplicate each pattern piece shown on pages 244 and 245. A ½-inch seam allowance is included in each pattern piece.

Step 2: Transfer the grain arrows to each pattern piece. Cut out the patterns.

Step 3: Place pattern piece D on a strip of the border print and cut out the first panel. Use this panel to cut the other five identical panels. Cut six identical D Reverse panels.

Step 4: Border print panels C and D must match at their mitered corners. Read "Working with Border Prints" on page 77 before you cut panel C. Pin the mitered edge of the D panel you cut in Step 3 onto pattern piece C, matching the miter in the fabric to the miter on the pattern piece. Place the pinned unit onto another strip of border print, matching the mitered end to the design at the cut miter. Cut the C Reverse panel.

Step 5: Use the C Reverse panel to cut five more identical pieces. Flip it over and cut five C panels.

Step 6: Cut 6 B panels from the red print. Cut 6 E panels, 6 F panels, and 6 F Reverse panels from the green fabric.

Making the Gores

Step 1: Refer to the **Skirt Assembly Diagram** on page 242 as you follow these directions. Use a ½-inch seam allowance as you sew. Sew a C and a C Reverse border print panel to each side of a red B center panel, ending the seam ½ inch from the mitered edge. Use a linc from the border print as your sewing guide.

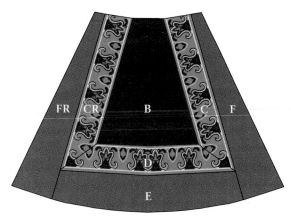

Skirt Assembly Diagram

S t e p   2 : Sew a D to a D Reverse. Press the seam open. Sew the resulting D panel across the bottom of the red B panel, stopping ½ inch from each mitered edge. Sew up the miters between the C and D panels. Press.

S t e p   3 : Pin the E band to the bottom of the gore. Sew the two pieces together. Press.

S t e p   4 : Pin the green F and F Reverse panels to the sides of the gore and sew together. Press.

S t e p   5 : Repeat, making five more identical gores.

S t e p   6 : Join three gores together to form the skirt front. Join three gores to form the skirt back. Press.

S t e p   7 : Continue making the skirt following your pattern instructions. To make a skirt like the one shown here, cut the yoke from the dark green fabric.

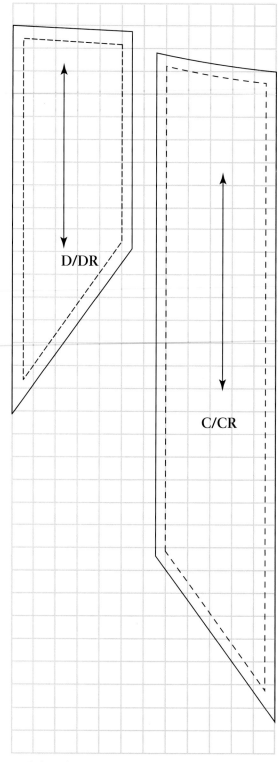

Holiday Skirt Patterns   One square = 1 inch

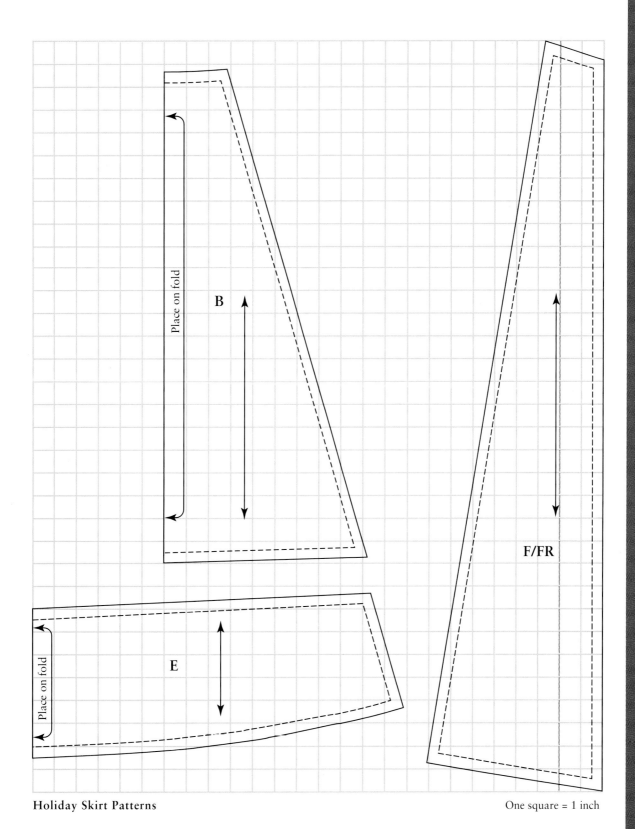

Place on fold

B

Place on fold

E

F/FR

Holiday Skirt Patterns

One square = 1 inch

Index

Note: Page references in *italic* indicate illustrations.
Boldface references indicate photographs.

A

Apples
  in Apple and Grape Table
    Tree, 180–83, **181**
  in Apple and Holly Boxwood
    Wreath, 126–27, **126**
  in Apple Plaque with
    Double Swag, 145–48,
    145, 146
  in Boxwood Wreath with
    Mixed Fruit, **118,** 128–29,
    128
  in boxwood wreaths, 124,
    124
  in Mantel Decoration with
    Greens and Mixed Fruit,
    184–86, **184–85**
  in Over-Doorway Apple
    Plaque with Pine Roping
    Trim, 142–44, **142,** *143,*
    144
Appliqué stitch, 37
Aprons, 207–12, **207,** 218–21,
  218
Assembly line piecing, of quilts,
  85, *85*

B

Backings, quilt, 88, *88*
Basting quilts, 88–89
Batting, for quilts, 87–88
Beautyberries, 121
  in Juniper Wreath with
    Woodland Materials,
    131–33, **131**
Betweens, for quilting, 72
Bias binding, for quilts, 91, *91*
Binding for quilts, 90–92, *91, 92*
  attaching, 92–93, *93*
Black, shading to, 3, 6, 7

Border prints
  in Border Print Mantel Trim,
    196–99, **196, 198**
  in Border Print Place Mat,
    202–4, **202**
  in Border Print Table Runner,
    203, 204–6
  in Border Print Throw
    Pillows, 213–16, **213**
  in Christmas Tree Border Print
    Tree Skirt, 174–77, **174,**
    175, 177
  in Flying Geese Border Print
    Tree Skirt, 168–73, **168**
  working with in quilts, 77–81,
    79, 80, 81
Bows, for Stairway Roping,
  191–93, *191,* **191,** *192*
Boxwood
  in Apple and Holly
    Boxwood Wreath, 126–27,
    126
  in Basic Boxwood Wreath,
    122–25, **122, 125**
  in Boxwood Wreath with
    Mixed Fruit, **118,** 128–29,
    128
  gathering, 124
  in Kissing Ball, 187–88,
    187
  in Miniature Boxwood Tree,
    162–63, **162**
Boxwood wreaths
  packing, 120
  uses for, 120, 125

C

Callicarpa spp., for wreaths, 121,
  131, 132, 190
Centerpiece, 180–83, **181**
Charm quilts, 13
Christmas colors
  palettes for, 6–8, **6–8**
  shading of, 1, 9
Christmas tree, 150–77
  miniature, 162–63, **162**

ornaments for, 152–57, **152,**
  158–61, **158–59**
skirts for (*see* Tree skirts)
Color palettes
  of Christmas colors, 6–8,
    6–8
  for quilts, 3, **3,** 7, 7
  for sweaters, 4, **4,** 5, **5**
Color planning, system for, 1–2,
  9
Colors, Christmas. *See* Christmas
  colors
Continuous bias binding, for
  quilts, 91–92, *92*
Cotton, for batting, 88
Cotton-polyester blends, for batting, 88
Crazy-patch quilting, 86–87, *87*
  for Miniature Stocking
    Ornaments, 160
Cutting mat, for quilting, 72

D

Darners, for quilting, 72
Designs, quilt, 87
Doorstop, 228–32, **228**
Drying quilts, 74

E

Equilateral triangles, drafting,
  167, *167*
Evergreens. *See also specific types*
  in Basic Evergreen Wreath,
    130

F

Fabrics for quilts, selecting and
  preparing, 73
Fair Isle technique, of using multiple yarns, 97
Foundations for quilts, 75–77,
  76, 77
Fruit
  in Boxwood Wreath with
    Mixed Fruit, **118,** 128–29,
    128

in boxwood wreaths, 124–25,
124, 125
in Mantel Decoration with
Greens and Mixed Fruit,
184–86, **184–85**

G

Gold, shading of, 7
Grapes, in Apple and Grape
Table Tree, 180–83, **181**
Grapevines
in Grapevine Wreath with Ivy
and Holly, 137, **137**
in Grapevine Wreath with
Lotus Pods, Rose Hips,
and Pomegranate, 134–36,
134
Green, shading of, 7
Greens. *See also specific types*
in Mantel Decoration with
Greens and Mixed Fruit,
184–86, **184–85**
for wreaths, 120–21

H

Hand piecing, of quilts, 81–83,
82, 83
Hand quilting, 89–90
Hemlock cones, in Juniper
Wreath with Woodland
Materials, 131–33, **131**
Holly
in Apple and Holly Boxwood
Wreath, 126–27, **126**
gathering and preparing, 127
in Grapevine Wreath with Ivy
and Holly, 137, **137**
for wreaths, 120, 121

I

Inside decorations, 178–99
found items as, 194–95, **194,
195**
projects for, 180–83, **181,**
184–86, **184–85,** 187–88,
187, 189–93, **189,** 196–99,
196, 198
Intarsia technique, of using multiple yarns, 97
Ironing, for quilting, 72

Ivy, in Grapevine Wreath with Ivy
and Holly, 137, **137**

J

Joining seams of knitted garments, 102, *102*
Juniper
for Basic Evergreen Wreath,
130
in Juniper Wreath with
Woodland Materials,
131–33, **131**
for pine roping, 141

K

Knitting, 94–117
joining seams in, 102, *102*
sweater projects, 98–117
using multiple yarns in, 96, 97

L

Lemons
in Boxwood Wreath with
Mixed Fruit, **118,** 128–29,
128
in boxwood wreaths, 124
Limes
in boxwood wreaths, 124
in Mantel Decoration with
Greens and Mixed Fruit,
184–86, **184–85**
Log cabin wreath, 120–21
Lotus pods, in Grapevine Wreath
with Lotus Pods, Rose Hips,
and Pomegranate, 134–36, **134**

M

Machine piecing, of quilts, 84, *84*
Machine quilting, 90
Mantel decorations, 184–86,
184–85, *186,* 193, 196–99,
196, 198
Mirrors, for quilting, 72, 81
Mock blanket stitch, for finishing
sweaters, 103, *103*
Mohair yarn, for sweaters, 96, 97
Muslin, for permanent quilt foun-
dations, 75

N

Nandina domestica, 190
Needles, for quilting, 72

O

Oranges
in Boxwood Wreath with
Mixed Fruit, **118,** 128–29,
128
in boxwood wreaths, 124
Ornaments, tree, 152–57, **152,**
158–61, **158–59**
Outside decorations, 138–49
projects for, 140–41, *140–41,*
141, 142–44, **142,** 145–48,
145, 146
for windowsills, 149, **149**

P

Palettes, color. *See* Color palettes
Paper, for removable quilt foundations, 75–76
Patchwork, 201–43
projects in, 154, 202–6, **202,
203,** 207–12, **207,** 213–16,
213, 218–21, **218,** 222–27,
222–23, 228–32, **228,**
233–39, **233,** 240–43, **240**
Piecing, in quilting, 81–85, *82,
83, 84, 85*
Pillow forms, making your own,
217
Pillows, 213–16, **213**
Pineapples
in Apple and Grape Table
Tree, 180–83, **181**
in Apple Plaque with Double
Swag, 145–48, **145, 146**
in Boxwood Wreath with
Mixed Fruit, **118,** 128–29,
128
in boxwood wreaths, 124–25,
125
in Over-Doorway Apple
Plaque with Pine Roping
Trim, 142–44, **142**
Pine boughs, in Mantel
Decoration with Greens
and Mixed Fruit, 184–86,
184–85

Pine roping, 140–41, *140–41*, **141**
    in Over-Doorway Apple
        Plaque with Pine Roping
        Trim, 142–44, **142**
Pins, straight, for quilting, 72–73
Place mats, 202–4, **202**, 222–24, **222**
Polyester, for batting, 88
Pomegranate, in Grapevine
    Wreath with Lotus Pods, Rose
    Hips, and Pomegranate,
    134–36, **134**
Potholders, 207, **207**, 212,
    222–23, **222**, 226–27
Pressing quilts, 72, 85

Q

Quilting. *See also* Quilts
    border prints for, 77–81, *79,
        80, 81*
    crazy-patch, 86–87, *87*, 160
    fabrics for, 73
    foundations for, 75–77, *76, 77*
    hand, 89–90
    machine, 90
    piecing basics for, 81–85, *82,
        83, 84, 85*
    string, 86, *86*, 155, 160
    strip, 86, *86*, 155, 160
    supplies for, 72–73
Quilts, 11–93. *See also* Quilting
    backings for, 88, *88*
    basting, 88–89
    batting for, 87–88
    binding for, 90–92, *91, 92*
        attaching, 92–93, *93*
    charm, 13
    design of, 87
    as inside decorations, 194, **194**
    pressing, 72, 85
    as projects, **12**, 13–21, **22**,
        23–25, **26**, 27–31, **32**,
        33–45, **46**, 47–53, **54**,
        55–61, **62**, 63–71
    signing, 93
    washing and drying, 73–74
Quilt tops, assembling, 87

R

Red, shading of, 6, 7
Right angles, for quilting, 72
Roping
    pine (*see* Pine roping)
    Stairway Roping, 189–93, **189**
Rosa eglanteria, for wreaths, 121,
    131, 132
Rose hips, in Grapevine Wreath
    with Lotus Pods, Rose Hips,
    and Pomegranate, 134–36, **134**
Rotary cutter, for quilting, 72
Rulers, for quilting, 72

S

Scissors, for quilting, 72
Seams, joining, in knitted gar-
    ments, 102, *102*
Setting in quilt pieces
    by hand, 83–84, *84*
    by machine, 84, *84*
Sewing machine, for quilting, 72
Shading, as color principle, 2, 3,
    9
Sharps, for quilting, 72
Shelves, decorations for, 193
Skirt, hostess, 240–43, **240**
Stitching, appliqué, 37
Stockings, 158–61, **158–59**,
    233–39, **233**
Straight-grain binding, for quilts,
    91, *91*
Straight pins, for quilting, 72–73
String quilting. *See* Strip quilting
Strip quilting, 86, *86*
    for Miniature Cat Ornaments,
        155
    for Miniature Stocking
        Ornaments, 160
Supplies, for quilting, 72–73
Swag, 145–48, **145**, **146**
Sweaters
    mohair yarn for, 96, 97
    as projects, 98–103, **98–99**,
        104–11, **104–5**, 112–17,
        112–13
    using multiple yarns for, 96,
        97

T

Sweet brier rose, 121
    in Juniper Wreath with
        Woodland Materials,
        131–33, **131**

T

Table runners, **203**, 204–6,
    222–23, **222–23**, 224–26
Teddy bears, as inside decora-
    tions, 195, **195**
Templates, for quilting, 73,
    74–75
Thimbles, for quilting, 73
Thread, for quilting, 73
Tops, quilt, assembling, 87
Tree, Christmas (*see* Christmas
    tree)
Tree skirts
    drafting equilateral triangles
        for, 167, *167*
    as projects, 164–66, **164**,
        168–73, **168**, 174–77, **174**
Triangles, equilateral, drafting,
    167, *167*

W

Washing quilts, 73–74
White, shading to, 3, 6, 7
Windowsills, decorations for,
    149, **149**, 193
Wool, for batting, 88
Wreaths, 118–37
    boxwood
        packing, 120
        uses for, 120, 125
    greens for, 120–21
    log cabin, 120–21
    as projects, **118**, 122–25, **122**,
        126–27, **125**, **126**, 128–29,
        128, 130, 131–33, **131**,
        134–36, **134**, 137, **137**

Y

Yarns, using multiple, 96, 97